THE BEATRICE INN's presence in New York City spans close to a century, and its history is ever changing, from one of New York's first speakeasies, frequented by Fitzgerald and Hemingway, to a beloved neighborhood Italian restaurant to one of the city's most notorious nightclubs. Angie Mar purchased the Beatrice Inn in 2016 and led the storied landmark into its next chapter. Mar transformed the space and the menu into a stunning subterranean den where guests are meant to throw caution to the wind and engage their most primal of senses.

Now, in Mar's debut cookbook, the Beatrice Inn experience will resonate with readers no matter where they live. *Butcher and Beast* invites them into this glamorous, gutsy, and forever-nocturnal world. Mar's unconventional approach to flavor profiles is captured in over 80 recipes, including **MILK-BRAISED PORK SHOULDER, DUCK AND FOIE GRAS PIE, VENISON CASSOULET,** and **BONE MARROW–BOURBON CRÈME BRÛLÉE.** Throughout are essays on Mar's controversial and cutting-edge dry-aging techniques, her adoration of Champagne, the reality of what it takes to lead in the New York City restaurant scene, and the love and loyalty of her tight-knit family. Visually arresting photography shot entirely on Polaroid film captures the elegant and ever-opulent world of the Beatrice Inn.

BUTCHER + BEAST

BUTCHER
+ BEAST

MASTERING THE ART OF MEAT

RECIPES + STORIES
FROM THE BEATRICE INN

ANGIE MAR

WITH JAMIE FELDMAR

PHOTOGRAPHS BY JOHNNY MILLER

CLARKSON POTTER/PUBLISHERS

New York

CONTENTS

SUMMER

AUTUMN

INTRODUCTION

I STARTED WRITING THIS BOOK IN 2013.

When I first met with my literary agent, we talked about a book that would showcase simpler versions of the food I cook at the Beatrice as well as entertaining ideas I might use in my own home. It seemed like a good idea at the time—no one knew me and I was under the impression this was the only idea that would sell to publishers and ultimately to the general public. I hadn't yet defined a sense of my creative self, nor had I found my voice in food, or even within the Beatrice Inn.

But that was then. And I've decided I'll leave that bullshit to the semihomemade set. Instead, this is the story of me, of the Beatrice Inn, of this family, and of the magic created within our walls.

I've torn up the table of contents for this book more times than I can count. I've cried, laughed, and had utter meltdowns. I've contemplated giving back the advance and not writing it at all, because I felt I couldn't handle the deadlines while running a business. During the process of completing this book, I've experienced extreme highs and extreme lows: I purchased a landmark piece of New York history, received a glowing two-star *New York Times* review, and was awarded *Food & Wine*'s Best New Chef. I've also been sued, extorted, had my face splashed across Page Six, and fired more managers, captains, and kitchen staff than most people who have been in the kitchen ten times longer than I have. I suffered the monumental loss of my father, and gained the monumental expense of having a different attorney for every day of the week. But most important, my team and I have achieved what most chefs and restaurateurs wait a lifetime for. We bet on the underdog, and came out on top—in New York City, no less. The words contained in these pages capture some of the gritty, ugly, gutsy, and beautiful moves we've made to get to where we are today, and the dishes we've created along the way.

MY PHILOSOPHY:
THE HUSTLE AND THE GAME

The Notorious B.I.G. once rapped about "The Ten Crack Commandments," and if you know anything about how the restaurant industry works, his rules for success will sound familiar. Bottom line: It's a business. Don't get high off your own supply. Don't think you are invincible. Don't shit where you eat. And never buy into your own hype and think you can coast, because you can lose it all in an instant. There will always be someone behind you willing to work longer hours, hustle harder, and play the game smarter than you.

Once upon a time, all you had to do was cook good food. Build it and people will come, they said. But now, to be successful in the restaurant industry, you have to do three things, and do them well. Having insanely good food is part of it, but only a small part of it. You also have to hustle hard, and you have to play the game—people often conflate these, but they're not the same.

The hustle is the easy part. Go, go, go—you can sleep when you're dead. Until then, coffee, military naps, and a plethora of energy drinks will keep you going. My brothers and I say that we came out of the womb hustling. I'm constantly working the floor at the Bea, shaking hands and kissing babies, even though it's not in my nature and I generally have to be dragged from the kitchen, kicking and screaming, to do it. I know how my regulars and even my semiregulars like their cocktails, what their wives like to eat, and what table their mistresses prefer. I am both a mother and a therapist to my four dozen employees, and I carry the weight of knowing that how hard I hustle directly affects getting asses into seats every single night so my staff can pay their rent and I can pay mine.

I wish I could tell you success was solely about raw talent and creativity, but the truth is that *money fosters creativity.* I don't know about you, but I find it massively difficult to be in my best creative mind when I can't pay the utility bills.

So, yes, the Beatrice Inn is a business and it is about making money—but it's about making the right kind of money. I generally spend my mornings on the phone with my publicist, agents, and managers declining deals and press opportunities that don't make sense, and working the fuck out of the ones that do. I take the Karl Lagerfeld approach: I will say no to money any day of the week and twice on Sundays if saying yes would mean I have to give up my image, who I am, or what I represent. We don't cheapen our brand, and we don't sell out—we do what we do every single day, and that means staying true to who we are, because our integrity is on the line.

At the end of the day, all we have is our integrity, and I'll be damned if anyone ever says I sold out. We put integrity into how we cook our food, how we run our floor, and how we run our business. A lot of people say compromise is key, but I prefer minimal compromise and the maximization of my vision: my way or the highway. I've always driven a hard deal, played the cards in my hand right, and played the players across from me even better, because success in this business truly is all about the long game. I've learned that there are two kinds of moves to make: ones that make you money, and ones that build your brand. Any other kind are a waste of time, and anyone who can't keep up should get out of the way; they're slowing you down. Just keep hustling.

The game is a bit more complex than the hustle. My dear friend and mentor Pat LaFrieda, the famed butcher and meat purveyor, once told me years before I did my first interview that I could become anyone I wanted to be because no one knew who I was yet. He told me not to be afraid to be different, to be raw, to be controversial, and to be myself. He said that one day I'd figure out who I was and what my vision is—but until that day came, I should keep a low profile, my personal life should remain mysterious, and my skills in the kitchen would do the talking. I am still that fiercely private person. Or at least I have been until now, when I'm finally putting my thoughts and feelings on paper.

I TAKE THE KARL LAGERFELD APPROACH: I WILL SAY NO TO MONEY ANY DAY OF THE WEEK AND TWICE ON SUNDAYS IF SAYING YES WOULD MEAN I HAVE TO GIVE UP MY IMAGE, WHO I AM, OR WHAT I REPRESENT.

Learning how to play the game is an entirely different skill from the business of hustling—it's one that requires years of practice, honing, and discipline, and one that I am *still* working on. I've spent the last decade cultivating relationships with press, purveyors, and guests alike, because I want to have a genuine connection to the people I do business with. My principle is simple: Do right by others because it's the right thing to do, and you will be paid back tenfold. It is perhaps more difficult in execution, especially at the beginning, and even now. Even as I was writing this book, there were people in the press who, by their own admission, did us wrong, and they've made our blacklist. I won't speak to them, won't do their panels, and sure as shit won't let them into our restaurant. You know who you are—I told you I wouldn't be your clickbait. Those rare cases aside, every person now in my phonebook is someone I've worked with to build a real relationship. We've helped each other's businesses and families, we've become friends, and those connections have served me well in times of both celebration and adversity.

The road to success is long, it's hard, and it's more emotional than I ever expected it to be. Both the press and the public are fickle, and that's without even getting into the politics you'll deal with inside your own house. In fact, I have logged an obscene number of hours in therapy just to help me cope with the pressure and quell the anxiety of constantly being under a microscope. But that's the trade-off, I suppose—dealing with the ups and downs. My manager says it the best: "You get five emotional minutes. But then you gotta go back to being gangster." Learning to have grace and humility in times of both hardship and triumph has been one of my greatest struggles and personal successes, and it has taken a long time for me to master.

A whole generation of aspiring restaurant professionals and cooks may be reading this, and feel their dreams being crushed. If that is you and this doesn't

"YOU GET FIVE EMOTIONAL MINUTES. BUT THEN YOU GOTTA GO BACK TO BEING GANGSTER."

sound like the dreamy romance you signed up for: Get out of this industry right now. We don't want you, and you don't want us. It's not fun, this hustle, this game—it's hard fucking work. It's a combination of empire building, the military, parenting, politics, imagination, self-reflection, artistry, world domination, and working harder than you ever thought possible.

Nothing can prepare you for ownership of a business, let alone ownership of a business that has been a New York establishment since the 1920s. The emotional weight of bringing something back from the dead and making it not only relevant but also creative, beautiful, and groundbreaking is so much harder than people realize. I have become my business—a 24/7 operation. I cannot afford to stop for one second, and why would I want to? The reason I do what I do, and why I go through everything I've gone through and would do it all again tomorrow, is because I fucking love my job and this industry.

BUTCHER + BEAST

I want the food on the pages of this book and the stories contained within to do for you what they do for me. I want this book to bring joy, I want it to bring happiness, I want it to bring comfort. I want it to bring anger because it's so fucking good. I want it to bring inspiration and truth—both to the plate, as well as to how you perceive my industry. I want this book and the sentiments contained within to be at times challenging, but always eye-opening, thought provoking, and essential.

Of course, there are recipes in this book—the food we cook and the food that brings people together—but you're also holding the story of how everything came to be. When I began this process, I wrote a bunch of recipes I thought home cooks would love to make on a Sunday. But then I thought, *That isn't who I am. That isn't what I want to teach people. Those are not the ideas I want to share, nor the reason why the dining room at the Beatrice is filled night after night.* Instead, I've written this book to share my real ideas, however mad they seem: It's the recipes that define this restaurant, the dry-aging techniques that polarized both national press and diners, and the stories we acquired along the way. At the end of the day, I want this book to bring you memories and experiences, because so many of my memories and experiences are bound up here, too. Whether you cook out of this book, or simply read the stories in it, I hope to give you a taste of what life is like in my world.

WELCOME TO THE BEAUTIFUL, CONFOUNDING MADNESS THAT IS MY MIND, AND THE WORLD WE HAVE WORKED SO HARD TO BUILD.

WINTER

THIS RECIPE IS HOME TO ME, and there is a reason it's the one I chose to share first in this book. It has roots; it has soul. I first made it when I was fifteen for Sunday supper for my family using a recipe I pulled out of one of my father's old Italian cookbooks. My dish was a disaster—the meat was tough as hell, the texture of the curds and whey was terrible—and my brothers teased me mercilessly. So I set about practicing it—using earnings from my after-school job at the mall for groceries—every Sunday for the next six months, until I had it mastered. I still make it for my family when I go home, where I serve it with rice, because in Asian culture, a meal isn't a meal until there's rice on the table (even if pasta and potatoes and other starches are present). One bite and I'm a teenager again, sitting with my family, swinging the lazy Susan around to claim the best bits.

When people think of the Bea, they think of steak or game meats and we do plenty of those, but for me, this dish is the most meaningful on the menu. When I started to cook professionally, I never served it because I wanted to keep it in my back pocket—I knew when I had my own kitchen, it would become my signature. It is the perfect embodiment of the way I look at the masculine and feminine influences on food—a big, beautiful piece of meat balanced with the soft, floral jasmine rice soubise, laced with fresh herbs and earthy mushrooms—with these contrasting flavors, textures, and temperatures coming together on one plate. It's sensual. It's visceral. It's deeply satisfying. And that, to me, is the ideal dish.

MILK-BRAISED PORK SHOULDER WITH JASMINE
RICE SOUBISE, MAITAKE MUSHROOMS, AND SAGE *Serves 6*

PORK SHOULDER
5 pounds (3 kg) boneless pork shoulder

Kosher salt

5 tablespoons (68 g) olive oil

1 (750 ml) bottle white wine, such as Chardonnay

4 cups (928 g) whole milk

2¼ cups (510 g) heavy cream

About 4 cups (840 g) Chicken Stock (page 283)

1 large onion, halved

1 sprig sage

3 sprigs thyme

2 bay leaves

1 head garlic, halved horizontally

JASMINE RICE SOUBISE
2 cups (440 g) uncooked jasmine rice

3 medium Spanish onions, sliced

Generous 1 cup (250 g) heavy cream

Kosher salt

GARNISH
8 ounces (226 g) unsalted butter

2 bunches sage, leaves picked (about 30 leaves)

Kosher salt

2 tablespoons (27 g) olive oil

12 ounces (340 g) maitake mushrooms, separated by hand

Recipe continues »

NOTE: *Season the meat a day in advance, and let it rest in its braising liquids for a full 24 hours. You can serve it immediately, but it's even better if you let it sit in the refrigerator overnight, then slowly reheat it in a low oven or on the stovetop.*

MAKE THE PORK SHOULDER: Season the pork shoulder on all sides generously with salt and place on a rack set over a rimmed baking sheet. Marinate in the refrigerator for at least 12 hours, or ideally, overnight.

Preheat the oven to 350°F.

In a large Dutch oven or heavy-bottomed pot, heat the olive oil over high heat. Season the pork lightly with salt once more and add it to the pot and cook it, turning, until deep golden brown on all sides, about 15 minutes total. Remove the pork to a plate to rest.

Drain the excess fat from the pot but try to keep any crispy bits on the bottom, and return the pot to medium heat. Add the white wine, bring to a simmer, and deglaze the pot, scraping up any browned bits from the bottom. Reduce the wine until ¼ cup remains, about 15 minutes.

Return the pork to the pot and add the milk, cream, and enough stock just to cover. Tie the onion, sage, thyme, bay leaves, and garlic in a square of cheesecloth, and add the sachet to the pot as well.

Cover with a cartouche (see page 293), then cover with a lid. Transfer to the oven and bake until the pork is tender and falls apart when pulled with a fork or picked with hands, about 2½ hours.

MAKE THE SOUBISE: Place the rice in a large pot. Cover it with the onions and 2 cups water; do not stir.

Bring to a boil over high heat, then cover with a cartouche (see page 293), reduce the heat to low, and cook until the rice is tender with a slight bite, about 30 minutes.

Working in small batches, spoon equal parts rice and onion into a food processor and pulse quickly with ¼ cup of the cream at a time, until the rice is coarse but creamy like polenta. Season lightly with salt. Transfer to a bowl and repeat with the remaining rice and onion.

JUST BEFORE SERVING, MAKE THE GARNISH: In a small pot, melt the butter over medium-high heat until it just begins to toast, about 12 minutes. As the foam subsides and the butter takes on a noisette color, working in batches, drop in 10 to 12 sage leaves and swirl the pot so they separate and begin to fry. When crispy and curled at the edges, 35 to 45 seconds, transfer to a baking sheet lined with paper towels and season with salt. Repeat with the remaining sage leaves, reserving the butter in the pot when you are done.

In a medium sauté pan, heat the olive oil over medium-high heat. Add the mushrooms and sauté until golden and just beginning to crisp, 5 to 6 minutes. Season with salt.

Serve family-style in a large serving bowl or cut the pork into 6 individual portions. Spread the rice soubise along the bottom of a platter or bowls, top with the pork shoulder, and spoon the braising liquid over everything. Garnish with the fried sage and mushrooms, and spoon the reserved brown sage butter on top of everything.

THE CAPTAIN'S WORD
IS LAW

MY MOTHER is from Taipei but grew up part of the time in Oxford, England, so between her and my Chinese American father, our dinner table was a mixed bag of East meets West meets Europe. One night we would have steamed bass with scallions and soy or chicken hearts with black bean sauce, and the next it would be shepherd's pie, a T-bone steak, or, on weekends, prime rib. But no matter what, there was always steamed jasmine rice. To this day, it's my comfort food, and what I crave most often. A family meal at the Beatrice without jasmine rice is a sure sign that hell has frozen over. There's a particular technique to cooking it, which my mother drilled into me just as I do my cooks now: Wash the rice until the water runs clear, cook it just through, and let it dry a bit before serving so the grains fall apart ever so slightly. It's very much an art form. My mother also instilled in me a profound adoration for British culture and cuisine, exposing me to my first fish and chips, Sunday roasts, and the firm belief that a pot of tea can fix just about anything.

My father is one of the biggest influences in my life. He was kind and thoughtful, and fierce in his love for his children and his family. He came up in the kitchen, working in my auntie's restaurant, the inimitable Ruby Chow's. He washed dishes alongside Bruce Lee, and shook hands with Warren Magnuson, Frank Sinatra, Sidney Poitier, and Sammy Davis Jr. He understood the long hours, the minuscule pay, the glitz and glory that is portrayed when the curtain goes up, and the grit and gusto it takes backstage to make it happen. He became a father figure to many of the people who knew him over the years, whether family or not—helping them stay in school, teaching them how to drive, coaching their basketball teams, and bailing them out when they were in a bind. My father was such a strategist that I didn't even realize that he played the long game until I was much older—when I could recognize it and learn from it myself. He'd often sit at the dinner table and tease one of us mercilessly until the other siblings joined in, but just when you thought you could tease your little brother without repercussion, he'd turn the tables on you instead, laughing endlessly at his own joke. It taught us to be quick-witted and on our toes, as he seemed to always get the better of us.

My brothers, Conrad and Chad, are everything to me, and God help any woman who crosses either of them. We grew up with such a sense of loyalty that sometimes I wonder if those teachings backfired on my mother and father, as we'd sooner die than rat each other out. Even today, we are in each other's corner—they designed my website, menus, and business cards, practicing what my father preached to us so long ago. They come to my events when I am traveling, and are always the first to cheer me on—and to put me in my place. When people ask me what I made as a young cook, they never hesitate to put me on blast and tease me about the time I made a smoked salmon dip the color of Pepto-Bismol. Our parents separated when I was fourteen; it was an incredibly hard time for the three of us. We understood why it was happening, but we all felt a bit lost in the shuffle. I took on the responsibility of raising my brothers, and much of the basis for my cooking was to take care of them when my parents were going through their divorce. We stuck together, through thick and thin, just as we had been taught. Although the three of us now live in different cities, we are closer than ever.

MY FATHER always encouraged me to follow my dreams, even if my dreams were misguided, and that meant he was bailing me out of trouble often throughout my teens and well into my twenties. He never asked for a thank-you—he only tutted in disapproval, then would sigh, tell me he loved me, and warn me that I better not fuck up again (which we both knew that I inevitably would).

I didn't actually get my shit together until I moved to New York at the end of 2008. I was making minimum wage as a line cook and in culinary school full time. I couldn't afford to take the subway, let alone eat, and I honestly think *that's* when my father truly got behind my career choice.

It has only occurred to me in retrospect that although my father sometimes worried about me, when I decided to become a chef he found a new respect for who I am. I was no longer the girl fucking up and calling him to help get her out of trouble. I was bailing myself out, as I had finally chosen a distinct path, and was working to attain something. I was doing what he and his siblings had done—starting from the bottom, and working my way up.

Beginning in 2015, every October he visited New York like clockwork for my annual James Beard dinner. He always requested Pat LaFrieda's beef and a reservation at Carbone: his two favorite things in New York. The year I bought the Beatrice, I made the mistake of wanting him to eat at the restaurant every night and canceled the reservation at Carbone. He was outraged.

"What do you mean we're eating your food *again*?" he bellowed. "I love Carbone—you know that, Angela! I've been eating your food all your life, and here I was excited to go to Carbone and have the lamb chops," he complained while eating caviar from the best table at the Beatrice.

I did not make the same mistake the following year. When we returned to Carbone, he was greeted with multiple decanters of Brunello and hugs from the entire staff. "Doctor Mar, it's so good to see you back here," said their GM. "We already have your lamb chops on the way."

"Well, you know, *she* tried to keep me away from here last year," my father replied, pointing to me with his dry, teasing-but-actually-serious smile.

My father brought laughter and light to everyone he encountered, and most of all to his family.

I treasure the time he spent in New York, even when it was against his doctor's orders, because his cholesterol was high, and he shouldn't have eaten with such gusto. My brothers and I would poke fun at him for how he'd try to fool the cardiologist by moving his appointments around, lying about what he ate on his trips here, and bingeing on lettuce to attempt to counteract the effects of a long, steak-laden weekend. He never lost his love for life and for living.

We lost my father in the spring of 2018 while I was in the midst of writing this book. I've included certain recipes as a tribute to him and the wonderful love of food that he gave to his children. And I've omitted others because I want them to remain mine and mine alone. I know he is still with me in spirit because his fingerprints are all over the Beatrice and his influence floods the pages of this book. The Sunday suppers of my childhood are here, in the prime rib, the rabbit stews, and the roasted hens, and that first dish that started it all for me, the milk-braised pork shoulder. My father's birth year is represented in the restaurant's Madeira collection, and those bottles are some of the last of their kind in the world, including one from 1927 that contains a nearly extinct grape. My father is at the bar, where my bar director Antanas keeps a bottle of Crown Royal on the shelf just for him. But he is best represented in the way we cultivate the family housed under our roof.

My father was a naval officer in his early twenties and neither the mentality nor the discipline ever left him. The week before I opened the Beatrice, I was walking through Portobello Road in London when I found the brass sign that hangs over our kitchen. It reads: "The Captain's Word Is Law." Many people think it refers to my absolute authority within our house, but the truth is that it's there in my father's honor. What I have tried to do every day is to follow his words of guidance, his examples of kindness, and his innate desire to bring our family up the right way, so we could not only be good people, but truly prosper together.

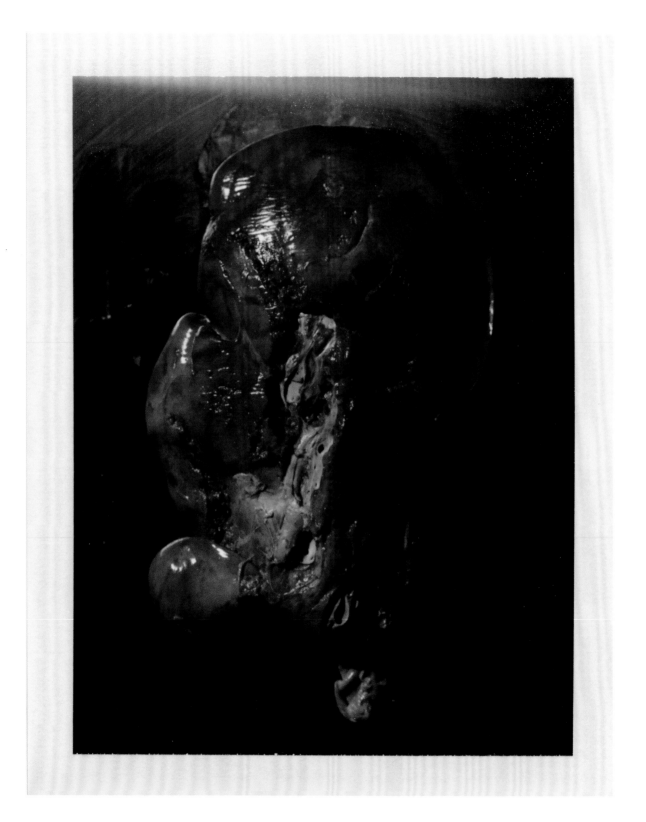

MY FATHER made a simple dish of liver, bacon, and onions when I was growing up, so I've always loved liver, especially when it's cooked to a perfect medium-rare, turning custardy and melty and utterly luxurious in the process. I find myself craving calf's liver often, especially when I need to feel nourished or revitalized after a period of intense creative work. My liver dish builds off of my father's classic take by adding an element of sweetness in the sauce to balance the liver's iron and earthiness. I love bordelaise—a sauce made of shallots, beef demi-glace, and an abundance of black pepper—and think it pairs perfectly and somewhat unexpectedly with cherries here. We make ours with bone marrow instead of butter, which adds a rich silkiness to the sauce without weighing it down.

FOIE DE VEAU

WITH SHALLOTS AND CHERRY BORDELAISE   *Serves 1*

CHERRY BORDELAISE SAUCE

3 tablespoons (42 g) unsalted butter

½ cup (79 g) diced shallots

1 cup plus 2 tablespoons (257 g) red wine, such as Cabernet Sauvignon

2 cups plus 1 tablespoon (433 g) Beef Stock (page 283)

¾ cup (140 g) dried cherries

LIVER

5 tablespoons (68 g) extra-virgin olive oil

2 shallots, halved

3 cipollini onions, halved

1 tablespoon (13 g) Chicken Stock (page 283)

½ pound (283 g) calf's liver

Kosher salt

FOR FINISHING

2 teaspoons (4 g) freshly ground black pepper

1½ teaspoons (5 g) thyme leaves

2 teaspoons (6 g) Rendered Bone Marrow (page 284)

NOTE: *When buying liver, look for pieces that are bright and vibrant, the color of rich jewels. Ask your butcher to peel off the membrane for you, unless you have masochistic tendencies (as I do).*

Recipe continues »

MAKE THE SAUCE: In a small saucepan, melt the butter over medium heat. Add the shallots and cook until softened with just a slight bite, 5 to 7 minutes. Increase the heat to medium-high and continue cooking the shallots until slightly browned, 1 to 2 minutes more. Add the red wine, bring to a simmer, and deglaze the pan, scraping up any browned bits from the bottom. Reduce the sauce until the liquid has almost all evaporated but it feels sticky, 3 to 5 minutes.

Add the beef stock and bring to a boil over high heat. Reduce the heat to a simmer, add the cherries, and cook until the liquid reduces by about two-thirds and the cherries rehydrate, about 20 minutes. The sauce should become quite sticky and coat the back of a spoon. It's important to simmer the sauce gently to make a clear, garnet-hued sauce that is not cloudy or muddy. Remove the pan from the heat and set aside somewhere warm, such as on top of the oven.

MAKE THE LIVER: Preheat the oven to 425°F.

In an ovenproof medium sauté pan, heat 3 tablespoons of the olive oil over medium-high heat. Add the shallots and onions and sear until golden brown, 5 to 6 minutes. Add the chicken stock and cook until it reduces and evaporates, 1 to 2 minutes.

Push the onions to the side of the pan and add the remaining 2 tablespoons oil. Generously season the liver with salt on both sides. Add the liver and sear on one side until golden, 1 minute, then flip and sear on the other side for 1 minute. Push the onions around the liver and transfer to the oven to finish cooking until medium-rare (a thermometer inserted in the center should read 108°F), 5 to 6 minutes. Remove the pan from the oven and let the liver rest in the pan for 3 minutes; the internal temperature will rise to about 118°F.

WHILE THE LIVER RESTS, FINISH THE SAUCE: Bring the bordelaise to a rolling boil over high heat, then turn off the heat. Add the black pepper and thyme and stir to combine. Stir in the rendered bone marrow, shaking the pot, so it naturally emulsifies and thickens the sauce.

To serve, arrange the liver and onions on a plate, then spoon the bordelaise over them.

A WHILE BACK, during an end-of-night meeting with the kitchen, I had asked each of my cooks to think of an old, forgotten French dish that they wanted to not only talk about but also perhaps workshop for our autumn menu. Duncan, who is a sauté cook, brought up pheasant Périgord. He talked about the history of the dish, its Escoffier origins, and its rise and fall in popularity. I loved his selection, because it was so true to the ethos of what the Bea is and the food that we cook.

Traditional pheasant Périgord is roasted in a Madeira sauce with truffles shaved into it, but our version exchanges Madeira for ruby port because I love the color and richness port provides alongside Périgord truffles. Instead of simply roasting a bird and saucing it, ours is decidedly more complex, and very hands-on for our guests, because there is nothing that I love more than food you're forced to interact with physically. We stuff the bird with truffles and savory and slow-cook it, basting it with butter, and seal it in a cocotte with pastry that will ultimately be used as a vessel to eat more sauce. This dish hits all the right notes: classic, new, messy, refined, and just a bit offensive. It really is everything that the Bea embodies, and I think it's one of the sexiest meals for two we've ever done.

PHEASANT PÉRIGORD EN CROÛTE *Serves 2*

1 whole pheasant
(3 pounds/1.35 kg)

7 sprigs savory

Kosher salt

½ cup (109 g) plus 5 tablespoons
(63 g) Truffle Butter
(page 273)

1 pound (453 g) unsalted butter

1½ cups (315 g) ruby port

4¾ cups (997 g) Duck Stock
(page 283)

½ teaspoon (2 g) cracked black
pepper

0.3 ounce (9 g) Périgord truffle

¼ recipe 50/50 Dough
(page 277)

1 egg, beaten

Position a rack in the center of the oven and preheat to 350°F.

Stuff the cavity of the pheasant with the savory and season the cavity with salt.

Tie the bird's legs together with butcher's twine (not a full truss, just the legs). Rub 5 tablespoons of the truffle butter under the skin of the breasts and thighs. Season on all sides with salt.

Place a Dutch oven or cocotte just large enough to hold the bird over medium-high heat, and melt together the butter and ½ cup of the truffle butter. Place the bird in the butter, on its side, to brown the thighs first, until golden brown, 8 to 10 minutes.

While it's browning, use a ladle to continually baste the bird with butter.

Flip the pheasant over and repeat on the other side, basting as you go. Since there's so much butter in the pan, the breasts will begin to cook as you brown the thighs. When both thighs are golden brown, flip the pheasant breast-side down to finish it to the same color, about 5 minutes.

Once the whole bird is a beautiful deep golden brown, remove it from the butter and set aside. Pour off the butter and reserve.

Return the Dutch oven to medium-high heat and add the port to deglaze the pan, scraping up any browned bits from the bottom. Add the duck stock and bring to a boil. Cook until the liquid reduces to sticky and glossy, and your finger leaves a distinct line when you run it down the back of a sauce-coated spoon, 25 to 30 minutes.

Slowly incorporate the reserved butter back into the sauce for gloss and sheen; it should emulsify beautifully. (The finished sauce will be thinner than this, but the bird will emit juices as it cooks, so we're accounting for that by making the sauce slightly too thick

at this stage.) Season with the pepper and remove from the heat.

Thinly slice the truffle and add the slices to the port wine reduction. Return the bird and any accumulated resting juices to the Dutch oven. Roll the dough out to a ribbon 2½ to 3 inches wide and long enough to wrap around the pot twice. Brush the dough with the beaten egg and press the dough onto the rim of the pot, egg-washed-side down, wrapping the pot entirely twice, and gently pressing the dough into the sides to seal. Brush the outside of the dough with the egg wash once more and then place the lid gently over the top, pressing down, ever so slightly, to seal.

Transfer to the oven and bake until the crust is golden brown, 20 to 25 minutes. Rest in a warm place for 10 minutes.

To serve, bring the Dutch oven to the table and use the back of a spoon to crack the pastry so it falls off. Remove the lid and carve the pheasant into pieces, and either return them to the pot or arrange on a platter, using half the sauce to garnish. Dip the pastry shards into the remaining sauce in the pot, using your hands.

THE STEAK THAT STARTED IT ALL

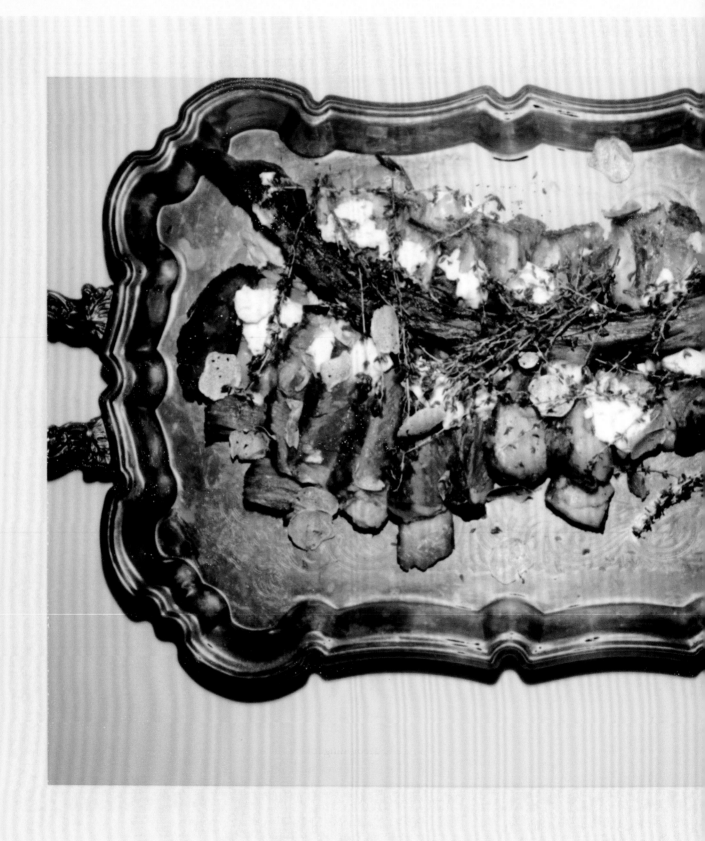

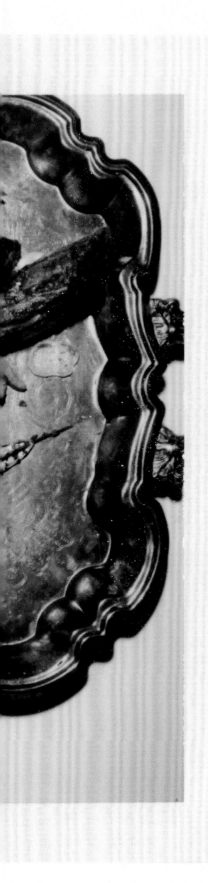

EVERY AUTUMN, WE RELEASE A NEW DRY-AGING TECHNIQUE AT THE BEA, AND WITHOUT FAIL IT BECOMES ONE OF THE MOST POLARIZING DISHES IN NEW YORK. THE 160-DAY DRY-AGED WHISKY BEEF WAS THE STEAK THAT STARTED IT ALL.

Years ago, when I was learning to butcher, one of my dear friends, Andrew Dorsey, fed me a steak that changed my life. We were sitting in the living room of his Brooklyn apartment and he had cooked me dinner: a pea salad, some roasted potatoes, and a hanger steak that he had aged in whisky for ninety days. I'll never forget how it tasted, and how it made me feel. I was truly floored by the flavors, texture and depth, and emotion that this steak stirred within me. I think that might have been the first piece of beef to actually make me cry.

I set about learning everything I could about the technique and found that it had never been done in a restaurant in the United States. Andrew had trained under famed Parisian butcher and bad boy Yves-Marie le Bourdonnec, from whom he learned the technique. When Andrew went back to Paris a few years later, I jumped at the chance to visit him and spend time in Yves-Marie's tiny *boucherie*. The technique changed the way I looked at dry-aging, and I put it into heavy production at the Bea while I was finishing negotiating its purchase.

Over the months that followed our opening and the release of this technique, the whisky-aged steaks became a magnet for the press. People created videos on the madness of the technique that racked up millions of views, fashion publications like *Vogue* wrote essays on them, and they were the catalyst for *Food & Wine* awarding me Best New Chef. The steak's notoriety finally hit me when I received a call asking for 250 pounds of the stuff packaged up and ready to go on a long flight overseas.

I, of course, obliged, and the next day an entourage of five black SUVs pulled up to the restaurant. Half of the dark-suited men built like linebackers wearing sunglasses and earpieces descended upon the Beatrice, leaving the other half to secure the perimeter. I explained to the gentlemen that I had packed it as best I could, but wasn't sure the airline would take a box this large. "It's going private, Chef," the man said. *Oh, silly me*, I thought. I later learned the steaks were for the royal family of Saudi Arabia, who had been in New York that week and heard about our creation. *Oh, okay.*

And of course, with the good came the bad. The whisky steaks were dissected and criticized. A food blogger turned critic (and I use the term "critic" loosely) wrote that I had veered toward catering to the one percent with the creation of this steak—yet he still noted that I had pioneered a new technique. He never actually tried the dish, which I think is an essential component of being a food critic. But I suppose I should take the opportunity to thank him, as I've never sold as many $1,000 steaks as after he wrote about how utterly ridiculous and extravagant they are.

The public and the press are quick to assign a dollar value to all food, as if it is all created equal. What most people fail to understand is that to creatives, the finished product has nothing to do with the logistics of the food's cost—to us, it's about the vision, the madness, the passion, the inspiration, and the realization of an idea on the plate. Whether you think a piece of food is good or bad, the process is more meaningful to its creator than whatever your opinion of it may be.

But still, it's important for me to acknowledge how controversial this dish has been—and to say that I've loved and reveled in every minute of it. All of the time and money and manpower that has gone into the development of this singular piece of beef has been both a source of pride and a point of frustration for me, the cause of misunderstanding for others, and the focus of tremendous love and care. I've never worked so hard to make something, and it's very special to me because of that. It has been called both innovative and outright mad; it's been dissected, debated, copied, and celebrated—but most important, and frankly all I care about, is that it has pushed the boundaries of the industry and moved it forward.

This is the first time I've ever committed the full process to the page. In truth, it's a simple technique, but it is time- and resource-intensive. To see the evolution of scarlet-hued fresh racks of sweetly scented beef to the deeply matured, beautifully jewel-toned colors and delicate aromas that this method of aging imparts is nothing short of thrilling for the meat-obsessed among us.

I often marvel at the collection of beef that lies dormant in our fridges, waiting for its turn to slink around our dining room floor on that stunning pewter tray. They are things of beauty, constantly changing, maturing, the embodiment of the masculine and feminine approach that we take with every dish we create, fragranced with notes of vanilla and oak, and a deep umami that further seduces with every bite.

WHISKY BEEF *Serves 3 to 5*

AGED BEEF

12 (750 ml) bottles whisky, ideally
    French single-malt

10 to 12 pounds (4.5 to 5.4 kg)
    rib-eye rack

Kosher salt

LOBSTER BUTTER

½ cup (31 g) cooked lobster meat

1 pound (453 g) unsalted butter

Seeds of 2 vanilla beans

1 teaspoon (3 g) kosher salt

———

NOTES: *Ask your butcher for a center-cut,
3-bone standing rib roast.*

*You can use any whisky that you'd drink,
though I am partial to Brenne, a French
single-malt that's aged in Cognac barrels,
adding a different dimension and layer of
sweetness that American whiskeys lack.*

AGE THE BEEF: Roll out a 12-foot length of cheesecloth and fold it like a piece of paper into four layers to create one thick sheet. Pour about one-half bottle of whisky into a medium bowl and dip the cheesecloth in, completely saturating it. (You can also put the whisky into a spray bottle and saturate the cloth this way.) Wring out any excess liquid, wrap the cloth tightly around the beef, and secure it with butcher's twine.

Place the meat on a roasting rack nestled inside of a baking dish. The meat will emit moisture as it ages, and it's good for this water to be able to drip off away from the meat.

Put the baking dish with the meat on the rack in the crisper drawer or back of the refrigerator, where it can sit undisturbed. Age for at least 90 days and up to 160. Once a week, remove and discard the cheesecloth and repeat the whisky-soaking process with fresh cloth, re-wrapping and tying the steak each time. As the meat ages, it will feel firmer to the touch and start to develop a moldy crust on the outside—this is a good thing; it means it's developing flavor.

After 90 to 160 days, unwrap the meat, discard the cheesecloth, and use a sharp knife to lightly trim the crust off, being careful not to slice too deeply into the meat. The meat should have a beautiful, deep oxblood hue, as opposed to the bright red of fresh meat.

Cut the rack into single bone-in steaks.

MAKE THE LOBSTER BUTTER: In a food processor, combine the lobster meat, butter, vanilla seeds, and salt and pulse into a thick paste.

COOK THE STEAK: Heat your grill to medium-high heat. Season the steak evenly with salt on both sides and sear on the grill, continually flipping it every 2 minutes. (I like to do this so the internal juices baste the steak and cook it evenly and slowly on both sides.) Cook until medium-rare (a thermometer inserted in the center should read 110°F), about 20 minutes. Remove the steak from the heat and let it rest for 10 minutes before serving.

To serve, carve the steak into ½-inch slices, transfer to a plate, and dollop with the lobster butter.

I OFTEN FANTASIZE about the nightclubs of old New York—the Stork Club, the Cotton Club, and of course, the Copacabana. The Copacabana opened in November of 1940 on East 60th Street, and was a notorious front for Frank "the Prime Minister" Costello of the Genovese crime family. I imagine showgirls, cigar smoke, Brazilian decor, and everything gold, gold, gold.

When I was writing our Autumn/Winter menu in 2018, I wanted it to pay homage both to the city of New York and to the era that my father grew up in. He often reminisced fondly over his glamorous nightlife past, so I very much let my imagination run wild.

This dessert embodies all of the flavors the Copacabana evokes for me—coconut in the custard, smoke in the whipped cream to emulate cigars, and a tropical vibe reminiscent of Brazil itself. It's fun to make, fun to look at, and a hell of a lot of fun to eat.

CUSTARD COPACABANA *Serves 6*

CAKE

8 ounces (226 g) unsalted butter, at room temperature

1¼ cups (250 g) sugar

½ teaspoon (1.5 g) kosher salt

5 large eggs

1 teaspoon (4 g) vanilla extract

3 cups (360 g) all-purpose flour

1¼ teaspoons (6 g) baking powder

2¼ cups (522 g) whole milk

CUSTARD

4 cups (765 g) coconut milk

1 cup plus 2 tablespoons (225 g) sugar

Seeds of ½ vanilla bean

1 teaspoon (3 g) kosher salt

⅓ cup (75 g) heavy cream

5 large egg yolks

⅓ cup (50 g) cornstarch

SMOKED WHIPPED CREAM

3 cups (675 g) heavy cream

2 tablespoons cherrywood chips

3 sheets (8 g) silver gelatin

4½ teaspoons (11 g) confectioners' sugar

½ cup (47 g) unsweetened coconut flakes, toasted (see Notes)

——

NOTES: *You will need a handheld smoking gun (see page 293) for this recipe.*

To toast the coconut flakes, spread them in a single layer on an unlined baking sheet. Lightly toast in a 350°F oven until golden brown, stirring occasionally, 4 to 5 minutes. Let cool completely before using.

MAKE THE CAKE: Preheat the oven to 325°F. Grease the bottom and sides of a 10-inch cake pan, then line the bottom with a round of parchment paper and grease the parchment as well.

In a stand mixer fitted with the paddle attachment, cream the butter and sugar together on high speed until light and fluffy, 6 to 7 minutes. Add the salt and reduce the speed to medium. Add the eggs, one at a time, beating until evenly incorporated after each addition. Add the vanilla. The mixture might look slightly broken, but don't worry. Scrape down the sides of the bowl using a rubber spatula. Beat for 30 seconds more on medium speed to ensure all the ingredients are incorporated.

In a small bowl, combine the flour and baking powder. Reduce the speed of the mixer to low and add the flour mixture in three additions, alternating with the milk, beginning and ending with the flour. Mix until combined, scraping down the sides of the bowl as needed.

Pour the batter into the prepared cake pan, smoothing the surface with a spatula and gently tapping the bottom of the pan against the counter to release any air bubbles. Bake until a tester inserted in the center comes out clean, 15 to 20 minutes. Let the cake cool completely in the pan.

WHILE THE CAKE COOLS, MAKE THE CUSTARD: In a large heavy-bottomed saucepan, combine the coconut milk, sugar, vanilla seeds and pod, salt, and cream and bring to scalding over medium-high heat, 6 to 8 minutes.

In a medium bowl, beat the egg yolks. Slowly whisk the scalded liquid into the egg yolks to temper them. Whisk in the cornstarch until smooth, whisking until there are no lumps. Return the mixture to the saucepan and return to medium-high heat. Whisking constantly, bring the mixture to a boil, 3 to 4 minutes, and continue whisking for 8 minutes to activate the cornstarch. The custard should thicken into a pudding-like consistency. Remove the pot from the heat and strain through a fine-mesh sieve to remove any solids.

Divide the custard into six 8-ounce martini or parfait glasses, filling each about one-third of the way, and smoothing out the top. Press plastic wrap directly onto the surface of each custard to prevent a skin from forming and refrigerate for 1 hour to set.

MEANWHILE, MAKE THE WHIPPED CREAM: Cold-smoke (see page 293) the cream with cherrywood chips for 20 minutes, until the cream has absorbed the smoky flavor. Chill in the refrigerator for 15 minutes.

Soften the gelatin sheets in cold water.

Place the smoked cream in a medium saucepan and bring to scalding over medium-high heat, about 4 minutes. Remove the pot from the heat. Wring any excess water from the gelatin and whisk the gelatin into the cream until dissolved, 1 to 2 minutes. Transfer the cream mixture to the bowl of a stand mixer and refrigerate for 20 minutes to chill.

Fit the stand mixer with the whisk attachment. Add the confectioners' sugar to the chilled cream and whisk on high speed until soft peaks form, 6 to 8 minutes. Return the bowl to the refrigerator for another 30 minutes to chill and to allow the gelatin to set.

TO ASSEMBLE: Unmold the cake from its pan and place on a cutting board. Using a cookie cutter or paring knife, cut three rounds the same width as the martini or parfait glass. Cut each round in half horizontally into ¼-inch-thick rounds.

Remove the plastic wrap from the custard glasses and press a cake round directly into each custard, cut-side down, ensuring there is no air between layers. Divide the whipped cream evenly on top of each cake round and level it out. Refrigerate to chill.

Serve the custard chilled, dividing the coconut flakes evenly among the glasses.

IT'S SATURDAY NIGHT IN NEW YORK MOTHERFUCKING CITY. WE DO WHAT WE DO.

THE SUMMER I purchased the Beatrice, I knew that as soon as we opened our doors in September, we'd attract the press. My cousin Melissa, with whom I own the restaurant, wasn't as optimistic: Autumn 2016 was a big season for restaurant openings by seasoned chefs and restaurateurs and she thought the *New York Times* would have a giant list of new restaurants to review before getting to ours. I was confident enough in my prediction that I was a nervous wreck. I had forgone things like eating (except to taste my own food while recipe testing), sleeping, the gym, makeup, and hair products. I had picked up the habit of chain-smoking, and was fully immersed in my obsession for perfect food, perfect service, and spotting Pete Wells (the *New York Times* dining critic) in our dining room.

We had barely been open for a month when I spent a night away from the restaurant for the first time, to cook dinner at the James Beard House, which I did every year. My father and brothers had flown in from the West Coast to attend, as they always did, and Melissa and her husband were also there. As I stood in the kitchen of the Beard House plating the first course of veal carpaccio, I was struck with an eerie sensation akin to a calm before a big storm. At that moment, my sommelier whirled by and yelled over the shoulder of his immaculately tailored suit: "Get your shit, we have to go!"

"Kyle, what are you talking about? Are you high? We're in the middle of a dinner," I said.

"Wells just walked into the restaurant. *Get your shit, we have to go. NOW,*" he yelled as the door of the Beard House shut behind him.

Fucking hell. I very quickly had to make a choice: continue to play to a respected organization that may or may not give me a nomination or award in the future, or walk out, forgoing all the good standing that had taken me many years and thousands of dollars in contributions and labor to acquire, to go back to my restaurant to cook for the one man who tells the entire world where and what to eat.

It wasn't even a choice. I handed the reins of the expediting station over to a chef friend who happened to be dining at the Beard House that evening, and I bolted down West 12th Street, making peace with myself and the culinary gods that I would probably never receive a James Beard Award.

I found the kitchen in a state of chaos. Our entire dining room was full, Wells had just sat and was looking at the menu, and I had been open for a grand total of about three weeks, so we were far from the well-oiled machine that we are today. I stopped the entire team and told them something that I still say to this day: "It's Saturday night in New York Motherfucking City. We do what we do."

That night, we put out 256 perfect meals, one of them for a table that happened to be occupied by the *New York Times* food critic. My family came into the bar after their dinner at the Beard House around midnight to see how I was doing. That evening, I stayed at the restaurant until 4:30 in the morning with my team because Wells stayed well past closing, hanging out on Table 14. I alternated between lying on the banquette in the bar, drinking whisky with my family, and going outside to chain-smoke. My father, never one to shy away from a bit of excitement, vowed to stay, too. "I'm waiting until this guy leaves!" my father proclaimed as he held out his glass to Antanas, my bartender.

Our *New York Times* review would be published on the early afternoon of October 25, 2016, two weeks later. I hadn't been able to sleep the night before so I went into the restaurant super early in the morning. In times of happiness, of sadness, and of strife, all I know to do is cook. I gathered all of the meat I could find in the walk-in, brought it into the kitchen, and told everyone to leave me be. I stood for hours at the stove in a trance, butchering, searing, and braising any piece of meat I could get my hands on.

Finally, around 11:30 a.m., my phone began to blow up. I knew the review had gone live. I pulled all of the meats off the stove and went around the corner to sit alone in my dining room. I pulled up the *New York Times* website, and there it was. "The Beatrice Inn: A Cuisine for Animals," read the headline, followed by a glowing love letter to our newly anointed two-star restaurant. Halfway through reading it, I began to cry. Pete's writing was beautiful.

This was the beginning of a new chapter for the restaurant. Until then, I had felt clouded by doubt and skepticism about my vision, about whether or not I was ready to lead, and secretly, about whether purchasing the Beatrice had been

the right move for me. I had been struggling to articulate my view on food—the masculinity, the femininity, the primal qualities that I wanted to evoke, and the emotions I wanted to draw out of diners. At that point in my career, I could only cook it, not explain it to others, as I couldn't even explain it to myself.

But that day, the review ushered in a new wave of confidence for me, one that I wasn't prepared for and hadn't expected to receive. Pete Wells seemed to understand what I was trying to articulate and the notions that I had put on the plate, perhaps before I even understood them myself.

WE WERE NOW COOKING TO CELEBRATE NOT ONLY THE ANIMALS ON THE SILVER PLATTERS THAT PARADE AROUND OUR DINING ROOM, BUT ALSO TO CELEBRATE OUR LIVES AND LIVING AS THE ANIMALS THAT WE ARE.

After that, we were flooded with people. All of a sudden our restaurant was busy—people wanted to be there because of what Pete Wells had written. Beyond full tables, I had also immediately gained a sort of notoriety in the restaurant industry, among my peers and people I looked up to.

Several months later, I was pulled into a meeting with Jordana Rothman, the restaurant editor of *Food & Wine* magazine. I was thrilled to meet her, as I had long admired her work, and *Food & Wine* is a publication that has been part of my reading repertoire religiously since I was seven years old. She invited me in for a simple get-together and I went willingly, excited to finally put a face to the name. After our chat, she promised we would get together soon, saying she could hopefully find a piece for me in the magazine sometime in the future. Just before I left, Jordana asked me to participate in a *Food & Wine* tradition of a short interview taped in their wine room. As I sat in front of a camera, Nilou Motamed, then editor in chief, asked me an array of questions, from my favorite hair product to what I love about New York. Nearing the end, she said, "And one more question before you go . . . How would you feel if I told you we've named you a *Food & Wine* Best New Chef?"

I was stunned, speechless, and simply began to cry. I was welcomed into a family and joined a category of chefs that I had always looked up to: Daniel Boulud, Thomas Keller, Eric Ripert, and so many others. They are all part of an amazing legacy that is *Food & Wine* magazine's Best New Chef, and I am still humbled and honored every day to be among them.

To those not in the restaurant industry, it's difficult to explain the importance of obtaining these two accolades. There are so many restaurants in New York, and the privilege of even cooking for the writers of these publications—let alone having them write about your creations—is something that many cooks wait a lifetime for. It's impossible to articulate my gratitude and to quantify the effect that these accolades have had on our business, and the way diners perceive what we truly do and what our food truly says. But what I do know is that without the amazing writers and critics who supported and stood by the Beatrice early on, I would not have had the confidence to continue to push the boundaries and cook the food I believe in today.

I LOVE SO MANY cuts of beef, but oxtail is very high on the list thanks to its silky, succulent texture; when braised correctly, it utterly melts in your mouth. I like to make it on a Sunday night, curl up next to the fireplace, and eat it with a spoon—then pick at the bones until my fingers and lips are coated in sticky-sweet, velvety collagen. Served over a bowl of rustic potato mash, it's a solitary pleasure for me, and deeply soul-soothing.

Pairing oxtail with Madeira and prunes is a beautiful marriage of meaty, sweet, savory, earthy, and creamy all at once. Prunes are, in my opinion, a vastly underrated ingredient. When cooked into a sauce like this they add an incredible depth of flavor. Regarding the meat, there may come a point, especially when you're braising something as tough and sinewy as oxtail, where it finally softens, but it's dry, and you become concerned

that you've overbraised it. Don't be. Let the oxtail simmer over gentle heat for 20 minutes past the point where you think it's done, and I promise some alchemy makes the oxtail finally throw up its last flag and submit into its final juicy, succulent, silken state.

OXTAIL WITH MADEIRA, MASH, PRUNES, AND ROSEMARY *Serves 4 to 6*

BRAISE

5 pounds (2.25 kg) oxtail

Kosher salt

2 tablespoons (27 g) extra-virgin olive oil

2 shallots, halved lengthwise

1 head garlic, halved

1 bunch rosemary

1 cup (214 g) Banyuls vinegar

½ bottle (375 ml) white wine, such as Chardonnay

15 pitted prunes

About 8 cups (1.7 kg) Chicken Stock (page 283)

MASH

3 pounds (1.35 kg) potatoes, peeled

Kosher salt

¾ cup (180 g) whole milk

⅔ cup (155 g) heavy cream

4 tablespoons (56 g) unsalted butter

1 small bunch Tuscan (lacinato) kale, center ribs removed, leaves cut into ribbons

1½ cups (325 g) Madeira

3 tablespoons (42 g) unsalted butter

NOTE: *The seasoned oxtail should sit for at least 6 hours, or ideally overnight, in the refrigerator. Plan accordingly.*

MAKE THE BRAISE: Season the oxtail generously all over with salt.

Preheat the oven to 325°F.

In a large Dutch oven or heavy-bottomed pot, heat the olive oil over medium-high heat. Working in batches, add the oxtail and cook, turning, until deep golden brown in color, 3 to 5 minutes per side. Remove to a plate, leaving any rendered fat in the pot.

In the same pot, over medium-high heat, cook the shallots and garlic until blistered and golden brown, about 2 minutes. Add the rosemary and fry until fragrant, 10 to 15 seconds. Remove and set aside with the oxtail.

Pour off the fat from the pot, but retain any seasoning that has accumulated at the bottom. Heat over medium-high heat, add the vinegar to deglaze the pan, scraping up any browned bits from the bottom. Reduce the vinegar until it is sticky and coats the back of a spoon like cough syrup, 4 to 5 minutes.

Return the oxtail, shallots, garlic, and rosemary to the pot and add the white wine, 5 of the prunes, and just enough chicken stock to cover by about ½ inch. Bring to a boil, then reduce the heat to low. Cover with a cartouche (see page 293) and a lid, transfer to the oven, and braise until the meat is tender and falling off the bone, about 2½ hours.

WHILE THE OXTAIL BRAISES, MAKE THE MASH: In a large pot, combine the potatoes with cold water to cover and add 1 tablespoon salt. Bring to a boil over high heat and simmer until the potatoes are knife-tender, about 20 minutes. Drain and return the potatoes to the pot. Add the milk and cream and mash with a large spoon until velvety, but with some lumps remaining. Add the butter and season to taste with salt. Fold in the ribbons of kale until they wilt a bit. Set aside, covered, to keep warm.

When the meat is finished, transfer it to a bowl and cover loosely with foil, adding a bit of the braising liquid so it doesn't dry out. Strain the remaining braising liquid, pressing on the solids to extract as much liquid and flavor as possible. Discard the solids.

Return the strained braising liquid to the pot it cooked in. Bring to a boil, then add the Madeira. Reduce the heat to medium and cook the liquid until reduced by three-quarters, about 20 minutes.

Return the oxtail to the sauce, adding the remaining 10 prunes, and gently simmer to heat through and reconstitute the prunes, 10 to 12 minutes. Add the 3 tablespoons butter, which gives the sauce an additional velvety texture and sheen. Serve the oxtail with the mash alongside.

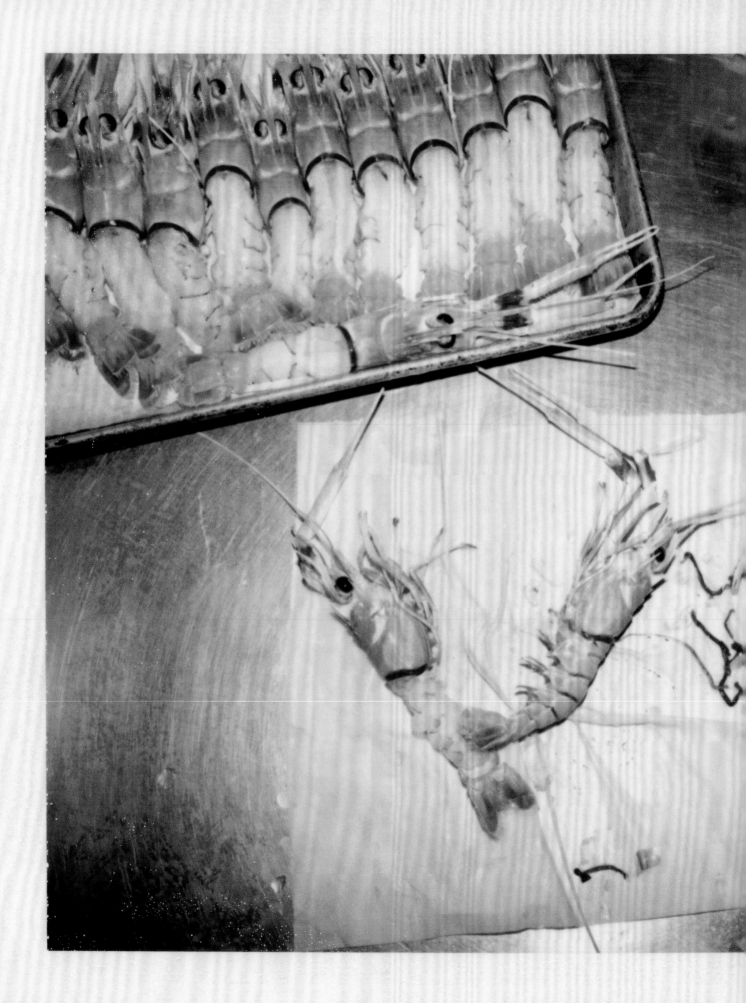

LE GRAND COQUILLAGE

(page 44)

IT'S NO SECRET that I've never been a lover of cooked fish. Instead, I tend to be drawn to shellfish, bivalves, and crustaceans. One of my favorite activities when I'm in France is to sit at Huîtrerie Régis in the 6th arrondissement at one of the sidewalk tables, drinking a very crisp Vouvray or Champagne, chain-smoking, and indulging in their amazingly fresh seafood. I tend to eat with my hands during these visits, throwing all caution (and any supposed protocol) to the wind. I love looking through the window to the kitchen inside at the cadre of sixty-something French men, all with hands like bear's paws, shucking oysters bare-handed, drinking wine, and smoking cigarettes at the same time. From the first time I arrived there, I knew I was in the right place, and have been very much in love with it ever since.

Le grand coquillage, or seafood platter, is something I like to eat in the winter to start a meal if I'm entertaining, or even as the entirety of my meal, if it's just me and one other person. Shellfish and crustaceans are at their best and sweetest in the winter when the waters are cold. There's so much pleasure to be found in cozying up with someone you love and a beautiful bottle of Champagne or white wine, eating perfectly chilled shellfish. I find it very intimate and very sexy.

LE GRAND COQUILLAGE *Serves 4 to 6*

6 head-on langoustines

6 head-on tiger prawns

8 razor clams

24 of your favorite oysters, shucked

8 cherrystone clams

2 ounces Marinated Anchovies (page 280)

1 pound cooked Alaskan king crab legs

½ pound cooked Jonah crab claws

Sea kelp, for garnish

¼ cup Yuzu Cocktail Sauce (page 281)

¼ cup Juniper Mignonette (page 281)

¼ cup Drawn Langoustine Butter (page 274)

¼ cup Roasted Garlic Aioli (page 280)

Crusty sourdough bread, for serving

Set up a large bowl of ice and water. Fill a large pot with 2 inches water, fit with a steamer basket, and bring to a boil over medium-high heat. Steam the langoustines until opaque and cooked through, about 6 minutes, and immediately plunge into the ice bath to stop them from cooking.

Over the same pot of boiling water, steam the prawns until opaque and cooked through, about 4 minutes, plunging them into the ice bath to stop cooking.

Slice the diggers off the razor clams and discard their stomachs. Rinse the shells and reserve. Slice the razor clam diggers on the bias and return them to their reserved shells for serving.

Arrange a three-tiered platter with the following: oysters, cherrystone clams, and razor clams on the bottom level; langoustines, prawns, and anchovies in the middle; king crab and Jonah crab on the top. Arrange the sea kelp to garnish.

Serve with bowls of cocktail sauce, mignonette, langoustine butter, aioli, and bread on the side.

MY LAVENDER-AGED BEEF is the yin to the yang of Whisky Beef (page 33), and a creation of which I'm very proud—it's a seductive steak inspired by the romance of Provence that feels decidedly more feminine than its booze-soaked counterpart while still evoking a deep, heady flavor. For the restaurant, we special-order a cut of beef called the 103—a tomahawk rib eye that includes the eye, spinalis dorsi, short plate, short rib, and deckle—which is common in France but difficult to find in the US. I like using the deckle—normally considered a utility cut that goes into burgers and stew meat—because it tenderizes beautifully during the dry-aging process. We cold-smoke the whole rack with French oak, then bury it in fresh lavender and age it for 90 days in our special refrigerators. We're the only restaurant in the US to practice this technique; it's important for us to constantly be pushing the boundaries of the industry forward.

You can lavender-age almost any cut of beef at home. I chose hanger steak for this recipe because I love its beefiness and big flavor—it stands up to the floral qualities that the lavender dry-aging process brings out. It's also a readily available cut and an easy process to manage at home.

Masculine and feminine; floral and earthy; light and deep—to have all of these contrasting elements in a single dish is a rare and beautiful thing indeed.

LAVENDER-AGED BEEF *Serves 2 or 3*

5 pounds (2.25 kg) hanger steak, untrimmed

Oak wood chips

3 bunches fresh lavender

½ cup (112 g) Herbes de Provence Butter (page 273), at room temperature

5 Don Bocarte anchovy fillets, roughly chopped

2 tablespoons (27 g) extra-virgin olive oil

Kosher salt

———

NOTE: *You will need a handheld smoking gun (see page 293) for this recipe.*

Cold-smoke (see page 293) the steak with oak wood chips for about 20 minutes, until the meat has absorbed the smoky flavor.

To age the beef, roll out 3 feet of cheesecloth and spread half of the lavender across it in a shape roughly the same size as the steak. Place the steak on top of the lavender and cover the top of the meat with the remaining lavender, essentially sandwiching the meat between two layers of the herb. Roll the cheesecloth tightly around the steak and tie the whole thing with butcher's twine.

Place the meat on a roasting rack nestled inside of a baking dish. The meat will emit moisture as it ages, and it's good for this water to be able to drip off away from the meat.

Put the baking dish with the meat on the rack in the crisper drawer or back of the refrigerator, where it can sit undisturbed. Age for at least 30 days and up to 45. As the meat ages, it will feel firmer to the touch and start to develop a moldy crust on the outside—this is a good thing; it means it's developing flavor.

After 45 days, unwrap the meat, discard the cheesecloth, and use a sharp knife to lightly trim the crust off, being careful not to slice too deeply into the meat. The meat should have a beautiful deep oxblood hue, as opposed to the bright red of fresh meat. Slice the whole thing in half lengthwise, through the silver skin, to yield 2 steaks.

Preheat the oven to 375°F.

In a small bowl, fold together the herbes de Provence butter and chopped anchovies.

In a large heavy-bottomed pan, heat the olive oil over medium-high heat. Season the steaks evenly with salt on both sides. Add the steaks to the pan and sear on one side for 3 minutes, then flip and sear on the other side until evenly browned, 3 minutes longer.

Transfer the steak to a wire rack set over a rimmed baking sheet. Roast until medium-rare (a thermometer inserted in the center should read 120°F), 7 to 9 minutes.

Remove from the oven and let the steak rest for about 10 minutes; the internal temperature should rise to about 130°F.

To serve, cut the steak against the grain into ½-inch-thick slices, transfer to a platter, and dollop with the herbes de Provence/anchovy butter.

PAT LAFRIEDA

PAT LAFRIEDA

PAT LAFRIEDA AND I met over the phone in the spring of 2013. It was 3:00 a.m. and I was calling to yell at him about the burger mix for the Spotted Pig, where I worked at the time. We hotly debated the grind for about 45 minutes until he realized I actually knew what I was talking about (even if it was a fraction of what he knew), and more important, that I thought the phone call was as ridiculous as he did. The burger grind was perfectly fine; I was just following the marching orders of my current master.

That 3:00 a.m. conversation, and our subsequent meeting, has turned into one of the most significant relationships I've ever had.

To the outside world, I suppose, our friendship is a given: He is a butcher. I am a meat cook. But our relationship has always been more than just beef and the procurement thereof.

When I was contemplating taking on the role of executive chef at the Beatrice, the restaurant had just received zero stars in the *New York Times* and no one wanted to eat there. I thought it would be career suicide, and had consistently turned the job down for two months straight when I finally called Pat for advice. He said, "Ang, you have the amazing opportunity of taking over a restaurant with an iconic New York name."

"It's already gotten a shit review, and no one wants to eat there. Everyone is going to think I am insane!" I responded.

"That's exactly why you are going to take the job, my dear," he said. "No one will be paying attention. Your friends will think you are crazy. The industry will think you are crazy. But you'll go and make mistakes on someone else's dime. You'll learn from them. And when you are ready, you will bring that restaurant back from the dead and it will make your career. And I will help you."

I took the job the next day.

A similar thing happened a year and a half later when I received the offer to buy the restaurant. I had already been contemplating leaving—I had put in my time and I was ready to own something, start writing a business plan and looking for investors. I was ready to cook my own food. With the offer on the table, I rang Pat so we could play out the many potential scenarios, as we often do. He didn't even let me finish before saying, "Buy it. What else is going on, babe?"

What? I whined about the bad press, how the history of the building was appealing, but it had been more negative than positive over the past ten years, and didn't I deserve a fresh start?

"You're not going to get any fresher than this, kid," Pat said. "A year and a half ago everyone thought you were insane for taking that job, and look how that worked out. Now you're doubling down on crazy. Buy the business."

I closed on the restaurant a year later, and the rest has been history—in the making.

Clearly, Pat has been one of my greatest mentors and one of the greatest influences on my career. We spend late nights handpicking and tagging racks of beef for the Bea; his dry-aging room is his pride and joy, and one of my favorite places on earth. Now, instead of debating burger grinds, we have conversations about setting up my business for the next twenty years; he advises me on how to buy my first house, and he talks me off the ledge when I am having an utter meltdown because I believe I am getting Lyme disease from the tick that jumped off the deer I am skinning (yes, that happened). Pat was there when the Bea earned its glowing review from the *New York Times;* he was also there when I was awarded *Food & Wine* magazine's Best New Chef. He has tracked down my stolen cell phones (twice, successfully); he has my kid brother on a standing delivery for Italian sausage and rib steaks from across the country, and he has been there for me and for my family in times of trouble and of loss. That's just who he is.

It's hard to express to people how much of my success I owe to him. He has helped shape who I have become, both personally and professionally, and selfishly, I was hesitant to write about our relationship as we are both very private people. But the truth is, he has taught me how to be a better person, a better mentor to the amazing team I lead, and how best to grow them and myself. Pat saw in me something I still can't describe even before I saw it in myself. He's been my supporter since before anyone knew who I was, or what I

was capable of. Perhaps even before I knew who I was, and definitely before I found my voice in the kitchen.

Sometimes I wonder why he has spent so much time cultivating me, protecting and promoting me—what did I do to deserve it? I asked him one day and he answered simply that my tenacity and work ethic remind him of himself. He saw that in me immediately, and thinks I've earned his support. His statement humbled me, made me tear up, and also warmed my soul. When it comes to us, I don't feel like I've earned anything, just that I am very lucky to have him in my life, and moreover I have come to realize that he is the one person who has my complete and utter admiration.

FROM START TO FINISH, this is truly a butcher's stew, featuring all of the parts that people generally dismiss, which are full of so much seductive flavor. If I were to rank the beef cuts I love most, rib eye would come first, but it's followed closely by oxtail, then tongue, and then tripe. We serve a very refined version of this dish at the Beatrice that's stewed with roast duck carcasses and topped with veal sweetbreads, and I encourage you to add either or both to this dish if you're keen. But the version you see here is the Butcher's Stew in its glorious original incarnation. Years ago when I met Pat LaFrieda, he mentioned that one of his friends made him a tripe stew that he adored. Naturally, I became quite competitive and invited Pat over for a dinner of this stew. Suffice it to say, my stew won, and it has become a favorite of ours to this day.

BUTCHER'S STEW *Serves 6*

1¼ cups (220 g) dried cannellini beans

2¼ cups (500 g) hot water

1 (2-pound/933 g) piece beef tongue

1 pound (453 g) tripe, sliced into ¼-inch-wide strips

¼ cup (54 g) extra-virgin olive oil

3 pounds (1.35 kg) oxtail, cut into 3-inch pieces

Kosher salt

6 ounces (176 g) pearl onions, peeled (about 1¼ cups)

5 garlic cloves, smashed

1 bunch thyme

2 bay leaves

1 cup (195 g) white wine, such as Chardonnay or white Burgundy

4 cups (840 g) Beef Stock (page 283)

NOTE: *If possible, make this stew a day in advance (through the step where it's simmered for 4 hours and the oxtail is very tender) and chill overnight, so the flavors have time to meld and you can remove the fat in one solid layer. If not, you can still make it and eat it day-of.*

In a large bowl, combine the cannellini beans and hot water. Set aside to soak.

Meanwhile, fill a large pot with water and bring to a boil over high heat. Add the beef tongue, then reduce the heat to medium-high and simmer until the skin on the tongue starts to burst and peel away, about 1 hour 30 minutes.

While the tongue simmers, add the tripe to a medium pot and cover with cold water. Bring to a boil over high heat and boil for 5 minutes, then drain. Repeat the process with fresh water. After the second blanch, drain the tripe and set aside.

In a large Dutch oven or heavy-bottomed pot, heat the olive oil over medium-high heat. Season the oxtail with salt. Working in batches, add the oxtail and sear, turning, until deep mahogany on all sides, 8 to 10 minutes. Transfer the oxtail to a plate.

Recipe continues »

Add the pearl onions and garlic to the Dutch oven and cook until light golden, 5 to 6 minutes. Add the thyme and bay leaves and fry until they crackle and blister, and are fragrant, about 30 seconds. Carefully pour off any fat, then return the oxtail and any accumulated juices to the pan with the onions.

Add the wine, bring to a simmer, and deglaze the pan, scraping up any browned bits from the bottom. Cook until the liquid is reduced by half, 8 to 10 minutes. Add the beef stock, bring to a boil, then reduce the heat to low and simmer, uncovered, until the sauce coats the back of a spoon, 5 to 7 minutes.

Remove the tongue from the water. When cool enough to handle, peel off the top layer from the muscle of the tongue and discard the skin. Cut the peeled tongue into ½-inch-thick slices. At this point, it won't yet be tender—don't worry. Add it to the pot with the oxtail. Cut the tripe into 1-inch pieces. Add it to the pot with the oxtail and tongue. Add the beans and their soaking liquid. The ingredients should be covered with liquid; if necessary, add more water, 2 to 3 cups.

Cover with a cartouche (see page 293), then cover the pot with the lid. Simmer over low heat until the oxtail is silky and starts to pull away from the bone, about 4 hours. Ideally, at this point the stew should be refrigerated overnight (see Note).

If making the day-of, remove the cartouche and lid and skim off as much of the fat as possible. Increase the heat to medium-high and cook until the liquid is reduced by about one-quarter and is slightly thickened, and just veils the back of a spoon, 10 to 12 minutes. Check for seasoning and serve.

ONE OF MY FAVORITE DESSERTS as a child was my Aunt Louise's lemon meringue pie. This tart is my nod to her famous dessert, albeit one that's slightly less . . . neon. I like to use a sabayon method for the rich filling, which involves cooking it in a double boiler and whisking in the butter—a technique that's similar to making hollandaise. The cardamom meringue topping makes it look like a toasted cloud. Quivering and silken, this tart has become a mainstay at my personal dinner parties and the Beatrice alike.

MEYER LEMON TART
WITH CARDAMOM MERINGUE   *Makes one 10½-inch tart*

NOTES: *I urge you not to miss out on Meyer lemon juice in the winter, but feel free to use regular lemons in other seasons so you can enjoy this tart year-round.*

The filling in this pie needs to chill for at least 6 hours and up to overnight to set, so plan accordingly.

If you don't own a handheld torch to brûlé the meringue, place the tart under the broiler for 5 minutes.

TART SHELL

¾ cup plus 2 tablespoons (177 g) sugar

12 ounces (330 g) unsalted butter, at room temperature

3 large egg yolks

Scant 3 cups (350 g) all-purpose flour

1 teaspoon (3 g) kosher salt

TART FILLING

1 cup plus 2 tablespoons (225 g) sugar

4 large eggs

4 large egg yolks

Juice of 5 Meyer lemons (⅔ cup)

1 teaspoon (3 g) kosher salt

6 ounces plus 1 tablespoon (187 g) unsalted butter, cubed

CARDAMOM MERINGUE

14 large egg whites

1⅓ cups (273 g) sugar

8 cardamom pods, shelled and seeds crushed in a mortar and pestle

Kosher salt

MAKE THE TART SHELL: In a stand mixer fitted with the paddle attachment, cream the sugar and butter on medium speed until light and fluffy, about 4 minutes. Slowly add the yolks and beat until evenly incorporated, about 30 seconds. Scrape down the sides of the bowl using a rubber spatula. Add half of the flour and the salt and mix on low speed until just incorporated, then add the rest and repeat. Avoid overmixing.

Transfer the dough to a 10½-inch tart pan with a removable bottom and, using your fingers, push it into the bottom and up the sides in an even layer. Trim any excess dough hanging over the side. Refrigerate for at least 30 minutes, or up to overnight, to chill.

Preheat the oven to 350°F.

Line the tart shell with foil or parchment paper, weight down with pie weights or dried beans, and parbake for 10 minutes. Remove the foil and weights and bake for 5 minutes more to dry out the surface of the shell. Set aside to cool completely, about 1 hour.

MEANWHILE, MAKE THE FILLING: In a large heatproof bowl, whisk together the sugar, whole eggs, and egg yolks until smooth, about 2 minutes. Set the bowl over (not in) a pan of simmering water over medium-low heat. Cook, whisking gently, until thickened to the consistency of crème anglaise, 10 to 12 minutes. Add the lemon juice in three increments, whisking to incorporate after each addition. Whisk in the salt.

Reduce the heat to low. Slowly whisk in the butter piece by piece until smooth and completely incorporated. The filling should thicken to a custard-like consistency.

Pour the filling into the cooled tart shell and gently tap the pan against the counter to remove any air bubbles. Refrigerate for at least 6 hours and up to overnight to set.

MAKE THE CARDAMOM MERINGUE: Place a large heatproof bowl or the bowl of a stand mixer over (not in) a pan of simmering water over low heat. Add the egg whites and half of the sugar. Using a handheld electric mixer, beat together until foamy and forming very loose peaks, with the sugar incorporated but not completely dissolved, 8 to 10 minutes. Transfer the mixture to a stand mixer fitted with the paddle attachment and add the remaining sugar 1 tablespoon at a time, along with the crushed cardamom seeds and a pinch of salt. Mix on high speed until thick and marshmallowy, about 5 minutes.

Spoon the meringue over the top of the chilled lemon tart (you may not need all of it) and use the back of a spoon to make light, airy swoops in the surface of the meringue—don't worry about making it too perfect, the beauty of this stunning tart lies in its imperfections. Brûlé the meringue with a handheld torch until golden. Serve immediately.

THIS DISH has been on the menu at the Bea since the day I bought the restaurant. It's my version of surf and turf: a tender bone-in rib eye, pan-roasted in its own marrow, with a delicate prawn-infused butter that whispers subtly of the sea. Combined with onyx-hued berries, just barely blistered in rich animal fat, this dish is tremendously sensual and sexy, perched neatly at the intersection of masculine and feminine that I find so compelling. Unlike the meat-and-sides you get at a traditional steakhouse, this plate is a fully composed thought. The vanilla in the prawn butter plays off the beautifully funky aged beef, adding nuance to a meal that's more than the sum of its parts. Luxurious ingredients aside, this is actually a very straightforward recipe to follow at home, perfect for a romantic night in or a special occasion for two.

DRY-AGED CÔTE DE BOEUF
WITH BLISTERED BLACKBERRIES, GARLIC CONFIT, AND CHARRED PRAWN BUTTER *Serves 2*

2 tablespoons (27 g) extra-virgin olive oil

2 large head-on tiger prawns

4 tablespoons (56 g) unsalted butter, softened

Seeds of ¼ vanilla bean

6 tablespoons (71 g) Rendered Bone Marrow (page 284)

1 (26- to 28-ounce/737 to 794 g) aged bone-in côte de boeuf or rib eye

Kosher salt

1 pint (170 g) blackberries

8 cloves Garlic Confit (page 280)

½ bunch fresh thyme

Freshly ground black pepper

NOTE: *When it comes to sourcing, seek out beef that's been aged for at least 45 days (at the Bea, 60 days is the minimum), which good butchers or online purveyors should be able to supply.*

Preheat the oven to 400°F.

In a small sauté pan, heat the olive oil over medium-high heat. Add the prawns and cook until deep brown and caramelized, turning once, about 5 minutes per side. Remove from the heat and roughly chop the prawns (including the shell). Transfer to a food processor and add the butter and vanilla seeds. Pulse to combine until smooth. Set aside.

In a large ovenproof sauté pan, heat the rendered bone marrow over high heat. Season the steak liberally on both sides with salt. Add to the pan and sear, turning once, for about 2 minutes per side. Transfer the pan to the oven and roast, turning 2 to 3 times, until medium-rare (a thermometer inserted in the thickest part of the rib eye, away from bone, should read 110°F), about 10 minutes.

Transfer the steak to a rack or cutting board (set the sauté pan aside but don't wash it yet) and let the steak rest for 10 to 12 minutes.

Set the reserved sauté pan over medium-high heat. Add the berries and garlic confit and sauté until blistered and just warmed through, about 90 seconds. Add the thyme at the end to fry and finish with a few cracks of black pepper.

Cut the steak against the grain into ¼-inch-thick slices and arrange on a platter. Spoon dollops of the prawn butter over the steak. Top with the berries, garlic confit, and thyme.

MY FIRST ENCOUNTER with poutine was at a food truck in Seattle when I was a teenager. I went with my two brothers, intending to get hamburgers, but instead we wound up sitting in my car, all of us fighting over this incredible combination of fries, gravy, and cheese curds. From that day forward, I was irrevocably changed—all I ever wanted was that cardboard box full of poutine. The version at the Bea is served on something just a bit sturdier and I've added foie gras, but for me, there's still absolutely nothing better than hanging at the bar and sinking in to this comfort food, with a glass of Brunello or Allagash ale for good measure.

GAME BIRD POUTINE *Serves 6*

1¼ pounds (563 g) russet potatoes, cut into ¼-inch batons

GRAVY

1½ tablespoons (22 g) duck fat

1 large squab (15 ounces/427 g)

Kosher salt

3 medium Spanish onions, thinly sliced

Scant 3 tablespoons (21 g) all-purpose flour

2½ cups (525 g) Duck Stock (page 283)

FRITES

Canola oil (about 4 quarts or 3.5 kg), for deep-frying

1 tablespoon (6 g) picked rosemary leaves

2 tablespoons (6 g) picked savory leaves

ASSEMBLY

1¼ pounds (560 g) foie gras

Kosher salt

1 duck egg

Freshly ground black pepper

8½ ounces (240 g) d'Affinois cheese, at room temperature

NOTE: *The potatoes need to soak for at least 3 hours or up to overnight, so plan accordingly.*

In a large bowl, cover the potato batons with cold water. Soak in the refrigerator for at least 3 hours or up to overnight.

MAKE THE GRAVY: In a large sauté pan, warm the duck fat over medium-high heat. Season the squab all over with salt. Add to the pan and sear, turning, until golden brown, 6 to 8 minutes. Remove the squab to a plate. Add the onions to the pan, season lightly with salt, and cook until beginning to caramelize, 12 to 15 minutes.

Return the squab and any accumulated juices to the pan. Add the flour, stir to coat the squab evenly, then add the duck stock. Bring to a simmer over medium heat, cover, reduce the heat to low, and cook until the meat starts to pull away from the bone and the onions are cooked down to a jammy consistency, 30 to 40 minutes.

Remove the squab and set aside until cool enough to handle, then pull the meat off the bones (discard the bones). Return the meat to the pan and increase the heat to medium. Reduce the gravy until it has a volume of about 3 cups and the liquid coats the back of a spoon like velvet, 10 to 15 minutes. Taste for seasoning, adjusting as necessary. Set aside off the heat.

MAKE THE FRITES: Preheat the oven to 250°F.

Drain the potatoes, pat them dry, and set on paper towels. Pour about 5 inches of canola oil into a countertop fryer, Dutch oven, or large heavy-bottomed pot with a thermometer clipped to the side. Bring the oil to 220°F over medium-high heat.

Working in batches, add the potatoes to the oil and fry until just cooked through and translucent, about 5 minutes. Transfer the potatoes to a baking sheet lined with paper towels to drain, arranging them in an even layer.

Bring the oil up to 400°F. Again working in batches, fry the potatoes a second time, this time until golden brown, 5 to 6 minutes. One minute before the frites are finished, add half of the rosemary and half of the savory. Remove the frites to a baking sheet lined with paper towels and set aside in the oven to stay warm.

FOR ASSEMBLY: Cut the foie gras into 6 even steaks, each about ¾ inch thick. Heat a large sauté pan over high heat. Season the steaks with salt and sear on one side for 1½ minutes, then flip and sear on the other side for another 1½ minutes, basting them in their own rendered fat. Turn off the heat but leave the pan on the burner for 3 to 4 minutes more, to allow the foie gras to just cook through from the residual heat. The finished foie gras should have some give when touched, and feel squishy and silken, but warm all the way through when tested with a metal skewer. Transfer the

foie gras to a plate and set aside, reserving the fat in the pan.

Return the pan to high heat and crack in the egg, being careful not to rupture the yolk. Cook, undisturbed, for 3 minutes, until the white sets and the edges are crisp. Season with salt and pepper.

To serve, stir the remaining savory and rosemary into the gravy. In a large serving bowl, arrange a layer of frites. Place

2 heaping dollops of d'Affinois cheese on top of the frites, one-third of the gravy, and 2 pieces of seared foie gras. Add a second layer of frites, cheese, gravy, and 2 pieces of foie gras on top of that. Build a third and final layer of frites, cheese, gravy, and foie gras, topping the pile with the duck egg and spooning any remaining gravy over the top. Serve immediately, and call your cardiologist in the morning.

**BONE MARROW-BOURBON
CRÈME BRÛLÉE** *(page 64)*

BONE MARROW–BOURBON CRÈME BRÛLÉE has become one of the most iconic dishes on the menu at the Beatrice. I came up with the idea when I was preparing for my first dinner at the James Beard House in 2015. I was so excited to be invited to cook there. I smuggled in kilos of illegal beef from Europe, hidden under sweaters in suitcases hand-carried by my friends running the risk of customs detention and imprisonment, all so I could cook something special. But what I didn't know is that no one would remember that heroic effort—and the defiance of mad cow disease warnings—because all anyone could talk about was the crème brûlée: Beef, bourbon, vanilla, sugar, and salt, served inside a hollowed-out bone that you can pick up with your hands and lick if you're quite keen. I mean, if ever there was a mic drop of a dish, this is it.

Since then, it has been cooed over by Pete Wells, "borrowed" by the chefs at Hawksmoor in London and put into their cookbook (they misspelled my name), and has consistently sold out every night at this restaurant. It is one of the dishes that no matter what else I make, I will always be tremendously proud of.

Presentation aside, the dish is a fairly traditional, beautifully silken crème brûlée with the addition of rendered bone marrow, which adds an unmistakable animal quality. It's a little bit familiar and a little bit weird all at once, which makes it perfect.

To serve it as I do, you need marrow bone cut into pipes (see Notes), which you use first for rendering the marrow for the custard and then empty for serving. This dish is a baller move, so if I am being honest, you should do it right or not at all.

BONE MARROW–BOURBON
CRÈME BRÛLÉE *Serves 6*

NOTES: *Ask your butcher to cut enough marrow bones to give you six 3½-inch-long pipes.*

For this recipe, I strongly encourage you to use the gram measurements. Pastry is a funny thing, and when dealing with fats and emulsification, grams are the most exact measurement and will yield the truest results.

This recipe takes 2 days to complete due to various chilling times, so plan accordingly.

If you don't own a handheld torch to brûlé the custard, place the bones under the broiler for 5 minutes.

6 marrow bones, 3½ inches long

1 tablespoon (13 g) bourbon

5 large egg yolks, at room temperature

¼ teaspoon (1 g) kosher salt

Seeds from ½ vanilla bean

2 cups (450 g) heavy cream

½ cup (95 g) dark brown sugar

Boiling water

⅓ cup plus 2 tablespoons (84 g) sugar

Flaky sea salt, to finish

Put the bones in a large bowl with enough cold water to cover and let them soak in the refrigerator. Drain and re-cover with cold water every hour for 3 hours to purge them of any blood.

Preheat the oven to 425°F.

Arrange the marrow pipes in a single layer on a rimmed baking sheet. Roast until deep brown in color and the marrow is no longer pink, 20 to 25 minutes. Remove the bones from the oven. Pour any of the marrow that has rendered into liquid form out of the pan into a bowl. When the bones are cool enough to handle, scoop out any solid pieces of marrow into a small saucepan. Set the bones aside.

Set the saucepan over low heat and slowly melt the marrow solids in the pan until liquid, then add them to the bowl with the other rendered marrow. Strain the liquid marrow through a fine-mesh sieve into a bowl to remove any solid particles or bone fragments. Measure out 3½ tablespoons (43 g) of the rendered bone marrow and set aside. (Store any remaining rendered marrow for another use; refrigerate in an airtight container for up to 2 weeks.)

In a small saucepot, heat the bourbon over medium-high heat, carefully ignite, and swirl gently until the flames extinguish and the alcohol burns off, about 30 seconds.

In a large bowl, combine the egg yolks and reserved rendered marrow fat. Using a handheld electric mixer, beat together until fully combined. Add the kosher salt, vanilla seeds, heavy cream, and brown sugar and beat until smooth and pale yellow in color. Refrigerate overnight or for up to 2 days to chill.

Preheat the oven to 300°F.

Pour the chilled custard into a medium baking dish and place neatly inside a larger baking dish. Pour boiling water into the larger baking dish to come up to the level of the custard in the smaller dish. Cover the whole thing with foil. Bake until the custard is set around the edges but quivers when gently shaken, 30 to 40 minutes. Remove the custard from the water bath and let sit at room temperature for 20 minutes to rest, then transfer to the refrigerator overnight to set.

To serve, transfer the custard to a pastry bag and pipe it into the marrow bones. Sprinkle the sugar evenly on top of the custard. Use a handheld torch to toast until golden brown. Finish with flaky sea salt.

SMOKED MANHATTAN *Makes 1 cocktail*

—ANTANAS SAMKUS, BAR DIRECTOR

"Obviously, we did not invent the Manhattan. The recipe we use is
from cocktail pioneer Jerry Thomas from over 125 years ago, so
it's very classic, although we do have a few tricks that make it ours,
primarily surrounding the presentation. Chef went to London and
came back with all of these beautiful antique silver plates and crystal
cake stands and cloches and asked me to come up with a creative way
to use them at the bar. I decided to fill the crystal with wood smoke
and put a drink on a silver platter beneath it, surrounded by a bed
of rosemary and thyme, like some shamanic ritual from the woods.
When we serve it, it's a show for all of your senses. You can just make
the drink, of course, but why miss out on the drama?"

2 ounces overproof rye whiskey

1 ounce Antica Formula Sweet Vermouth

¼ ounce Grand Marnier

3 dashes of Angostura bitters

1 dash of orange bitters

Ice

3 maraschino cherries sprayed with Laphroaig Islay Scotch, for garnish

1 bunch rosemary, for serving

1 bunch thyme, for serving

Cherrywood chips, for smoking

NOTE: *You will need a handheld smoking gun (see page 293) for this recipe.*

Combine the whiskey, vermouth, Grand Marnier, both bitters, and ice in a cocktail shaker. Shake hard for 30 seconds. Strain into a chilled rocks glass with one large ice cube. Garnish with the maraschino cherries.

Place the glass on a platter and arrange the herbs around it. Cover the platter with a cloche and, using a smoking gun, fill the chamber with cherrywood smoke. Open the cloche as you serve the drink so the aromatic smoke wafts out in dramatic fashion.

I LOVE TARTE TATIN, but instead of using the traditional apple or pear, I reach for quince in the winter months, which I believe to be one of the sexiest sorts of produce to exist. This rare fruit must be cooked to be consumed and I love the way it turns from ecru when raw to a deep reddish-blush color when poached, finally taking on a beautiful deep crimson hue upon baking. Quince is sweet, but still has a tartness, so the effect isn't cloying.

I don't bother peeling the fruit because I like the rusticity of the skin, which, as it cooks, caramelizes into candy-like bits that stick to your teeth. When the *New York Times* writer Tejal Rao tasted this dish, she told me a story about Mary, Queen of Scots "cooking" candied quince in her faux kitchen to impress guests (of course, her staff did the actual work). As someone who's always been fascinated by historical references in food, I love this story and am grateful to Tejal for sharing it with me, as it has entertained countless dinner guests of my own since.

At the restaurant, we like to turn the pastry out onto a platter, top it with vanilla ice cream, and flambé Calvados to pour over everything. The dramatic presentation is recommended but not strictly necessary if you're less fond of playing with fire.

QUINCE TARTE TATIN *Serves 6*

1 (750 ml) bottle white wine, such as Chardonnay

¾ cup (157 g) Calvados

18 ounces (522 g) honey

2½ cups (500 g) plus 3 tablespoons plus ½ teaspoon (42 g) sugar

1 teaspoon (2 g) juniper berries

1 vanilla bean, split

1 cup (236 g) maraschino cherry liquid (optional)

1 teaspoon (3 g) kosher salt

6 quince

2½ tablespoons (34 g) unsalted butter

1 sheet store-bought puff pastry, trimmed into a 10-inch round

Vanilla ice cream, for serving

2 cups (320 g) crème fraîche, for serving

NOTE: *Leftover poaching liquid can be used to store leftover quince, to poach other fruits in, reduced into a syrup for use in a cocktail, or discarded.*

In a large pot, combine the wine, Calvados, 6 cups water, the honey, 2½ cups of the sugar, the juniper, vanilla, maraschino cherry liquid (if using), and salt and bring to a boil over high heat.

Add the whole quince to the boiling liquid and reduce the heat to medium-low. Cover with a cartouche (see page 293) and simmer until the fruit has turned a pinkish-blush color and is just knife-tender, 35 to 45 minutes. Remove the pot from the heat and let the quince rest in the poaching liquid until cool enough to handle.

Preheat the oven to 400°F.

Halve the quince lengthwise, leaving the seeds and skin intact.

In a 10-inch ovenproof skillet, combine the remaining 3 tablespoons plus ½ teaspoon sugar, the butter, and 4 tablespoons of the reserved poaching liquid. Set over medium-high heat and swirl the pan to combine—do not stir, as stirred sugar crystallizes. The caramel will bubble and brown; keep swirling to achieve an even color, until the caramel is a deep, burnished copper, 5 to 7 minutes.

Remove the skillet from the heat. Place one quince half cut-side down in the center of the pan, and surround it with the remaining quince halves, also cut-side down, as tightly as they can fit.

Return the pan to medium heat and continue to cook, undisturbed, until the quince begins to caramelize slightly and turns to deep red, 8 to 10 minutes. The caramel will bubble up around the quince and meld the fruit into a cohesive mass.

Remove the skillet from the heat and place the puff pastry over it. Trim any excess dough (there should be no overhang, and it should fit just inside the walls of the skillet). Prick a few holes in the pastry using the tines of a fork.

Transfer to the oven and bake, rotating front to back once halfway through, until the puff pastry is a deep golden brown and the caramel is incredibly fragrant, 20 to 22 minutes.

Remove the pan from the oven. Immediately cover the pan with your serving platter and flip out the tarte Tatin.

It's difficult to cut this sticky Tatin into individual pieces, which also ruins its beautiful appearance, so I like to serve it in the middle of the table with several spoons for guests to dig in at will, and bowls of vanilla ice cream and crème fraîche alongside.

I CRAVE CAVIAR at all waking hours, and while there's a time and place for traditional service with chopped eggs, blini, and crème fraîche, what I truly love is the taste of naked caviar in its purest form. At the Bea, we work hard to source the highest-quality caviar (usually kaluga or sturgeon from American Caviar Co.) that it would almost be a shame to dilute the pleasure of eating it by serving it with too many accoutrements. So I am adamant that when we serve caviar it come only with sliced brioche (cut into triangles, as it's a belief of mine that luxurious food tastes better in triangle form) that's been toasted in beef drippings and butter. It's the perfect way to start an evening—or to end one, preferably with a glass of your favorite Champagne in hand.

A SNACK OF
CAVIAR AND BRIOCHE *Serves 6*

8 ounces (226 g) unsalted butter

¾ cup (144 g) Rendered Bone Marrow (page 284)

6 slices (1½-inch) brioche

3 ounces caviar (or as much as you can eat)

In a large sauté pan, melt 4 ounces of the butter and half of the rendered bone marrow over medium heat until frothing. Add half of the brioche to the pan, being sure not to splatter the fat, and toast, turning once, until golden brown, about 2 minutes per side. Set aside on a paper towel to drain. Wipe the pan clean and repeat with the remaining butter, rendered bone marrow, and brioche.

Cut the toasted brioche into triangles and arrange on a platter. Serve the caviar in a small dish in the middle, with a small mother-of-pearl spoon.

WHEN I BOUGHT THE BEA, I wanted to cook the food that spoke truest to me, and that meant no cooked fish, no vegetables, and absolutely no chicken under any circumstances. It was a new chapter for me and for the Bea, though, so I decided on a policy of "zero fucks given" for 90 percent of the menu, and the 10 percent of the menu that had to be more "pedestrian" would be done tongue in cheek. That means refusing to call this dish chicken and using the beautiful Bresse breed from France. They're a bit gamey in flavor, with darker meat throughout.

There's a classic French recipe called *poulet roti grand-mère*, grandmother-style roast chicken, a light roast that yields no color, with glazed and perfectly turned pearl onions, mushrooms, potatoes, and lardons. As much as I adore that dish, I knew I would rather do something that was the antithesis of classic. Hence, *poulet petite fille:* the rebellious rock-and-roll granddaughter hen. It has a dark sauce and big flavors, and I like to serve it claw-on for maximum visual shock.

POULET PETITE FILLE

WITH CHERRIES, TRUFFLES, AND VANILLA   *Serves 2*

1 whole chicken (3½ pounds/ 1.6 kg)

3 tablespoons (43 g) Truffle Butter (page 273)

1 bunch thyme

1 bunch savory

5 bay leaves

¼ cup (54 g) extra-virgin olive oil

Kosher salt

1½ cups (214 g) Bing cherries, pitted

1½ vanilla beans, split lengthwise

1 cup plus 3 tablespoons (249 g) Chicken Stock (page 283)

4 ounces (110 g) butter, cubed

Périgord truffles, for serving

Preheat the oven to 425°F.

Starting at the top of the bird, near the neck where the skin is already broken, use your fingers to gently separate the skin from the breast meat. Rub the breast meat with the truffle butter as evenly as possible, being careful not to tear the skin. Stuff the thyme, savory, and 2 of the bay leaves under the skin as well. Truss with butcher's twine, then rub the bird evenly over the skin with olive oil and season all over with salt.

Place the bird in a large heavy-bottomed ovenproof skillet, transfer to the oven, and roast until the juices run clear when poked and a thermometer inserted in the thickest part of the breast reads 155°F, 50 to 60 minutes. Transfer the bird to a plate to rest. Don't wash the skillet.

Place the skillet from the chicken over high heat. Add the cherries, the remaining 3 bay leaves, and the vanilla beans and cook until the cherries are blistered and shiny and their skins begin to burst, 3 to 4 minutes. Be careful to not overcook. Using a slotted spoon, transfer the cherries to a plate.

Pour off the fat from the skillet and return it to high heat. Add the chicken stock, bring to a simmer, and deglaze the pan, scraping up any browned bits from the bottom. Reduce the heat to medium-high and cook until the liquid is reduced by two-thirds, 5 to 6 minutes. You should have a rich, dark sauce with a beautiful mahogany color. Turn off the burner. Whisk in the butter until emulsified, to thicken the sauce and give it a lustrous sheen.

Return the bird to the sauce, along with the cherries and vanilla beans. Serve directly out of the skillet, shaving Périgord truffles over the top.

**VENISON WELLINGTON WITH
ESCARGOTS, WILD MUSHROOMS,
AND BLACK CURRANT JAM**

(page 76)

FOR AS MUCH as I love beef, I consider filet a bit of a shameful cut. It just doesn't have enough fat or flavor for me, which isn't surprising, as it's a muscle that isn't worked that much. It's great when eaten raw for tartare or carpaccio, but otherwise, I don't have much use for beef filet.

But venison loin is another story. In the winter, when Pat LaFrieda comes home with these kills, it's great for us—we break down the whole deer and use it for pies (see page 208), braises, and cassoulets (see page 88); but one of the first things I always make is a Wellington out of the tenderloin. Venison's flavor is delicate and sweet and I think this is the best way to highlight the animal.

I love serving this alongside a chilled black currant jam. Having a beautiful medium-rare piece of meat wrapped in a hot flaky crust with the earthiness of mushrooms is enhanced only by a bite of chilled jam for contrast in flavor, texture, and temperature. The sweetness and acidity of the jam cuts through the richness, providing balance to a luxurious dish.

VENISON WELLINGTON
WITH ESCARGOTS, WILD MUSHROOMS, AND BLACK CURRANT JAM   *Serves 4*

BLACK CURRANT JAM

6½ cups (1 kg) fresh black currants

1¼ cups (250 g) sugar

½ teaspoon (1.5 g) kosher salt

Juice of 1 lemon

DUXELLES

4¾ ounces (133 g) unsalted butter

½ cup (65 g) finely chopped Spanish onion

12 ounces (335 g) black trumpet mushrooms (5 loose cups), finely chopped

3 ounces (85 g) finely chopped escargots (about 1 cup)

2 tablespoons (6 g) finely chopped black truffle

1 tablespoon (8 g) finely chopped fresh thyme leaves

½ cup (121 g) white wine, such as Chardonnay

½ teaspoon (3 g) truffle salt

1 teaspoon (3 g) kosher salt

1 tablespoon plus 2 teaspoons (23 g) truffle oil

VENISON

13 ounces (385 g) venison loin, cold

Kosher salt

2 tablespoons (27 g) extra-virgin olive oil

Flour, for dusting

½ recipe 50/50 Dough (page 277)

2 eggs, beaten

NOTES: *The duxelles are best made 1 day in advance, so plan accordingly.*

The black currant jam must be chilled in the refrigerator to set for a minimum of 3 hours, or ideally overnight, but can be stored for up to 3 days.

MAKE THE BLACK CURRANT JAM:
In a heavy-bottomed medium
pot, combine the black currants,
sugar, and salt. Clip a candy
thermometer to the side and bring
to a boil over medium-high heat.
Constantly stir until the berries
have started to burst and release
their juices, about 10 minutes.
Increase the heat to high and bring
to 104°F, 2 to 3 minutes more.
Squeeze in the lemon juice and
boil at 104°F for 2 minutes.

Remove from the heat and strain
well through a fine-mesh sieve
into a small bowl, using a ladle
to push down all of the solids,
extracting all of the juice. There
should be no solids whatsoever
in this mixture—this is intended
to be a clear, beautifully wobbly
jam. Refrigerate the jam until set,
a minimum of 3 hours, or ideally
overnight.

MAKE THE DUXELLES: In a large
sauté pan, melt the butter over
medium heat. Add the onion and
sauté until translucent and just
barely colored around the edges,

8 to 10 minutes. Add the black
trumpets, escargots, truffle, and
thyme and cook until soft and
fragrant, 8 to 10 minutes. Add
the white wine to deglaze the
pan, scraping up any browned
bits from the bottom. Continue
to cook until all of the liquid
from the wine and mushrooms
has evaporated, 5 to 6 minutes.
Season with the truffle salt and
kosher salt. Transfer the mixture
to a food processor and pulse to a
rough chop while streaming in the
truffle oil. Transfer to a bowl and
chill until cool, at least 3 hours, or
ideally overnight.

ON THE DAY OF SERVING:
Preheat the oven to 375°F. Line
a baking sheet with parchment
paper.

Season the venison on all sides
with salt. In a large sauté pan,
heat the olive oil over high until
shimmering. Sear the venison on
all sides until just golden brown,
about 10 minutes. Remove the loin
to a plate.

On a clean floured board, roll
out the dough to a rectangle
large enough to wrap the loin,
about 13 × 15 inches and ¼ inch
thick. Spread the chilled duxelles
mixture over the surface, leaving
a 1-inch border uncovered on
all sides. Place the venison loin
along a long side, on top of the
mushrooms (leaving the border
open) and roll tightly once. Fold
the edges of the dough on the ends
underneath the venison to seal.
Brush with the beaten egg and
place on the lined baking sheet.

Transfer to the oven and bake
until the pastry is golden brown
and the internal temperature of
the venison reaches 110°F, about
18 minutes. Remove the pan from
the oven and let the Wellington
rest for 10 minutes; the internal
temperature will rise to about
125°F. Cut it into 2½-inch-wide
slices and serve with the chilled
black currant jam on the side.

THIS DISH GIVES ME visions of Paul Revere riding through the night, hay and smoke perfuming the sky. It's a romantic fantasy, to be sure, but the combination of mutton that's roasted with fresh hay and herbs, velvety earthen mushrooms, and savory glacéed chestnuts tends to have that effect on my imagination. It's a period piece of a dish, and it will take you back to a time of lush whole-animal feasts.

The dish is cooked en cocotte (or in a Dutch oven) and it's fairly simple—once you sear the meat, nestle it into a nest of hay and aromatics, and add just a bit of Champagne for steam. You can sauté the mushrooms in the same pan you used to sear the meat, then make the sauce in the same pan as well. By the time that's done, the meat will have cooked through to a stunning medium-rare. I cannot overemphasize how magical this dish is when paired with Madeira, the fortified wine our country's forefathers drank generations ago.

MUTTON BLADE CHOP
WITH CANDIED CHESTNUTS AND CHANTERELLE CREAM   *Serves 2 to 3*

CANDIED CHESTNUTS

1¾ cups (367 g) Chicken Stock (page 283)

Scant 1 cup (193 g) sugar

2 teaspoons (5 g) kosher salt

1 pound (456 g) peeled chestnuts (about 3 cups)

1 bunch thyme

MUTTON

1 (2½-pound/1.125 kg) bone-in mutton blade chop

2 cups (22 g) hay

1 bunch oregano

1 bunch thyme

1 bunch rosemary

3 tablespoons (42 g) extra-virgin olive oil

Kosher salt

2 heads garlic, scalped (see page 293)

1 cup (193 g) Champagne

CHANTERELLE CREAM

4 ounces (112 g) chanterelles (about 2 cups)

Kosher salt

1 tablespoon (3 g) chopped fresh savory

¼ cup (50 g) Champagne

½ cup (105 g) Chicken Stock (page 283)

¾ cup (169 g) heavy cream

1 tablespoon (14 g) unsalted butter

1 teaspoon (5 g) chopped fresh parsley

NOTES: *The chestnuts can be made several days in advance. In winter, I like to make extra and always have some on hand to dress meats.*

Cooking in hay adds a layer to this dish—it's not so much a barnyard funk, but rather a sweet, musty flavor. The best hay for cooking, believe it or not, comes in sterilized bags at the pet store.

MAKE THE CANDIED CHESTNUTS: In a small saucepan, combine the chicken stock, sugar, and salt and bring to a boil over high heat. Add the chestnuts and thyme and simmer, swirling the pot occasionally, until the chestnuts are tender, about 15 minutes. Transfer to a small bowl to let the chestnuts cool in their liquid.

MEANWHILE, PREPARE THE MUTTON: Tie the blade chop with twine to hold its shape and allow to sit at room temperature for at least 30 minutes before cooking. In a cocotte or large Dutch oven, build a nest of rustically intertwined hay, oregano, thyme, and rosemary.

Preheat the oven to 425°F.

In a large sauté pan, heat the olive oil over high heat. Season the mutton chop all over with salt. Add it to the pan and sear on all sides, turning until a deep golden brown, 8 to 10 minutes. Transfer the mutton to the nest of hay and herbs.

Return the sauté pan to medium heat. Add the garlic and sear the scalped ends until golden brown, 1 to 2 minutes. Transfer the garlic to the nest with the mutton. (Set the sauté pan aside without washing it.) Add the Champagne to the cocotte, cover, and transfer to the oven. Roast to medium-rare (a thermometer inserted in the center should read 120°F), 12 to 15 minutes. Remove the cocotte from the oven and let the meat rest with the lid on.

MEANWHILE, MAKE THE CHANTERELLE CREAM: Return the sauté pan to medium-high heat. Add the chanterelles and sauté until golden, 1 to 2 minutes. The chanterelles will absorb flavor from the pan, so they will only need a light seasoning with salt if any at all. Add the savory and stir to combine until fragrant, a few seconds. Pour off most of the fat from the pan, leaving the mushrooms in the pan.

Add the Champagne to the pan off the heat and use a spatula to scrape up the browned bits from the bottom of the pan. Return the pan to medium-high heat and cook until the liquid is reduced by half, 1 to 2 minutes. Add the stock and cook until reduced by half, about 3 minutes, then stir in the cream and candied chestnuts (drained of their liquid before adding). Simmer until the sauce thickens and coats the back of a spoon, 3 to 5 minutes.

Add the butter and swirl the pan to emulsify it until the sauce thickens and takes on a beautiful gloss, 1 to 2 minutes. Stir in the parsley. Transfer to a serving bowl.

Serve the mutton in the cocotte with a carving knife and fork and the sauce in a bowl alongside.

BUYING THE BEATRICE

IN THE SPRING/SUMMER of 2013, I was running the kitchen of the Spotted Pig, a popular West Village gastropub. The hours were long, I didn't particularly like the kitchen culture or anyone who worked there, but I was putting in my time, learning what I could, making my contacts, and building a résumé. I only knew the Beatrice Inn as a restaurant that was down the street—I had never been there, I hadn't read its recent zero-star *New York Times* review, and I sure as hell never even had an inkling of a dream that the restaurant would one day be my own.

I received a call one day from my friend Peter Pavia. We had worked together, and he had fast become one of my favorite people—a cranky, charismatic, quick-witted, and very old-school bartender. He let me know that the owners of the Beatrice were looking for a new head chef, so I went in to do a tasting. I made the milk-braised pork shoulder, *boudin noir*, a burger, and the chicken liver pâté—dishes I knew were irrevocably mine. I got offered the job, but turned it down, as I was not yet ready to take the leap. For two months, the owners called me, and for two months, I kept turning them down. It wasn't until a conversation with my friend and mentor, Pat LaFrieda, that I finally changed my mind.

Fast-forward: I had been executive chef for a year and a half when the Bea's then-owner and the then editor in chief of *Vanity Fair*, Graydon Carter, and his partners came to me with the proposition for purchasing the Bea. I thought they were insane. Although I had made some great improvements, the restaurant was still not functioning at the level I wanted it to. I had been thinking of leaving—I was again putting in my time, and felt just about ready to begin to pave the road to owning my own business. Graydon and his partners wanted out, but they wanted the restaurant in the hands of someone who would love it as they had, who would care for it and do right by it. I called Pat once again for advice, who, without skipping a beat, told me I had to buy it. I called my father and spoke to him at length. He warned me that owning a restaurant would be hard, but that if I was going to do it, I had his support.

Neither my cousin Melissa nor I come from a lot of money, but we both had comfortable childhoods, spending summers together in Seattle. We both moved to New York in our twenties, struggled to make ends meet as all New York transplants do, and were now coming into our careers, me in restaurants, and her in public relations. When I met her for coffee one afternoon, I hadn't been planning to ask her to partner with me; we were just overdue for a catch-up.

I MENTIONED TO HER THAT I WAS THINKING OF BUYING THE BEATRICE, AND BEFORE I COULD EVEN FINISH THE STORY, SHE SCREAMED, "LET'S DO IT! OUR PARENTS WILL BE SO PROUD OF US!"

Our partnership was born. We scraped together money, hired attorneys, plotted over wine and cigarettes, and negotiated a shrewd deal for ourselves. We were doing what our parents had always said to do: If you make money, you make it for the family. If you start a business, you start it with the family. You protect each other and stick together, always.

Nearly a year later, we sat in my general attorney's office in midtown Manhattan, in the 47th-floor boardroom, looking out over the city and an impending storm. The date was April 8,

2016—Melissa and I had been adamant about closing on the 8th, as in Chinese culture eight is the luckiest number. We insisted the purchase be made quietly, not even telling our friends or regular customers, only letting our closest family know. I wanted to operate as per usual, and give myself time to get my ownership sea legs, since I knew that as soon as the story broke, it would send shock waves through the restaurant community. More important to me, I knew that as soon as the news went public, the *New York Times* would want to re-review us and I only wanted that attention once I was actually ready for it. I needed to change the menu, change the service, and get out of the headspace that I had been in for the past two and a half years. I had been making food the owners wanted on the menu. Now, it was time to figure out who I was, and what my vision would be for the next chapter of the Beatrice. And so we said nothing.

Of course, there was a catch. Most people would have purchased the restaurant and shut it down immediately to get themselves sorted; I, however, did not. We had spent all our money purchasing the restaurant and we needed the income to pay the rent while we planned for our revamp. In order to do that, I needed an operational liquor license, and in order to obtain one of those, I had to have a bill of sale for the restaurant. So there we sat: me, Melissa, our attorney, and the current owners of the Beatrice. My liquor attorney was patiently awaiting my arrival in Harlem, holding our place in line at the State Liquor Authority's office, with a stack of paperwork on deck for me to complete.

Before the ink was even dry on the purchase agreement, I bolted out onto 47th Street into the torrential rain to hail a cab. Racing to Harlem, I felt emotional: exhilarated and terrified all at once. I had just done something arguably insane. As my cab pulled up on Frederick Douglass Boulevard, I ran into the rain, shielding the paperwork as best I could, but when I entered the lobby of the building, my heart sank—my liquor attorney had given me the wrong address. I rang her, got the correct address, and did it all again, all the while cursing Mother Nature. I finally arrived at the window, three minutes before the SLA office closed, dripping wet and panting. Thankfully, nothing else went wrong.

License in hand, I ran back downtown so we could open our doors for service that evening. As I entered the restaurant, beaming, the entire staff was banging pots and pans as if it were a wedding, and I burst into tears—Melissa and I had purchased a piece of New York history.

SAVAGE BEAUTY *Makes 1 cocktail*

—ANTANAS SAMKUS, BAR DIRECTOR

"A classic Vesper is made of gin, vodka, and Lillet. It's what James Bond infamously orders as 'shaken, not stirred.' I wanted to make something that retained those floral, fragrant elements, but with more interesting ingredients. I use Hophead—hops-infused vodka—which has a nice, sweet, almost grassy taste, combined with ESP Noho gin, which has saffron, cardamom, and orange flavors. The gin gives this Vesper a mesmerizing golden-green hue, and there's a lot going on in each sip with all of those different fragrances and botanical flavors. Chef gave me the idea to garnish this with a flower blossom, and we named it in homage to the final collection of one of her favorite fashion designers, Alexander McQueen."

2 ounces Hophead vodka

¾ ounce ESP Noho gin

¾ ounce Mancino Bianco Ambrato vermouth

2 dashes of lemon bitters

Ice cubes

White ranunculus blossom, for garnish

Combine the vodka, gin, vermouth, lemon bitters, and ice in a shaker and stir. Strain into a coupe glass. Garnish with a ranunculus blossom.

I TYPICALLY SPEND a month each year in Europe, binge-eating squab at the River Café and St. John Bread and Wine and gorging myself on whole roasted bird, served with only a knife to assist me in tearing it apart.

At the Bea, we've taken the idea of whole squab and decided to vine-roast it with Pinot Meunier vines from France, which I discovered while cooking in London a few years ago. At home, you can achieve a similar effect with cold-smoking. What I love about these vines is that they arrive all twisted and beautiful, and when you light them on fire, they burn very hot, fragrant, and the brightest white. If you can't find Pinot Meunier vines, cherrywood or applewood are good substitutes, though it's worth asking local vineyards near you if you might have access to some of their vine clippings.

VINE-ROASTED SQUAB
WITH APPLES AND JUS   *Serves 6*

NOTES: *The squab take 3 days to cure, so plan accordingly.*

You will need a handheld smoking gun (see page 293) for this recipe.

Lady apples are a small, sweet-tart variety that I like to cook whole. You can substitute Honeycrisps, cut into wedges, if you cannot find Ladies.

CURED SQUAB

6 whole squab (8 to 10 ounces/225 to 280 g each)

½ cup plus 2 tablespoons (125 g) granulated sugar

7 tablespoons (82 g) dark brown sugar

5 tablespoons (44 g) kosher salt

2¼ teaspoons (20 g) pink curing salt (see page 292)

¾ teaspoon (6 g) smoked salt

2 tablespoons (12 g) juniper berries

JUS

Reserved squab necks

5 quarts (3.36 kg) Duck Stock (page 283), cold

FOR SMOKING AND ROASTING

¼ cup Pinot Meunier vines or cherrywood or applewood chips, for smoking

2 bunches thyme

2 bunches savory

APPLES

2 tablespoons (34 g) duck fat

10 ounces (290 g) lady apples (about 18 apples), whole and unpeeled

4½ tablespoons (64 g) unsalted butter

1 cup plus 3 tablespoons (237 g) granulated sugar

2 teaspoons (5 g) kosher salt

1 cup plus 3 tablespoons (249 g) Duck Stock (page 283)

Recipe continues »

CURE THE SQUAB: Remove the necks from the birds. Reserve the necks and refrigerate (they are used later to make the jus). In a large bowl, combine the granulated sugar, brown sugar, kosher salt, curing salt, smoked salt, and juniper berries. Divide the cure evenly among the 6 birds, rubbing them all over the outside and inside the cavity. Place the birds in an airtight container and refrigerate for 3 days to cure them, flipping them halfway through.

MAKE THE SQUAB JUS: Place the reserved squab necks in a dry large pot over medium-high heat. Cook, turning, until deep golden brown on all sides, about 10 minutes. Add the duck stock, bring to a boil, then reduce the heat to medium and cook until the liquid is reduced by three-quarters and becomes glossy, about 1 hour. Strain the solids and discard. The jus can be made 1 day in advance.

On the day of serving, position racks in the upper and lower thirds of the oven and preheat to 320°F. Fill a large baking dish with 2 inches water and place it on the lower rack of the oven as it's preheating.

PREPARE TO SMOKE AND ROAST: Remove the birds from their cure and shake off any excess. Cold-smoke (see page 293) with vine clippings or wood chips for 20 minutes, until the meat has absorbed the smoky flavor.

Stuff each squab with equal portions of thyme and savory, and truss them.

Place the squab on a wire rack set on top of a rimmed baking sheet. Place on the upper oven rack, above the baking dish with water (since the squab is cured, almost like a ham, it's important that it cook with some moisture). Roast until hot all the way through, about 125°F when pierced in the deepest part of the breast, 15 to 20 minutes. Remove and set aside to rest for 5 to 10 minutes.

MEANWHILE, PREPARE THE APPLES: In a large sauté pan, melt the duck fat over medium-high heat. Add the apples and cook, turning, until golden and blistered, 6 to 8 minutes. Add the butter, swirling the pan to melt it, then add the sugar and salt. Continue to swirl the pan as the sugar melts to create a golden-brown caramel, 5 to 6 minutes. Swirl in the duck stock. Reduce the heat to medium and continue to cook the apples until they're just barely fork-tender, about 15 minutes.

Arrange the rested squab on a platter along with the apples, and spoon about 1 cup of the jus over the squab just before serving. Serve extra jus in a small bowl alongside.

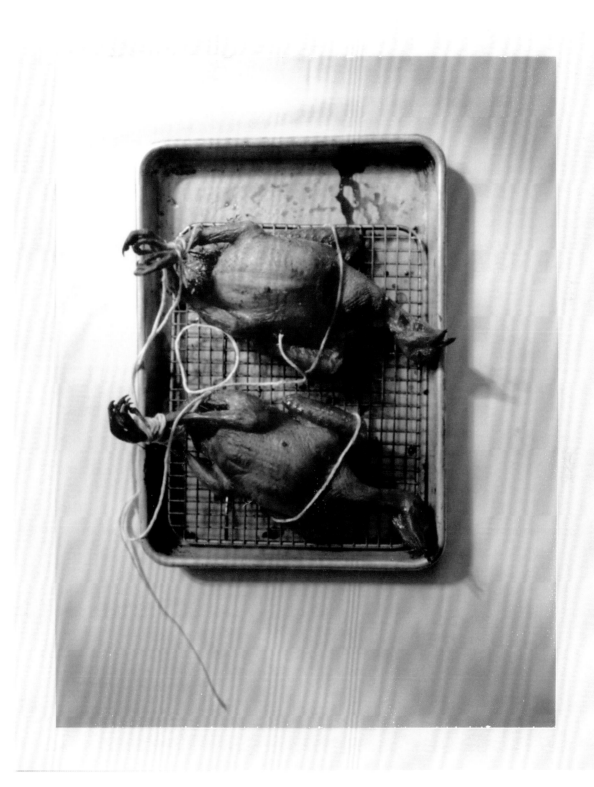

ONE OF THE THINGS I most look forward to in autumn and winter is hunting season, because I know that when Pat LaFrieda is hunting, I will be lucky enough to receive the first deer of the season. Typically, meat deliveries happen at the Bea early in the morning before most people are out and about. So one day when Pat told me he had a gift for me, I was incredibly excited for my early-morning venison. I waited all morning—all day—but to no avail. Finally, at about 4:30 in the afternoon, the delivery driver said, "Chef, you need to come outside, I can't bring in this whole thing by myself." When I walked up the stairs and onto West 12th Street, I found a giant 8-point buck, lying on a wooden pallet—on display for the whole neighborhood.

It required five grown men and over an hour to carry it inside, the whole time during which I feared a concerned neighbor was going to call the U.S. Fish & Wildlife Service about the giant dead deer on their block. When that (thankfully) didn't happen, with my new friend safely inside, I immediately got to work breaking it down, fantasizing about all of the beautiful things I could make with this gift. That's how I found myself at this cassoulet, which Pete Wells ate the weekend he came in to review us for the *New York Times*. This is the recipe I served him. Today, I have that deer's head hanging in the foyer of my apartment.

VENISON CASSOULET
WITH BOUDIN NOIR AND ANCHOVY-BONE MARROW CRUMBS *Serves 6 to 8*

NOTE: *Venison is available from D'Artagnan.*

3½ cups (642 g) dried cannellini beans

1 (1-pound/453 g) beef shank, trussed

1 pound (453 g) boneless pork shoulder, cut into 4 pieces

1½ pounds (661 g) venison shoulder, cut into 6 pieces

Kosher salt

6 ounces (174 g) bacon, cut into 1-inch pieces (1 cup)

1 cup (127 g) diced Spanish onion (about ½ large)

5 garlic cloves, smashed

2 bay leaves

1 bunch thyme, tied with string

1 (750 ml) bottle white wine, such as Chardonnay

4 cups (840 g) Chicken Stock (page 283)

3 links (522 g) Boudin Noir (page 166)

ANCHOVY BREADCRUMBS

7½ ounces (209 g) unsalted butter

¾ cup (180 g) extra-virgin olive oil

6 loose cups (172 g) brioche innards, hand-torn into 2- to 3-inch pieces

⅓ cup (61 g) finely chopped anchovy fillets (about 14)

2 tablespoons (10 g) finely chopped fresh parsley

Kosher salt

Place the beans in a bowl and add hot water to cover by 2 inches and set aside to soak. Season the beef shank, pork shoulder, and venison all over with salt.

Preheat the oven to 325°F.

In a large Dutch oven or heavy-bottomed pot, cook the bacon over medium heat until golden brown but not crisp and the fat has rendered, 5 to 6 minutes. Set the bacon aside, reserving the rendered fat in the pot. Increase the heat to medium-high. Working in batches, add the beef shank, pork shoulder, and venison and brown, turning, on all sides, 8 to 10 minutes per batch. Set the meat aside with the bacon, and reserve all of the accumulated fat in the pot.

Reduce the heat to medium. Add the onion and garlic to the pot and cook, stirring occasionally, until the onions are translucent and the garlic is blistered and golden, 3 to 5 minutes. Add the bay leaves and thyme and cook, stirring, until fragrant, 1 to 2 minutes.

Increase the heat to high and add the white wine to deglaze the pan, scraping up any browned bits from the bottom. Add the cannellini beans and their soaking water. Arrange the beans in an even layer on the bottom of the pan. Return the bacon and all the meats to the pot, along with any accumulated juices, arranging them on top of the beans. Add the chicken stock and bring to a boil. Cover with a cartouche (see page 293), then cover with a lid.

Transfer to the oven and braise until all the meat is tender and the beans are fully plump, about 3½ hours. A layer of fat will rise to the top, helping to keep the beans down and allowing them to cook more evenly; do not skim during cooking.

Remove the pot from the oven and return it to the stove over medium heat. Using a ladle or large spoon, skim and remove as much fat as you can from the top. Remove and discard the bundle of thyme. Bring to a simmer and cook uncovered to reduce the liquid by about one-eighth, about 10 minutes; about 3 minutes in, nestle the boudin noir links in between the other meats and simmer until cooked through, 7 to 9 minutes.

MEANWHILE, MAKE THE ANCHOVY BREADCRUMBS: In a large sauté pan, melt together the butter and olive oil over medium-high heat. Add the brioche breadcrumbs to soak up all the liquid and cook, tossing, until just golden, 7 to 8 minutes. Add the anchovies and cook, continuing to swirl the pan and stir, until the bread is golden brown. Remove the pan from the heat, stir in the parsley, and season to taste with salt. Transfer the breadcrumbs to a baking sheet lined with paper towels to drain.

To serve, arrange half of the breadcrumbs on top of the cassoulet in the pot, with the other half in a small dish on the side for guests to add to taste.

SAUCE JOINVILLE is an old and somewhat obscure sauce invented by French chef and writer Auguste Escoffier, traditionally served over fish. I came across it one day when I was researching historic menus of New York, and read about the *Great Gatsby*–themed parties the Waldorf-Astoria once threw. This dish is evocative of something Salvador Dalí might have cooked. It's dark and complex, with that *jolie laide* quality—so ugly it's beautiful. This dish is best eaten with your hands and a really beautiful baguette to mop up the sauce, plus a beautiful Burgundy or Rhône wine to wash it down.

RABBIT À LA JOINVILLE   *Serves 2*

1 whole rabbit (3¾ pounds/1.7 kg), cut into 7 pieces (see Notes)

Kosher salt

4 quarts (3.5 kg) canola oil

3½ ounces (100 g) fresh porcini mushrooms, halved if large

5 tablespoons (60 g) Champagne

½ cup (105 g) Duck Stock (page 283)

3 tablespoons (42 g) unsalted butter

8 whole crayfish, purged (see Note), or 1 ounce (25 g) crayfish tail meat, picked clean

Black truffle, for shaving

1 tablespoon (3 g) roughly chopped fresh tarragon

4 tablespoons (60 g) Langoustine Butter (page 274)

NOTES: *You can break down the rabbit yourself into 4 legs, shoulder, saddle, and backstrap, or ask your butcher to do this for you.*

To purge whole crayfish: Fill a large bowl with ice water. Place the crayfish in a separate large bowl and sprinkle them with a handful of kosher salt. They will start kicking wildly. After 1 to 2 minutes, plunge the salted crayfish into the ice water and gently stir with a wooden spoon—the salt will force the crayfish to expel all of their mud. Repeat the purging process twice. Crayfish can be cooked whole in this recipe.

To confit the rabbit, season the rabbit all over with salt. Refrigerate, uncovered, for a minimum of 3 hours, or ideally overnight.

When ready to cook, preheat the oven to 300°F.

Place the rabbit in a large Dutch oven or heavy-bottomed pot and add enough canola oil to submerge completely. Cover with a cartouche (see page 293) to keep the rabbit under the oil, then cover the pot and transfer to the oven. Cook the meat until tender and the hind legs (the thickest part) start to pull away from the bone, about 4 hours. Remove the rabbit from the oven and let it cool in its oil for 2 hours. Remove the meat from the bones and set aside. Reserve the confit oil for future confits, if desired.

In a large sauté pan, heat 5 tablespoons of the confit oil over medium-high heat until just smoking. Add the rabbit and cook, turning, until browned all over, 12 to 15 minutes. Transfer the meat to a platter.

Add the porcini to the pan and sauté, stirring, until soft, about 5 minutes. Pour off any remaining fat, reserving the mushrooms in the pan. Return the pan to medium-high heat and add the Champagne to deglaze the pan, scraping up any browned bits from the bottom, about 1 minute. Add the duck stock and cook until reduced by half and sticky and viscous, 5 to 7 minutes.

Add the butter and crayfish. Swirl until the butter is melted and the crayfish are heated through, about 1 minute. Remove the pan from the heat. Shave as much black truffle as you desire (I desire a lot) into the sauce and stir in the chopped tarragon.

Return the rabbit to the pot, along with any juices that have accumulated, and use a large spoon to baste the sauce all around. Transfer to a serving platter, dollop with langoustine butter, and serve immediately.

A COLD-WEATHER dish native to the French Alps, *tartiflette* is essentially a rustic potato gratin cooked with an abundance of Reblochon cheese and melted onions. The version we make at the Beatrice involves caramelizing the onions in bone marrow to impart a beefier-than-usual flavor, swapping the Reblochon for deliciously nutty, creamy d'Affinois cheese, and adding a bit of sage to softly contrast some of these heavy flavors.

Though we serve the dish as a side at the restaurant, it could certainly stand on its own as a meal, ideally with a glass of Châteauneuf-du-Pape or a flute of Champagne to help cut through all that richness. *Tartiflette* is intended to be rustic—there's no need to fuss with peeling the potatoes—so just focus on getting the most sumptuous cheese possible.

TARTIFLETTE

WITH MARROW-ROASTED ONIONS, SAGE, AND D'AFFINOIS *Serves 2 or 3*

4 tablespoons (45 g) Rendered Bone Marrow (page 284)

1 medium onion, thinly sliced

2 teaspoons (5 g) kosher salt, plus more to taste

¾ teaspoon (5 g) sugar

6 tablespoons (72 g) white wine, such as Chardonnay

2 or 3 sprigs sage, leaves picked and cut into a chiffonade

2 medium unpeeled russet potatoes (440 g), boiled, cooled, and cut into ¼-inch slices

Freshly ground black pepper

4 tablespoons (40 g) crème fraîche

1 pound (450 g) d'Affinois cheese, at room temperature

Preheat the oven to 400°F.

In a medium sauté pan, melt the bone marrow over medium-high heat. Add the onion and salt and cook until the onion releases its liquid, 8 to 10 minutes. Stir in the sugar. As the onion begins to brown and the sugars begin to caramelize, 6 to 8 minutes, add 3 tablespoons of the wine, bring to a simmer, and deglaze the pan, scraping up any browned bits from the bottom. Cook the onion until golden and soft and the liquid is reduced by half, 4 to 6 minutes. Add the remaining 3 tablespoons wine and reduce again, scraping as necessary, until the onions are a rich brown and jammy, 4 to 6 minutes. Stir in the sage, then remove the pan from the heat.

In a large terrine or soufflé dish, spread one layer of potatoes evenly over the bottom. Season with salt and pepper to taste and spread half of the onions over the top. Add another layer of potato, then the remainder of the onions. Spread the crème fraîche across the surface. Slice the cheese in half crosswise, then cap the potato-onion mixture with both pieces of the cheese, rind side up.

Bake until golden brown and bubbling, about 20 minutes. Serve directly from the terrine.

MY MOTHER grew up bouncing between Oxford, England, and Taipei, Taiwan, and as a result, British cuisine was a natural part of our family's dinner table. Shepherd's pie is near and dear to my heart, reminding me of trips to London with my mother, who would let me eat pasties while we walked the old streets in between church and museum visits. At the time, I didn't know anything about beef suet crust, of course—I just knew British meat pies were the best thing I'd ever had the pleasure of eating. Now, I like to make this version—my version—of shepherd's pie on very cold nights, when it feels exceptionally rich and comforting.

SHORT RIB AND BEEF CHEEK PIE
WITH RED WINE GRAVY AND BONE MARROW   *Serves 8*

NOTES: *I usually make this pie with only a thick top crust, but you can roll out a thinner bottom crust for a more traditional pie as well. If you want both, make a full recipe of the dough for beef suet crust.*

The key to this dish is to make the beef filling a day in advance to give the flavors time to meld. Be sure the filling is cold before going into the dough, otherwise it will melt the crust before it even has a chance to bake.

FILLING

3 tablespoons (40 g) extra-virgin olive oil

1½ pounds (675 g) boneless short rib, cut into 2-inch cubes

1½ pounds (675 g) beef cheek, cut into 2-inch cubes

Kosher salt

½ pound (220 g) pearl onions (2 cups), peeled and trimmed

8 garlic cloves, thinly sliced

½ cup (60 g) all-purpose flour

1⅓ cups (258 g) white wine, such as Chardonnay

5 cups (950 g) Beef Stock (page 283)

1 bunch thyme

2 bay leaves

13 ounces (370 g) fingerling potatoes

ASSEMBLY

½ recipe Beef Suet Dough (page 276)

1 (3½-inch) marrow bone pipe

1 ounce (25 g) Cambozola cheese

1 egg, beaten

Flaky sea salt, for finishing

MAKE THE FILLING: Preheat the oven to 350°F.

In a large Dutch oven or heavy-bottomed pot, heat the olive oil over high heat. Season the short rib and beef cheek all over with kosher salt. Working in batches, add the meat and cook, turning, until golden, 6 to 8 minutes. Transfer the meat to a plate, leaving behind the rendered fat and oil in the pot.

Reduce the heat to medium-low and add the onions and garlic. Cook until the onions are golden brown and the garlic is blistered and golden, 8 to 10 minutes. Return the meat and any accumulated juices to the pot and stir to combine. Sprinkle the flour evenly over the mixture and toss to coat. Cook until the flour starts to brown, 3 to 4 minutes.

Increase the heat to medium-high, add the wine, bring to a simmer, and deglaze the pan, scraping up the browned bits from the bottom. Add 4 cups of the stock, the thyme, and bay leaves and bring to a boil. Cover, then transfer the pot to the oven and braise until the meat is tender and can be pulled apart with a fork, 2½ to 3 hours.

Meanwhile, in a large pot, combine the potatoes with enough cold water to cover by 1 inch and salt it like the sea. Bring to a boil over medium-high heat, then reduce the heat to medium-low and simmer until the potatoes are fork-tender, 20 to 25 minutes. Drain immediately. When the potatoes are cool enough to handle, slice them into obliques.

Remove the meat from the oven, stir the potatoes into the pot, and check for seasoning and consistency. The gravy should have reduced a great deal to thickly coat the back of a spoon, and it should have a velvety texture. If the filling seems dry, add the additional 1 cup stock to loosen it up. Cover and refrigerate the filling until well chilled, a

minimum of 4 hours, or ideally overnight.

ASSEMBLE THE PIE: Preheat the oven to 350°F.

Roll the dough into a 12-inch round ¼ inch thick. Place the marrow bone, sticking up, in the middle of a deep 9- or 10-inch pie dish and surround it with the chilled short rib mixture and all of the gravy. Dot the Cambozola evenly on top of the filling.

Cover the pie with the dough, slicing a small hole for the marrow bone to poke through. Trim any overhang and use a fork to crimp the edges, brushing liberally with the beaten egg.

Bake until the crust is golden brown, 40 to 45 minutes. Let the pie rest for 10 minutes, then sprinkle the top of the bone marrow with flaky salt and serve.

THE BEATRICE BURGER

FROM LOWBROW TO HIGH-END, the burger is probably the one true American dish—one that transcends all generations and circumstances. When I took the helm under former owner Graydon Carter, he and his partner's one condition was that I have a burger on the menu. It was a staple of his diet and meals here (and it's still one of his favorite dishes that I make). So in October 2013, one of my first orders of business was an eager phone call to Pat LaFrieda with a recipe for a burger blend that I intended to debut on the menu. It was one that I had been holding in my back pocket for quite some time, and had never shared with anyone.

When I moved to New York, my girlfriends and I were struggling to pay our rent, go to school, find a job, find a lover, but we always made supper together every Sunday at my apartment. We couldn't afford much back then, so it was generally pasta and two-dollar bottles of wine from Trader Joe's. When we could afford it, we would spring for a luxe mac and cheese: I'd braise oxtails in red wine, then pull the collagen-laden meat from its bones, reduce the braising liquid, and layer it in with cavatappi pasta, rich with Gruyère and béchamel sauce. Those are the flavors that inspired the garnish of my burger at the Beatrice Inn.

Pat worked with me for weeks on altering and improving the recipe: a little more rib eye here, a little less short rib there, a little more age, alteration after alteration. Finally, the blend became what it is today, the Birkin bag of burgers: simple, elegant, coveted, and decidedly well aged.

That's how a simple demand from Graydon Carter became the Beatrice Inn's burger. The Bea is where New York's literati and cultural luminaries come to be nourished, body and soul. Many of them are featured in the following pages, eating, drinking, and living life, as only we can do here—and with this iconic dish.

BECAUSE I FEEL THAT I OWE SO MUCH OF ITS SUCCESS TO PAT, I ASKED HIM TO JOIN ME IN SHARING THE STORY OF ITS CREATION WITH YOU:

"I'm often asked when America's burger craze will end. It's a silly question, given that the burger is part of American history, and I think it's an example of a dish that can truly portray who a chef is. It often reveals their innermost desires, thoughts, cravings, and vision. Most chefs have an idea of their own perfect burger, but diners want to see what a chef's spin on the American classic is. In a city like New York—a place where excellence is required, especially for restaurants like the Beatrice—the burger needs to flourish, change the game, stand on its own, be unique, and above all, be delicious.

A burger is the ultimate economy cut, depending on the economy of its ingredients. If it's made with the scraps and trimming of whatever is left behind from a butcher's production, it will be the cheapest food cost on the menu. But it won't taste like much, and it definitely won't do any of the things I just described. If instead it's made with special care, meticulous technique, and the perfect combination of ingredients, magic happens. A burger can be the one item that keeps a restaurant at the top of the list for diners to revisit. Customers will yearn for a great burger again and again, as their basic American comfort instinct has been satisfied.

When Angie called me in 2013, it was at the peak of the burger boom. We had been making proprietary blends with the idea that two restaurants on the same street in New York could offer two very different experiences. The Beatrice, although it had been through several owners, was our company's longest-lived client, and Angie was going to get whatever she demanded.

What she asked for was unusual in several ways. Usually, a chef and I will review the different possibilities and price points, make a few samples, and adjust from there. But Angie was giving me very specific cuts to blend based on her personal beef preferences. We made samples, tweaked the aging, and the rest is history. The ingredients are not cheap compared with other burgers, but you get an aged-steak experience at a fraction of what an aged steak would cost. I think, therefore, it's one of the best bargains in the city. It's certainly one of the most unique blends in the world, and one of my very favorites.

Anyone who doubts the Beatrice Burger's magic needs only one bite to have their mind changed. But perhaps more important, by eating this burger, we get a glimpse into Angie's heart and her vision. This one American staple has given the Beatrice an identity and the confidence that whatever Angie is cooking, we are lucky to eat."

–PAT LAFRIEDA

THE BEATRICE BURGER *Serves 6*

2 pounds (942 g) 45-day
   dry-aged rib eye, cut into
   1½-inch cubes

3 ounces (85 g) 45-day dry-aged
   sirloin, cut into 1½-inch cubes

3 ounces (85 g) chuck flap, cut
   into 1½-inch cubes

3 ounces (85 g) brisket, cut into
   1½-inch cubes

RED WINE ONIONS

½ cup (110 g) extra-virgin
   olive oil

6 medium Spanish onions, thinly
   sliced (about 12 cups)

1 bunch thyme, wrapped in a
   cheesecloth

¼ cup (52 g) sugar

2 (750 ml) bottles red wine, such
   as Cabernet Sauvignon

4 teaspoons (12 g) kosher salt

6 teaspoons (14 g) freshly ground
   black pepper

BURGERS

Kosher salt

6 brioche buns, halved
   horizontally

8½ ounces (240 g) d'Affinois
   cheese, at room temperature

NOTES: *The red wine onions can be made a day in advance, but be sure to bring them to room temperature before cooking the burgers.*

The burger patties must be chilled for at least 8 hours and up to overnight before cooking, so plan accordingly. You should cook them from a cold temperature.

I like to use a 4½-inch ring mold to form the patties—burgers are all about density, so packing the meat in a ring mold helps it keep its shape.

Toss all the meat together and freeze for 30 minutes. Grind the meat twice: first through a large die, then again through a medium die.

Divide the ground meat into 6 equal portions (7 to 8 ounces each) and form into patties 1½ inches thick. Place the patties on a parchment-lined baking sheet and refrigerate for at least 8 hours or up to overnight.

MAKE THE ONIONS: In a large heavy-bottomed pot, heat the oil over medium-low heat. Add the onions and thyme and cook, stirring occasionally, until the onions are translucent and beginning to turn golden brown, 35 to 45 minutes.

Stir in half of the sugar and continue to cook until the onions turn deeper in color, 10 minutes more. Add half of one bottle (375 ml) of red wine to deglaze the pan, scraping up any browned bits from the bottom. Continue cooking slowly, stirring occasionally, until all of the wine has evaporated, and the onions are starting to brown on the bottom, about 10 minutes. Add the second half of the bottle (another 375 ml), stir in the remaining sugar, and repeat the deglazing process. Repeat two more times until all of the wine has been used. Season

with the salt and pepper. The onions should be cooked down and very soft and jammy.

COOK THE BURGERS: Heat your grill to high (or about 500°F). Season the cold burger patties with salt and immediately place them on the hot grill. Sear on the first side for 2 minutes, then flip and sear on other side for another 2 minutes. Flip every 1½ minutes thereafter, cooking for a total of 10 to 12 minutes for medium-rare. Set aside to rest on a rack for 5 minutes, flipping the patties once halfway through.

Toast the brioche buns cut-side down on the grill. Place a patty on each bun and top each with a plentiful dollop of d'Affinois and red wine onions. Serve immediately.

TOP: MARC ACHILLES; ANGIE MAR IN THE *NEW YORK TIMES*; EVYN BLOCK, ADAM SACHS
MIDDLE: NATALEE SCOTT
BOTTOM: WHISBE

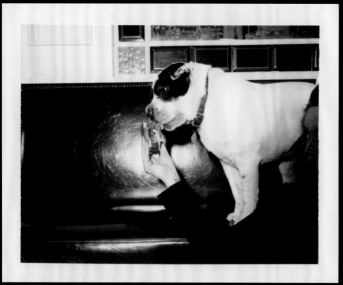

SPRING

SPRING LAMB is one of my favorite things to eat, and I love the Barnsley chop: a British cut that, in America, we call a double porterhouse. A chop like this is the perfect dinner for two, ideally served with the meat carved and the bone arranged on the platter for gnawing on. The flavors here are very much a take on a classic steak au poivre, with lamb in lieu of beef, and a fresher, more feminine twist with pink peppercorns.

BARNSLEY CHOP *Serves 2*

POACHED RHUBARB

1 (750 ml) bottle Sauternes

1 tablespoon plus 1 teaspoon maraschino cherry liquid

3⅔ cups (723 g) sugar

1 tablespoon (6 g) freshly ground black pepper

2 bay leaves

2½ stalks (251 g) rhubarb, cut into 3-inch batons

LAMB

1 (2¼-pound/1 kg) lamb chop, cut 2 inches thick

Kosher salt

2 tablespoons (27 g) olive oil

2 tablespoons (30 g) unsalted butter

1 tablespoon (5 g) lavender, picked

SAUCE

3 tablespoons (11 g) pink peppercorns

½ cup (105 g) Beef Stock (page 283)

1 tablespoon (15 g) butter

3 tablespoons (8 g) finely chopped fresh mint

2 tablespoons (30 g) Vanilla Butter (page 274), for serving

MAKE THE POACHED RHUBARB:
In a small pot, combine the
Sauternes, maraschino cherry
liquid, sugar, pepper, and bay
leaves and bring to a simmer
over medium-high heat. Turn
off the heat, leaving the pot on
the burner, and add the rhubarb.
Cover with a cartouche (see page
293) to hold the rhubarb under
the liquid. Allow it to poach in the
residual heat until just fork-tender,
10 to 15 minutes. Remove the pot
from the stove entirely and hold
the rhubarb in the poaching liquid
until ready to use, at which point
you will remove the stalks from
the liquid.

PREPARE THE LAMB CHOP:
Preheat the oven to 350°F.

Season the lamb on all sides
with salt. In a large ovenproof
sauté pan, heat the oil over high
heat. Add the lamb chop with
the fat cap down and sear on all
sides until golden brown, about
2 minutes per side. Continually
flip the lamb onto each side every
minute to ensure even cooking,
for 4 minutes total.

Transfer the pan to the oven and
roast to medium (a thermometer
inserted into the thickest part of
the lamb should read 120°F), 6 to
8 minutes.

Remove the pan from the oven
and return it to medium-high
heat. Add the butter and lavender.
The butter will melt and smell
nutty; the lavender will crackle,
releasing its fragrance. Using a
large spoon, baste the chop with
the melted butter continuously for
about 2 minutes. Place the lamb
on a rack with a plate underneath
to rest for about 10 minutes.
Reserve the fried lavender.

MAKE THE SAUCE: Drain fat
from the sauté pan and return it to
medium-high heat. Add the pink
peppercorns and lightly toast,
stirring, about 45 seconds. Add
the beef stock, bring to a simmer,
and deglaze the pan, scraping
up any browned bits from the
bottom. Bring the liquid to a boil
and cook until reduced by half,
3 to 4 minutes. Add the butter and
swirl the pan until it's melted and
the sauce is thickened, then pour
in any of the lamb resting juices.
Remove the pan from the heat
and taste for seasoning. Stir in
the mint.

To serve, carve the lamb into
¼-inch slices and arrange on a
platter. Dollop the vanilla butter
on top of the slices, garnish with
the poached rhubarb stalks, and
spoon over the sauce. Garnish
with the reserved fried lavender.

THE FIRST TIME we plated this dish in the restaurant, it reminded me of *Pride and Prejudice*. It contains everything I imagine would have been in Mr. Darcy's beautifully manicured English gardens—rabbits, herbs, snails, rhubarb, elderflower, and so on. It's a whole mess of spring ingredients that elegantly come together. At first glance, it seems quite precious—the vibrant pink of the rhubarb, the golden hue of the rabbit—but serving this animal in its entirety gives me a primal urge to pick it up with my hands and rip it apart right then and there. Seeing the rib cage glistening with butter, smelling the floral aromas—it's hard not to indulge in this dish passionately. This is a dish for lovers, and for those who seek sensuality with their food.

CONFIT RABBIT
WITH POACHED RHUBARB, SNAIL BUTTER, AND ELDERFLOWER *Serves 2*

NOTES: *The rabbit needs to be salted at least 3 hours in advance or ideally overnight, so plan accordingly.*

The rhubarb can be poached and chilled 1 day in advance and brought to room temperature before serving.

1 whole rabbit (3¾ pounds/ 1.7 kg), cut into 7 pieces (see Notes, page 91)

Kosher salt

4 quarts (3.5 kg) canola oil

1 head garlic, scalped (see page 293)

1 tablespoon (14 g) extra-virgin olive oil

Freshly ground black pepper

POACHED RHUBARB

½ cup (110 g) St-Germain elderflower liqueur

½ cup (118 g) maraschino cherry liquid

⅓ cup (20 g) green cardamom pods

2 tablespoons (12 g) juniper berries

3 tablespoons (20 g) black peppercorns

1¼ cups (250 g) sugar

1 pound 5 ounces (596 g) rhubarb, cut into 3-inch pieces

FOR FINISHING

5 fresh bay leaves

2 tablespoons (30 g) Snail Butter (page 273)

1 bunch elderflower, for garnish

Season the rabbit all over with salt and refrigerate, uncovered, for at least 3 hours, or ideally overnight.

Preheat the oven to 300°F.

Place the rabbit in a large Dutch oven or heavy-bottomed pot and submerge completely in the canola oil. Cover with a cartouche (see page 293), then cover the pot. Transfer to the oven and braise until the meat is tender and the meat on the hind legs (the thickest part) starts to pull away from the bone, about 4 hours.

One hour before the rabbit is done, dress the garlic with the olive oil and salt and pepper to taste, wrap in foil, and place in the oven to roast until the cloves are golden and soft.

MEANWHILE, POACH THE RHUBARB: In a medium pot, combine 3 cups water, the St-Germain, maraschino cherry liquid, cardamom, juniper, peppercorns, and sugar. Bring to a simmer over medium-high heat, then turn off the heat, but leave the pot on the burner, and add the rhubarb.

Cover with a cartouche (see page 293) to hold the rhubarb under the liquid. Allow to sit in the hot syrup until the rhubarb is just fork-tender, 10 to 15 minutes. Transfer the rhubarb and the poaching liquid to a clean plastic container with a lid. Place the container in the refrigerator immediately to chill. The sudden jolt of chilled air will brighten and lock in the color of the rhubarb to a bright pink hue.

Remove the rabbit from the oven, uncover, and let the rabbit cool in its oil at room temperature for 1½ to 2 hours. When completely cool, remove the rabbit parts. Reserve 3 tablespoons of the confit oil, discarding the remainder or saving it for another use (see page 280).

FINISH THE DISH: In a large sauté pan, heat the reserved 3 tablespoons confit oil over medium-high heat. Add the rabbit in a single layer and cook, undisturbed, until golden brown and crisp, 8 to 10 minutes. Flip and cook on the other side for 8 to 10 minutes more. The rabbit will naturally release from the bottom of the pan when it's ready. In the last minute of cooking, add the garlic cloves and bay leaves to the pan. Use a spoon to baste the rendered fat up around the meat and aromatics until they are fragrant, 30 to 45 seconds.

Transfer the rabbit and aromatics to a serving platter and dot with the snail butter and stalks of poached rhubarb. Garnish with fresh elderflowers. Serve immediately.

LIFE ON WEST 12TH STREET

IT'S A CHALLENGE TO CONVEY in words the magic between the walls of the Bea. From the second you walk through our doors, the vibe and the energy alone will intoxicate you. I could live in furs, eat dry-aged beef with my hands, and curl up by the fireplace even during the muggiest August day in Manhattan. When you find that fluorescent pink and green sign on West 12th Street and descend the staircase into the underbelly of Number 285, you've entered the den of one of New York's first speakeasies, founded in the home of a former mobbed-up Italian joint, the exclusive party spot for It Girls and actors, and the last place where Heath Ledger was seen alive.

But now, there is Sinatra in the early evenings followed by '80s hits and '90s rap pounding through the speakers as the hours pass, plus vintage, Victorian-style silver trays spilling over with roasted meats. You'll wonder, "What era am I in? Who are these people? Have I gone mad and entered an alternate universe where ambiance is king, everything is smoked or on fire, being a vegan or pescatarian is outlawed, and the chef is proclaiming, with Marie Antoinette–like authority, *'Let them eat suet!'*?" There's so much going on, you may not know where to look first.

My team are true entertainers. Sitting at the bar is like watching a beautifully choreographed ballet meet a Metallica concert. The crowd is typically eight deep while the boys throw ice cubes over their shoulders, catching them in cocktail shakers. They light Chartreuse on fire and pour it from glass to glass. It's effortless; it's completely in sync. Inevitably at some point during the evening, random girls will crawl over the bar to give them a kiss on the cheek; that is the moment that I look out from my perch in our tiny kitchen and think to myself, "I have the best damn bar team in Manhattan."

The dining room is a different beast entirely. Champagne and even our wines by the glass flow out of magnums, because if we are going to do something, we do it big and we do it right. Pick a dish and it's most likely on fire, being unveiled from beneath a smoke-filled vintage crystal cloche, or presented whole for tableside carving—prime ribs, hay-roasted mutton shoulders, the occasional cameo by a five-pound lobster Thermidor. We strive for a service that is unpretentious and welcoming, but also showstopping, always evoking an air of celebration and refinement.

You may lose all of your inhibitions, throw caution to the wind, and party like Kate Moss in the days when the Sevignys ruled the roost.

It's an honor for me to be a part of the next chapter in the history of this magnificent New York name. And part of my goal in this new chapter of the Beatrice is for the restaurant to represent this great city. New York has welcomed me, embraced my oddities, fed my neuroses, and nurtured my creativity.

WHAT I HAVE ALWAYS LOVED ABOUT NEW YORK IS THAT ITS INHABITANTS COME FROM ALL WALKS OF LIFE AND IT EMBRACES US ALL REGARDLESS.

Melissa and I bought the Beatrice with the intention of bringing everyone to the table—literally and figuratively. At its best, food transcends race, gender, political beliefs, and generations, tying us all together with a bite, a shared moment, and if we are very lucky, an entire meal—all with joy and abandon.

LA PARISIENNE *Makes 1 cocktail*

–ANTANAS SAMKUS, BAR DIRECTOR

"This is my take on a classic French 75, which, although typically thought of as a Champagne and gin cocktail, was originally made with Cognac. I love the warm, full-bodied flavor of Cognac, and I wanted to combine that with a newer classic, the Breakfast Martini, which is an orange marmalade-infused gin martini developed by London bartender Salvatore Calabrese. The result is a sparkling cocktail with depth and complexity, perfectly balanced between sweet and sour, refreshing all the way through. We named this cocktail for the Parisian actress Brigitte Bardot—it's sexy, feminine, and the ultimate bombshell."

1 ounce Pierre Ferrand Cognac

½ ounce Amaro Nonino

¾ ounce Grand Marnier

½ ounce lemon juice

2 bar spoons orange marmalade

Ice cubes

3 to 4 ounces Henri Giraud Champagne

Maraschino cherry, for garnish

Combine the Cognac, Amaro, Grand Marnier, lemon juice, and orange marmalade in an ice-filled cocktail shaker. Shake hard for 30 seconds. Strain into a Champagne flute and fill to the top with Champagne. Garnish with a cherry.

NOTE: *Use a high-quality orange marmalade with some rind intact. Though the rind will be strained out, it imparts excellent flavor in this cocktail.*

SPRING IS THE TIME of year to get together with friends, especially in New York. We typically come out of hiding from the cold, the sun begins to shine, and the days begin to get just a bit longer. And with the change in temperature, I like to indulge in something a bit lighter on the palate, but still complexly flavored. This dish does the trick, with different layers of salinity, thanks to the anchovy and the salt, plus unexpectedly heady notes from the coffee and vanilla, and a hazelnut gremolata that brings a tremendous freshness and texture to the plate.

VEAL CARPACCIO
WITH BLACK ANCHOVIES AND HAZELNUT GREMOLATA *Serves 10*

VEAL

¾ cup (52 g) ground coffee

2 tablespoons (16 g) porcini powder

Seeds of 2 vanilla beans

1 tablespoon (6 g) juniper berries

14 sprigs thyme, picked

1 teaspoon (3 g) kosher salt

1 (3- to 4-pound/1.36 to 1.80 kg) veal knuckle, peeled and trimmed of any silver skin or sinew

GARLIC PUREE

1 loosely packed cup (124 g) peeled garlic (about 30 cloves)

⅔ cup (160 g) whole milk

1 tablespoon plus 1 teaspoon (18 g) shirodashi (see page 292)

3 tablespoons (40 g) oil from Garlic Confit (page 280)

HAZELNUT GREMOLATA

5 tablespoons (27 g) finely chopped fresh parsley

1 tablespoon (3 g) finely chopped fresh marjoram

1 tablespoon (6 g) finely chopped fresh rosemary

1 tablespoon (3 g) finely chopped fresh savory

½ cup (66 g) finely chopped hazelnuts

⅓ cup (60 g) finely chopped salt-cured anchovies (about 14 fillets)

⅓ teaspoon (1 g) kosher salt

½ cup plus 3 tablespoons (150 g) extra-virgin olive oil

FOR GARNISH

Parsley

Marjoram

5 anchovy fillets, such as Don Bocarte

NOTES: *The veal must be marinated for 24 to 48 hours and then frozen for another 3 to 4 hours before proceeding with this recipe, so plan accordingly.*

The garlic puree and gremolata can both be made the day before.

PREPARE THE VEAL: In a small bowl, combine the coffee, porcini powder, vanilla seeds, juniper berries, thyme, and salt. Rub the mixture thoroughly all over the veal knuckle. Tightly wrap the knuckle in plastic and refrigerate for at least 24 and up to 48 hours.

On the day of serving, transfer the veal, still wrapped, to the freezer to firm up for easier slicing, 3 to 4 hours before serving.

MAKE THE GARLIC PUREE: Bring a small pot of water to a boil over high heat and add the garlic. Boil for 5 minutes to remove the bitterness, then drain.

In the same pot, bring the milk to a simmer over medium heat. Add the garlic and cook until softened, 8 to 10 minutes, then remove the pot from the heat (do not drain).

Transfer the garlic and milk to a food processor, add the shirodashi, and blend until smooth. With the machine running, stream in the garlic confit oil until the mixture is light and creamy. Transfer the mixture to a small bowl and cover with plastic wrap, pressing it directly onto the surface to prevent a skin from forming. Refrigerate for a minimum of 3 hours or up to overnight.

MAKE THE HAZELNUT GREMOLATA: In a small bowl, toss together the parsley, marjoram, rosemary, savory, hazelnuts, anchovies, and salt. Add the olive oil and stir to combine. The gremolata can be made up to 1 day in advance and stored in an airtight container in the refrigerator.

To serve, spread the garlic puree in an even layer to coat the bottom of a serving platter. Remove the veal from the freezer and unwrap it. Using a very sharp knife, cut the veal into tissue-thin slices.

Arrange the veal on top of the garlic puree in concentric circles, working from the outside in. Dollop the hazelnut gremolata across its surface, using all of it, and garnish with fresh herbs and anchovy fillets.

WHEN I WAS A TEENAGER, my parents split up, and feeding my younger brothers became one of my responsibilities, so I had to learn how to cook out of necessity. One of the easiest things for me to make was pasta with shrimp, garlic, lemon, and chile, a favorite of my brothers. As I entered my late teens and early twenties, I still made this dish for my family and for my friends. Now as an adult, I still love those flavors, though I've given this recipe a bit of an upgrade from the bodega noodles and frozen shrimp of my adolescent years. This whole dish comes together in under 20 minutes, using mostly pantry ingredients, and takes about half that long to eat. It's the perfect Sunday lunch for two, in my house often consumed in pajamas in the comfort of my bed or on the floor—soul-satisfying and deeply delicious.

BLACK SPAGHETTI
WITH LANGOUSTINES AND PINK PEPPERCORNS *Serves 2*

Kosher salt

½ cup plus 1 teaspoon (113 g) extra-virgin olive oil

½ pound (225 g) squid ink spaghetti

3 large garlic cloves, thinly sliced

½ teaspoon (1 g) chile flakes

1 teaspoon (3 g) pink peppercorns, lightly crushed

1 tablespoon (8 g) fresh lemon juice

½ cup plus 1 tablespoon (108 g) Champagne

5 head-on langoustines

2 tablespoons (14 g) grated Parmesan cheese

3 tablespoons (50 g) Langoustine Butter (page 274)

1 tablespoon plus 2 teaspoons (25 g) unsalted butter

2 tablespoons (10 g) chopped fresh parsley

Bring a large pot of water seasoned like the sea to a boil over high heat. Add 1 teaspoon of the olive oil. Add the spaghetti and cook until just under al dente, 1 to 2 minutes less than the time on the package directions. Drain, reserving ¼ cup of the pasta cooking water.

In a large sauté pan, heat the remaining ½ cup olive oil. Add the garlic and chile flakes and cook, stirring continuously, until the garlic just starts to turn golden, 3 to 5 minutes. Add the pink peppercorns and stir briefly to toast them, about 1 minute.

When the garlic is golden, add the lemon juice and Champagne to stop it from browning. Add the langoustines, cover the pan, and steam until the langoustines are just barely cooked through, about 3 minutes.

Add the Parmesan, langoustine butter, and regular butter. Season with salt, and when the butter and cheese are melted and everything is coming up to simmer, about 2 minutes, add the cooked pasta and reserved pasta cooking water, shaking the pan and tossing until all the pasta is coated. Finish with the parsley, give it one last toss, and serve immediately.

ON THE RARE NIGHT we didn't have a T-bone steak on the table when I was growing up, there was beef stroganoff. It came out of a package that also called for canned cream of mushroom soup; we ate it with white rice in lieu of noodles, and it was absolutely delicious. When I'm feeling nostalgic and missing my dad, I find myself craving that very stroganoff, in all of its preservative-laden glory. But I've tweaked my father's recipe to make use of veal osso buco, whose braised marrow bone adds a distinct richness to the dish, and some of my favorite fresh mushrooms, which are decidedly better than the canned stuff. You could serve this with rice instead of the noodles—either way, it's a perfect hearty meal.

VEAL STROGANOFF
WITH WILD SPRING MUSHROOMS   *Serves 2*

4 ounces (112 g) bacon

1½ pounds (680 g) bone-in veal shank

Kosher salt

1 cup (119 g) diced Spanish onion

5 garlic cloves, smashed

6 medium cremini mushrooms (158 g), halved if large

3½ ounces (95 g) chanterelle mushrooms (1½ loosely packed cups), halved if large

3½ ounces (95 g) morel mushrooms (1½ loosely packed cups), halved if large

¾ cup (144 g) Champagne or white wine

4 cups (840 g) Beef Stock (page 283)

1 bunch thyme, tied with string

1 cup (225 g) heavy cream

3 tablespoons (40 g) unsalted butter

⅓ cup (60 g) crème fraîche

5 cracks black pepper

½ bunch parsley, chopped

½ recipe Duck Egg Yolk Pasta (page 279), cut into pappardelle, cooked, and drained

In a large Dutch oven or heavy-bottomed pot, cook the bacon over medium heat until it is golden and the fat has rendered, 6 to 7 minutes. Remove the bacon to a plate, reserving the rendered fat in the pot.

Meanwhile, truss the veal shank and season it all over with salt.

Increase the heat to medium-high and add the veal to the rendered bacon fat and cook, turning, until browned on all sides, about 10 minutes total. Set the veal aside with the cooked bacon, reserving the bacon and veal fat in the pot.

Reduce the heat to medium. Add the onion and garlic and cook until soft and translucent, 5 to 7 minutes. Add all of the mushrooms and stir to combine. (Don't season anything yet—the vegetables will pick up salt from the bacon and veal fat.) Continue cooking until the onions are golden and the mushrooms are softened and have absorbed all of the fat, 5 to 7 minutes.

Return the bacon and veal shank to the pot, along with any accumulated juices. Increase the heat to high and add the Champagne to deglaze the pan, scraping up any browned bits from the bottom. Reduce the heat to medium, add the beef stock and thyme, and bring to a simmer. Cover with a cartouche (see page 293), then cover the pot with the lid. Simmer over medium-low heat until the veal is tender, about 3 hours 15 minutes.

Remove the thyme from the pot. Remove the veal, remove the string, and set the meat aside in a bowl with a few ladles of its own braising liquid to keep it from drying out. Cover with foil and place somewhere warm.

Increase the heat under the braising liquid to high and cook until the liquid has reduced by one-quarter, 8 to 10 minutes. The liquid should lightly coat the back of a spoon. Stir in the cream and return the liquid to a simmer to thicken and reduce by one-quarter again, until it thickly coats the back of a spoon, 5 to 7 minutes more. Add 1½ tablespoons of the butter and the crème fraîche, swirling to incorporate, and season with black pepper to taste. Return the veal shank to the pot and check for seasoning. Finish the sauce with half of the parsley.

Add the remaining 1½ tablespoons butter and the remaining parsley to the pot of cooked pasta, swirling to coat each strand. Serve the pasta family-style, topped with the veal stroganoff.

ONE OF MY greatest pleasures in life is sitting inside the dining room at Chez l'Ami Louis in Paris, drinking Champagne, and eating all different types of liver. My meal there always starts with a very straightforward duck liver pâté—chilled, seasoned with salt and black pepper, and served with a baguette. I often find the most pleasure in simplicity.

At the Beatrice, though, I love to make this *torchon*. Foie gras and truffles rank second only to beef, so we often have bits and pieces of both around; when we have enough scraps saved up, they feature beautifully in this dish. With a bit of pink curing salt, it cures for days, and is then served nearly raw to preserve its integrity. The foie gras turns a beautiful rosy hue, and the aroma of the truffles shines through. We serve it with brioche sautéed in butter, but it would be equally delicious with a fresh baguette and a bit of jam.

FOIE GRAS AND TRUFFLE TORCHON *Serves 10 to 12*

1 (25-ounce/706 g) piece foie gras, at room temperature

2 g pink curing salt (see page 292)

1 tablespoon plus ½ teaspoon (10 g) kosher salt

¼ ounce (8 g) white truffle, finely chopped

⅛ teaspoon (3 g) truffle oil

Freshly ground black pepper

NOTES: *When dealing with charcuterie recipes that involve pink curing salt, I urge you to work in grams, as the amount called for is typically quite small, and you need an exact quantity.*

The torchon *must chill for 5 days, so plan accordingly.*

Gently press down on the foie gras and separate the lobes, exposing the veins. Gently pull out the veins. Break the foie gras apart into small pieces and transfer it to a medium bowl.

In a small bowl, combine the pink curing salt, kosher salt, and white truffle. Working in 3 batches, sprinkle the mixture onto the foie gras and use your hands to gently fold it in until evenly incorporated.

Pull out an 18-inch length of plastic wrap and place it the long way on your work surface. Transfer the foie gras to the plastic and, leaving a 4-inch space along the bottom of the plastic, gently pat the foie gras with your hands into a rectangle 12 × 8 inches and ½ to ¾ inch thick. Lightly drizzle the truffle oil over the top. Gently pull the plastic overhang up to push the foie gras forward onto itself, as if you were making a sushi roll, rolling the foie gras gently and continuing to use the plastic to shape the foie gras into a log about 12 inches long and 2 inches thick.

Lay out a fresh 24-inch length of plastic wrap. Place the plastic-wrapped foie gras log in the fresh plastic and, holding the loose edges of the fresh plastic, roll the log across the countertop to create friction, helping compress the log. Use a cake tester to prick 12 to 15 holes in it to allow air to escape, then continue to roll it across the countertop 8 to 10 more times, twisting the ends to compress it further, into a log about 10 inches long.

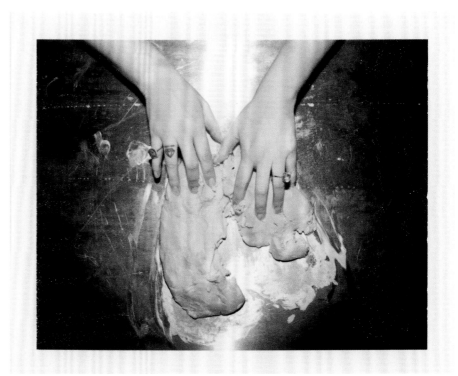

Tuck in the sides of the plastic and wrap the log one more time in a clean 18-inch piece of plastic wrap to ensure no air can get in. Roll the log one more time, twisting the edges tightly, and tying with butcher's twine to seal.

Using a piece of butcher's twine, hang the *torchon* vertically in the refrigerator to cure for 4 days.

Set up a large bowl of ice and water. Bring a large pot of water to a simmer over medium-high heat. Drop the wrapped *torchon* into the boiling water and poach for 1 minute to just set. Quickly shock the *torchon* in the ice bath. Return to the refrigerator and hang vertically for 12 more hours.

To serve, cut the *torchon* into ¼-inch-thick slices and season with black pepper.

**ROSE-SCENTED VERRINES
WITH LYCHEE AND PINK
PEPPERCORN MERINGUE**

(page 130)

WHEN I WAS VERY YOUNG, my family would drive up to Vancouver, British Columbia, for day trips. One of my earliest memories is of my mother buying giant quilts in Vancouver's Chinatown so she could smuggle bushels of lychees back across the United States border for us to feast on at home. I used to try to grow them in our backyard in Seattle, burying the seeds after we'd enjoyed the fruit, perpetually feeling frustrated that my lychee garden refused to bloom. Lychee is a very nostalgic flavor for me, so I came up with this beautifully light, airy dessert that's perfectly sweet but not too sweet. You can make these verrines in individual ramekins, though in the restaurant, we serve it in vintage crystal coupe glasses, which feel appropriately celebratory.

ROSE-SCENTED VERRINES
WITH LYCHEE AND PINK PEPPERCORN MERINGUE
Serves 6

PINK PEPPERCORN MERINGUE

6 large egg whites

1 cup plus 2 tablespoons (225 g) sugar

½ cup (36 g) pink peppercorns, roughly cracked

VERRINES

2½ cups (600 g) heavy cream

½ cup plus 2 tablespoons (122 g) sugar

Seeds of 1 vanilla bean

2 tablespoons (26 g) syrup from canned lychees, plus 12 lychees, for garnish

3 tablespoons (40 g) rose water

Grated zest of 1 lemon

3 tablespoons (46 g) lemon juice

MAKE THE PINK PEPPERCORN MERINGUE: Preheat the oven to 200°F. Line a baking sheet with parchment paper.

In a stand mixer fitted with the whisk attachment, whisk together the egg whites and sugar until stiff peaks form, about 10 minutes. Spread out the meringue in a thin layer on the prepared pan and sprinkle the peppercorns evenly across the surface.

Transfer to the oven and bake until the meringue is beginning to set, about 5 hours. At the 5-hour mark, crack the oven door open with tongs or a wooden spoon to

let some heat escape, in order to reduce the oven temperature to about 160°F. Cook until the meringue is set but does not take on any color, about 1 hour more. Set aside to cool completely. Meringue will harden as it cools.

MEANWHILE, MAKE THE VERRINES: In a heavy medium saucepot, combine the heavy cream, sugar, vanilla seeds, and lychee syrup. Clip a thermometer to the side of the pot and bring to a boil over medium heat, stirring constantly until the mixture reaches 220°F. Add the rose water, lemon zest, and lemon juice, stirring to incorporate. Boil for 1 minute, then strain through a fine-mesh sieve into a bowl. Ladle the mixture evenly into six 6-ounce ramekins or coupe glasses. Refrigerate until set, 3 to 5 hours.

To serve, break the meringue into jagged pieces of varying sizes. Top half of each verrine with the meringue (leaving half of the cream exposed), and garnish each verrine with 2 lychees.

CHAMPAGNE

—THERA CLARK, WINE DIRECTOR

"I BELIEVE CHAMPAGNE is so special, specifically at the Beatrice, not only because it's a versatile wine, but also because the whole air of the restaurant is celebratory—which is why we see a lot of people drink it here. As soon as you walk down those stairs, you're transported. You see the fireplace roaring and smell the unmistakable aromas of grilled meat and fresh herbs, and catch a glimpse of the sumptuous dishes emerging from the kitchen on real silver platters. The whole environment emits sensuality—this contrast of masculine-feminine aesthetics, ideas, and flavors.

The food itself is more complex than what you would find in a usual chophouse. But no one ever accused the Bea of being usual. In addition to beef and pork, we've got rabbit, we've got oxtail, and we've got all these different kinds of opulent preparations. Champagne works very well with *all* of that. This is a restaurant that encourages throwing caution to the wind and eating with abandon. There's a carnal sort of energy here—even if you're just sitting at the bar and having a cherrywood-smoked Manhattan and a burger, you're still indulging in something. And Champagne is always an indulgence.

From a pairing perspective, it works well with the food. For example, we always recommend starting a meal with seafood. When you're eating oysters and caviar off an icy tower, it screams for Champagne. But we can pair an entire meal—from oysters to bone marrow crème brûlée—with bubbles. Of course, we have an incredible wine list and a Madeira program, too, but we like to show people that Champagne can carry you from start to finish. It's not just something you drink in the beginning to get out of the way. Our bottles bring out the best in the food, even with meats you'd traditionally think to drink with red wine. I can tell you that when you sit down with a glass of barely aged Pinot Noir made into Champagne with our steak, or when you tuck in to our Rabbit à la Joinville (page 91) with a rosé Champagne, you will be a very happy person. It will work because of the acidity, and the balance in the food; it's all there.

We look at Champagne as something important to the restaurant's identity, and also as part of its history. The Beatrice has always been associated with luxury and glamour, whether during the glittering nights of yesteryear or its more recent heroin-chic past. I often imagine Zelda and F. Scott Fitzgerald sipping Champagne cocktails at the bar during the Prohibition era, and also the wild parties that infuriated the neighbors during the restaurant's nightclub era. In our current form, we like to evoke the air of celebration as an everyday occurrence—a joie de vivre that whisks you into an alternate universe as soon as you set foot in the bar.

And Champagne is something that just tastes delicious with what's coming out of our kitchen—we view it less as a pairing, and more as an essential part of the dining experience. We have an incredible selection. And we frequently pour it out of magnums, which is very much in line with our over-the-top style. Trust me when I say we go through a lot of Champagne.

We pour a lot of Billecart-Salmon, which is one of the oldest Champagne houses in existence that is still family owned, meaning somebody tied to that initial marriage of the Billecart and Salmon families actually runs the Champagne house.

Henri Giraud is a style we use to take a stand. It's bigger, it's heavier, and it's made mostly from barrel-aged Pinot Noir. It's a more luxe Champagne, which, again, works with the food in the restaurant because you're going head-to-head with a lot of strong, layered flavors in the food. We like their Code Noir, which I describe as the Cindy Crawford of Champagnes. The bottle itself is golden, and it's shaped like a torpedo—it screams sexy. You look at the bottle and you just want to touch it.

Krug is a real favorite. It's like the Lamborghini of Champagne. It's luxurious, it's precise, every time they put out a vintage it has depth, it's iconic, and it has that kind of personality that works well with our food. We also serve plenty of Dom Pérignon, which only produces vintage Champagnes, which are very special.

I would love to see people drink more Champagne with their meals, and I'm doing my part to make that happen. Coco Chanel had it right when she said, 'I only drink Champagne on two occasions: when I am in love and when I am not.' That's the kind of attitude we like to encourage here at the Bea."

A ROASTED CAPON is a lovely dinner for two, accompanied with mushrooms and Madeira—a classic pairing that dates back to the era of Escoffier. Many people associate Madeira with after-dinner drinks, but I love using it in savory cooking applications for depth, and as a pairing for meats—it is, after all, what our founding fathers toasted with upon signing the Declaration of Independence. The sauce here is a bit savory and a bit sweet—I like swirling in crème fraîche at the end, as it provides the perfect touch of lightness and acidity this dish needs. The combination of lavender, parsley, and tarragon is bright, feminine, and fresh, which contrasts brilliantly against the depth of the Madeira and the richness of the cream.

ROAST CAPON WITH MORELS, MADEIRA, AND LAVENDER CREAM   *Serves 2*

NOTE: *Allow the butter to sit at room temperature until it is a good, spreadable consistency.*

- 1 whole capon (4 to 5 pounds/ 1.8 to 2.25 kg)
- 4 tablespoons (55 g) unsalted butter, at room temperature, plus 1½ tablespoons (22 g) for the sauce
- 1 bunch thyme
- 1 bunch lavender, plus ¼ teaspoon (1 g), roughly chopped
- 3 tablespoons (40 g) extra-virgin olive oil
- Kosher salt
- 3 ounces (84 g) morel mushrooms (1½ loosely packed cups), halved if large
- 1 vanilla bean, split lengthwise
- 2 tablespoons (27 g) Cognac
- ¾ cup (157 g) Chicken Stock (page 283)
- ¼ cup (56 g) heavy cream
- ⅓ cup (71 g) Madeira
- ½ teaspoon (1 g) freshly ground black pepper
- 2 tablespoons (19 g) crème fraîche
- 1 teaspoon (1 g) finely chopped fresh tarragon
- 1 tablespoon (5 g) finely chopped fresh parsley

Preheat the oven to 375°F.

Using your fingers, starting at the neck of the capon, gently separate the skin from the meat of the breasts. Slide the 4 tablespoons butter in between, flattening it as evenly as possible.

Stuff the cavity of the capon with the bunches of thyme and lavender, then truss the bird with butcher's twine. Rub the olive oil all over the bird's exterior and season generously with salt. Place the bird in a large ovenproof sauté pan, transfer to the oven, and roast until the skin is golden brown, the juices from the thigh run clear when poked, and a thermometer inserted in the thickest part reads 150°F when pricked with a knife, about 40 minutes.

Transfer the capon to a wire rack to rest. Discard all but about 4 tablespoons of the rendered fat and juices from the sauté pan.

Place the pan over medium-high heat, add the morels, and sauté until tender, 3 to 5 minutes. Add the vanilla bean halves and cook until blistered and crackling, about 30 seconds.

Remove the pan from the heat and add the Cognac to deglaze the pan, scraping up any browned bits from the bottom, until the liquid has reduced by half to form a glaze, about 1 minute.

Return the pan to medium-high heat, add the stock, and cook until reduced by half, about 2 minutes. Add the cream and reduce by one-quarter, about 2 minutes more. Stir in the Madeira and pepper, then add the remaining 1½ tablespoons butter to thicken and add sheen to the sauce, swirling the pan to melt and incorporate it. Add the crème fraîche and taste for seasoning. Add the chopped lavender, the tarragon, and parsley and swirl once more to incorporate.

To serve, carve the bird, arrange it on a serving platter, then spoon the sauce over it.

MY MOTHER occasionally fed my brothers and me frozen Marie Callender's chicken potpies for dinner, which I developed a true love for. She couldn't really cook anything but Chinese food, and these reminded me of the ones we'd get in London every year. I hadn't had a chicken potpie for many years, frozen or otherwise, until a trip to London recently, when I stopped into a pub that served beautiful chicken and leek pies, which immediately took me back to those Marie Callender's nights. When I returned to New York, I knew I wanted to re-create it, or rather, make my own version to pay homage to the frozen delights of my childhood.

TRUFFLED HEN AND LEEK PIE *Serves 4 or 5*

NOTES: *Gallus brun hens are a French breed, raised for more than one hundred days to have darker, more flavorful meat. You may substitute a pheasant for similar results if it is not readily available to you.*

The key to this dish is to make the filling a day in advance to give the flavors time to meld. But be sure the filling is cold before going into the dough, otherwise it will melt the crust before it even has a chance to bake.

At the Beatrice, we get quite fancy with our pastry work, and this pie is one example. We roll out extra dough, cutting it into the shape of leaves to adorn the crust. If you wish to do this, you'll need to make a double recipe of the dough. But if you choose not to, the single-layer crust will be equally delicious.

1 whole Gallus brun hen or pheasant (1¼ pounds/555 g), boned, cubed, skin removed and reserved

½ teaspoon (4 g) truffle salt

Kosher salt

1 leek, cut on the bias into 1½-inch slices

5½ tablespoons (78 g) Truffle Butter (page 273)

½ cup plus 2 tablespoons (81 g) all-purpose flour

1½ cups (315 g) Chicken Stock (page 283), warmed

1¾ cups (393 g) whole milk

1 cup (225 g) heavy cream

¼ Spanish onion

1 bay leaf

½ teaspoon (1 g) grated nutmeg

Single or double recipe (see Notes) 50/50 Dough (page 277)

2 eggs, beaten

Season the hen meat with the truffle salt and a bit of kosher salt, and set aside.

In a medium sauté pan, cook the reserved hen skins, undisturbed, over medium heat to slowly render their fat, until the skins are golden but not crisp, 8 to 10 minutes. Remove the skins and chop into bite-size pieces. Pour off all but about 2 tablespoons of the rendered hen fat from the pan.

Increase the heat to medium-high and add the leek to the pan. Cook, stirring often, until soft but without color, about 15 minutes. Season to taste with kosher salt and set aside.

In a medium pot, melt the truffle butter over medium heat. Add the flour and whisk until the mixture is grainy like wet sand but has not taken on any color; this is a blond roux. Slowly ladle in the warm chicken stock, whisking constantly until thickened, about 5 minutes.

In a small pot, combine the milk and cream and warm over low heat. Slowly ladle this into the roux until combined into a smooth velouté, about 3 minutes.

Wrap the onion and bay leaf in a square of cheesecloth to make a sachet. Add the sachet to the velouté and bring to a simmer over medium heat, stirring so no flour sticks to the bottom. Simmer until the velouté is thick and your finger leaves a mark when you run it down the back of a spoon, 10 to 25 minutes. Season with the nutmeg and kosher salt to taste, and leave at a simmer over low heat.

Add the hen meat to the velouté and poach until just cooked through, 8 to 10 minutes. Drain the leeks of any excess fat and stir in to the velouté to incorporate, along with the chopped chicken skin. Transfer the filling to the refrigerator to chill completely, a minimum of 4 hours, or ideally overnight.

Preheat the oven to 350°F.

If using the single recipe of dough, divide it in half. (If making the extra dough for decorations, divide the dough into 4 equal portions and refrigerate or freeze one portion for a future use. The remaining 3 portions are for the 2 crusts and the decorations.) Roll each portion of dough into a round about 12 inches in diameter and ⅛ inch thick.

Press one of the rounds into the bottom and up the sides of a 10-inch pie dish, leaving a 1-inch overhang around the rim. Ladle in all of the velouté. Gently place a second round of dough on top and trim around the edges so it fits neatly over the filling. Brush a little of the beaten egg around the edge of the top crust and fold the bottom crust over it to seal. Brush more egg wash across the surface of the pie.

If making the optional decorations, using a 2 × 1-inch leaf-shaped cutter or a paring knife, cut decorative leaves out of the third piece of dough. Starting from the outside and working in, make concentric circles out of the leaves, alternating the direction they are pointing in with each layer. Brush with more egg wash and leave a small hole in the center for venting steam.

Bake until golden brown, 25 to 30 minutes. Allow the pie to rest for 10 minutes before serving.

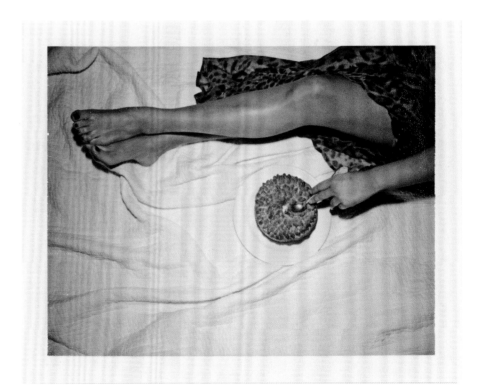

ONE OF my great indulgences is eating pâté with a beautifully aged port or Madeira. This recipe combines those flavors—instead of sealing the pâté with lard or fat as we normally would, we create a gelée using a forty-year aged tawny port. The result is perfect for a crisp spring day, when you want nothing more than to curl up next to the fireplace with a good book, a beautiful bottle of wine, and a tremendously rich, unctuous snack.

PORK LIVER PÂTÉ WITH PORT AND JUNIPER GELÉE   *Serves 6*

1 pound 2 ounces (507 g) unsalted butter

4 sprigs savory

1 tablespoon (6 g) juniper berries

4 cups thinly sliced Spanish onion (about 1 large)

1 pound (471 g) pork liver

Kosher salt and freshly ground black pepper

¾ cup (64 g) rosé Champagne

3½ sheets (9 g) silver gelatin

1½ cups (315 g) aged tawny port

½ teaspoon (3 g) sugar

FOR DECORATION

3 juniper berries

2 sprigs savory

NOTE: *Pâté must chill in the refrigerator overnight before serving, so plan accordingly.*

In a large sauté pan, combine the butter, savory, and juniper over medium heat. Once the butter is all melted and the herbs are starting to crackle and release their natural aromas and oils, strain out the herbs and discard, and return the butter to the pan.

Add the onions to the pan and sauté over medium heat until they are soft, but haven't taken on any color, about 15 minutes. Increase the heat to medium-high and add the pork liver to sear on each side, until it's cooked just under medium, 6 to 8 minutes. Season with salt and pepper to taste. Add the Champagne to deglaze the pan, scraping up any browned bits from the bottom. Allow the contents of the pan to sit, off the heat, for 5 minutes.

Meanwhile, in a small bowl of cold water, soften the gelatin. In a small saucepot, bring the port, ½ teaspoon salt, and the sugar to a boil over medium-high heat, then remove from the heat. Squeeze out the residual water from the gelatin and whisk the sheets into the port mixture to dissolve. Set aside to cool to room temperature while you blend the pork.

Transfer everything in the pork pan to a food processor and puree until smooth, about 6 minutes. Scrape the contents out into a 20-ounce terrine or soufflé dish, and tap it on the counter to even out the top and remove any air bubbles.

Gently pour the room temperature port mixture on top of the pork. Refrigerate for 45 minutes so the gelée starts to set, then remove and gently push the whole juniper berries and savory sprigs into the surface of the gelatin. Return to the refrigerator to set overnight, then enjoy the next day with a crusty baguette.

IN THE early spring, when it's still a bit chilly in the morning, I like to make this tart because it's savory and warming, with a light crust. What's interesting about this tart is that it tastes meaty, thanks to the sultry flavors of bone marrow and stock, but there's no actual meat in it. It fulfills my beef cravings without requiring me to sit down for a steak. It's an ideal lunch, with a bottle of Châteauneuf-du-Pape and creamy, nutty, perfectly tempered Cremont cheese on the side.

SHALLOT TART WITH MARROW AND
BEEF SUET CRUST   *Serves 8 to 10*

½ cup plus 1 tablespoon (112 g) Rendered Bone Marrow (page 284)

2 pounds 5 ounces (1.1 kg) shallots, halved lengthwise (about 6½ cups)

1 bunch thyme

1 tablespoon (8 g) kosher salt

1 tablespoon (14 g) sugar

2¾ cups (577 g) Beef Stock (page 283)

15 cracks black pepper

½ recipe 50/50 Dough (page 277)

20 cloves Garlic Confit (page 280), skins removed

1 (5-ounce) wheel Cremont cheese, at room temperature

In a large sauté pan, melt half of the bone marrow over medium-high heat. Add half of the shallots, cut-side down, and cook until golden brown, 10 to 12 minutes. Flip the shallots over and brown their other side, 5 to 7 minutes. Add half of the thyme, season with half of the salt and half of the sugar, and allow to caramelize, 5 to 6 minutes. Add half of the beef stock ½ cup at a time, scraping up any browned bits from the bottom, and allowing the liquid to reduce all the way down between additions, 5 to 6 minutes per ladle. Set the mixture aside and repeat the process with the remaining bone marrow, shallots, thyme, salt, sugar, beef stock, and pepper. Combine both batches, pick out the thyme and discard, and set aside to cool to room temperature.

Preheat the oven to 350°F.

Roll the dough out to a round ⅛ inch thick. Fit into a 12-inch fluted tart pan with a removable bottom, pressing the dough into the sides. There will be some overhang—roll a rolling pin over the top to remove it evenly.

Fill the tart shell with the cooled shallot mixture and its juices, and dot with confited garlic all around.

Bake until the crust is cooked through and the shallots are burnished and bubbling, 35 to 40 minutes. Remove from the oven and set on a wire rack to cool to room temperature.

To serve, cut the tart into wedges and serve with a wheel of Cremont on the side for people to garnish with as they wish.

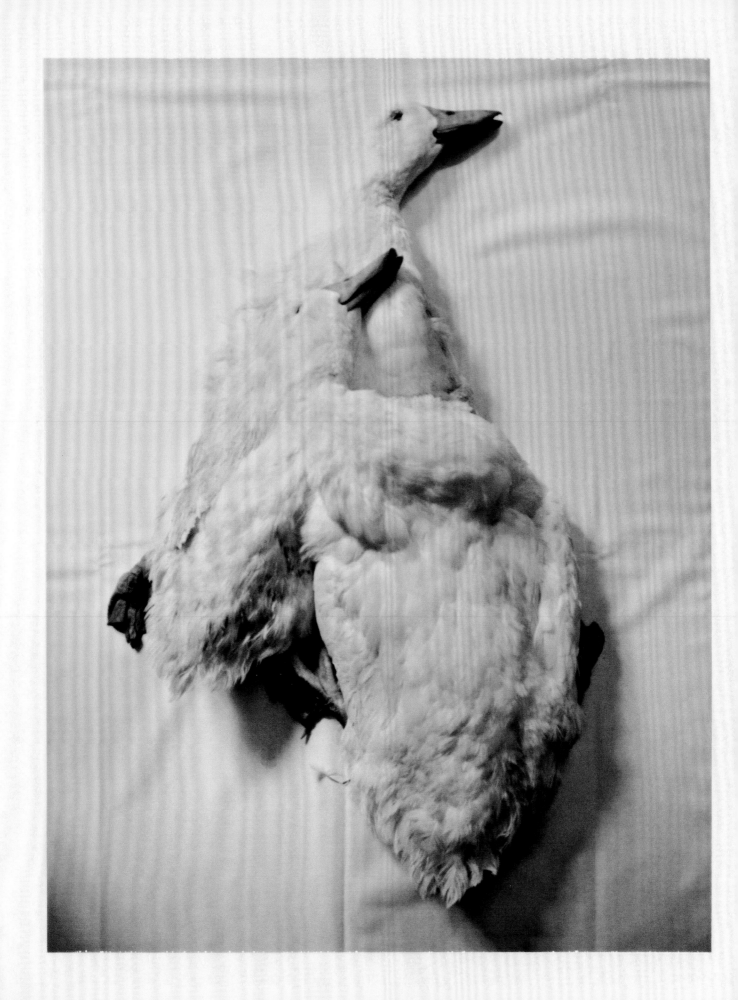

WHEN I EAT THIS PIE, it brings me back to one of my fondest recipe-creating sessions to date. It was early spring, and I had been clinging to the last days of winter like my life depended on it. I had nearly resigned myself to the fact that I would have to usher in the warmer weather. But defiant to the end, I wanted to create a "Spring/Summer Pie" that wasn't quite as deep or heavy as my cold-weather pies, but would still feel like the Bea. The result was this pie, filled with delicate duck meat and a lighter gravy—more silken than velvety. My team and I all gathered around the oven as it finished baking, spoons ready. One steaming bite of crust, gravy, and succulent meat—and a cigarette immediately thereafter—and a new Beatrice classic was born.

DUCK AND FOIE GRAS PIES
WITH TARRAGON GRAVY   *Makes 6 individual pies*

1 pound (450 g) duck legs, from about 6 pieces

Kosher salt

2 tablespoons plus 2 teaspoons (27 g) all-purpose flour

½ bottle (375 ml) white wine, such as Chardonnay

2 quarts (1.7 kg) Duck Stock (page 283)

1½ pounds (759 g) fingerling potatoes

12 cipollini onions, peeled and quartered

50/50 Dough (page 277)

1 egg, beaten

1 lobe (1 pound 10 ounces/ 739 g) foie gras, cut into 6 equal pieces

1 tablespoon (15 g) unsalted butter (optional)

1 tablespoon (3 g) finely chopped fresh tarragon

1 tablespoon (5 g) finely chopped fresh parsley

NOTES: *The duck legs must be salted for at least 6 hours or up to overnight, and the filling must be chilled completely in the refrigerator before assembling the pies, at least 6 hours or ideally overnight. Plan accordingly.*

You can of course make this pie in the winter, too, substituting winter herbs like savory, rosemary, or thyme for the tarragon.

Season the duck legs generously with salt, and let sit, uncovered in the refrigerator, for 6 hours or overnight.

Preheat the oven to 275°F.

Heat a large dry Dutch oven or heavy-bottomed pot over medium-low heat. Working in batches, add the duck legs, fat-side down, and cook, without moving, until deep golden brown and the fat has rendered, 10 to 12 minutes.

Transfer the seared duck legs to a plate. Pour off the rendered duck fat into a medium bowl and reserve.

Return the duck legs and any accumulated juices to the pot, sprinkle the flour over the top to evenly coat, then increase the heat to medium and cook, turning, until the flour is browned, 3 to 4 minutes. Increase the heat to medium-high and add the white wine to deglaze the pan, scraping up any browned bits from the bottom. Cook until the liquid has reduced by half, 5 to 7 minutes.

Add the duck stock and bring to a boil, then reduce the heat to low, cover, and transfer to the oven to braise until the joint of the duck leg is very giving and the meat is knife-tender but still intact on the bone, about 3 hours.

Recipe continues »

Meanwhile, in a medium pot, combine the potatoes with cold water to cover by 1 inch. Salt the water generously and bring to a simmer over medium heat. Cook until knife-tender, about 20 minutes. Drain the potatoes and set aside to cool.

In a large sauté pan, warm 1 tablespoon of the reserved duck fat over medium-low heat. Add the onions and sauté until they are translucent and light golden, 12 to 15 minutes. Chill completely in the refrigerator before assembling the pies, at least 3 hours, or ideally overnight.

When the duck is finished braising, skim the fat off the top (there won't be much since it was rendered before braising). Chill completely in the refrigerator before assembling the pies, at least 6 hours, or ideally overnight.

Preheat the oven to 375°F.

Divide the potatoes and onions evenly among 6 individual 20-ounce soufflé dishes. Place one duck leg in each dish and angle it upward so the bones stick out. Ladle in ½ cup of the cooled braising liquid. Reserve any remaining liquid.

Divide the dough into 6 equal pieces. Roll out each piece into a round slightly larger than the ramekins, about 7 inches across and ⅛ inch thick. Drape the dough over the top of each ramekin, slicing a small hole so the duck leg can stick out through it. It's okay if there is some dough draped over the sides—these pies are meant to be rustic. Press to seal against the rim of the dish with your fingers.

Brush the dough with the beaten egg and bake until the crust is golden brown and the filling is heated through and bubbling, 35 to 40 minutes. Remove the pies from the oven but leave the oven on. Let the pies rest for 10 minutes.

Meanwhile, cook the foie gras. Heat a large ovenproof sauté pan over high heat. Season the foie gras with salt. Add it to the pan and sear on one side for 1½ minutes, then flip and sear on the other side for another 1½ minutes, basting it in its own rendered fat. Transfer the pan to the oven to just cook the foie gras through, 1 to 2 minutes. The finished foie gras should have some give when touched, and feel squishy and silken, but warm all the way through when tested with a cake tester.

In a small pot, bring the reserved braising liquid to a simmer over medium heat, reducing if need be, so that it lightly coats the back of a spoon. If desired, add the butter to give the gravy additional thickness. Add the tarragon and parsley.

Top each pie with a piece of seared foie gras. Evenly divide the gravy over the tops and serve immediately.

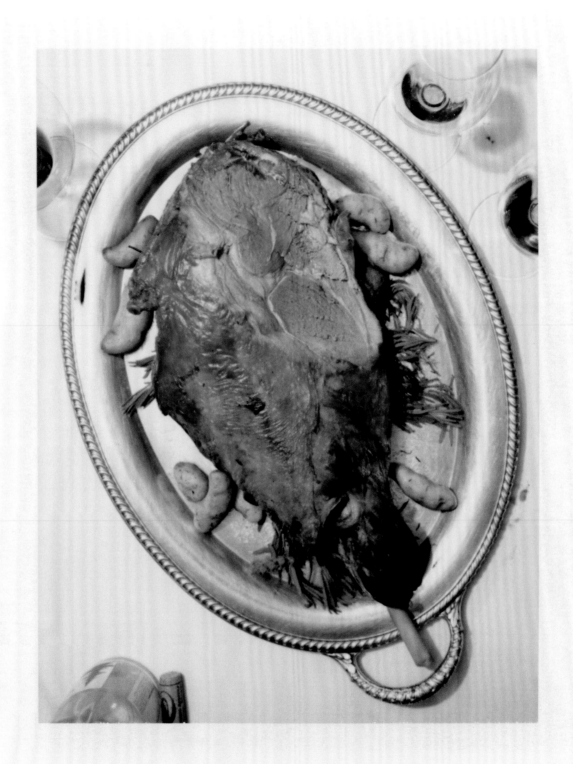

WHEN I WAS A CHILD and my family traveled to France, I fell in love with the whole-roasted birds turning on spits at the market, which dripped delicious fat onto a tray of potatoes below. I was inspired to do something similar here—the potatoes serve as a sort of resting rack so the underside of the lamb has airflow and cooks evenly, but then turn into a beautiful side dish at the end. This is a great way to showcase a larger cut for a dinner party that's filled with jewel-hued medium-rare meat.

SMOKED LEG OF LAMB
WITH LAVENDER-SCENTED FINGERLING POTATOES *Serves 6*

1 (12- to 15-pound/5.4 to 6.8 kg) bone-in leg of lamb

Pinot Meunier vines or cherrywood or applewood chips, for smoking

15 garlic cloves

Kosher salt

2 pounds (900 g) small fingerling potatoes

2 bunches lavender, plus more for garnish

2 bunches rosemary, plus more for garnish

_____

NOTES: *The lamb cures overnight and needs 5 to 6 hours to come to room temperature before cooking, so plan accordingly.*

You will need a handheld smoking gun (see page 293) for this recipe.

Cold-smoke (see page 293) the lamb with vines or wood chips for 30 minutes, until the meat has absorbed the smoky flavor.

Make 15 small incisions all over the lamb with a sharp knife. Push a clove of garlic into each incision. Season all over heavily with kosher salt and rest overnight, uncovered, in the refrigerator.

On the day of cooking, remove the lamb from the refrigerator and let come to room temperature, 5 to 6 hours.

Preheat the oven to 475°F.

In a roasting pan, combine the potatoes, lavender, and rosemary. Place the lamb, fat-side up, on top of the potatoes and herbs. Transfer to the oven to sear for 20 minutes.

Remove the lamb from the oven and reduce the oven temperature to 275°F. Allow the lamb to rest for 20 minutes in a warm place, then return to the oven and cook for another 20 minutes, uncovered. Remove the lamb again and allow to rest for

20 minutes. Repeat the 20 minutes in/20 minutes out cooking process 3 to 4 times total, or until the thickest part of the lamb reaches an internal temperature of 115°F. This in-and-out cooking method helps ensure the meat cooks evenly to a perfect medium-rare and stays rosy pink throughout.

Remove the lamb to a wire rack to rest for 20 minutes; the internal temperature will rise to about 125°F. All of the beautiful lamb fat should have seeped down to cook the potatoes and the herbs should smell amazing.

To serve, arrange the potatoes in a bowl and carve the leg tableside, holding the shank bone as a handle, into ¼-inch-thick slices, working your way around the bone so that everyone gets some salty end bits. Garnish with lavender and rosemary.

THE BAR ROOM

WHEN I TOLD MY FATHER I had decided to buy the Beatrice, the first words out of his mouth were, "Watch the bar! You're either going to make a ton of money or go broke if you don't watch the bar, Angela." I quickly realized how right he was. But I wasn't worried about employees drinking our money away—I was trying to figure out how to make the bar at the Beatrice one of the most coveted seats in the house.

I first met Antanas Samkus in 2014, when we both worked for the Bea's old owners. He had the funniest résumé I'd ever seen; it featured a photo of himself with a cartoon bubble above his smiling face that read, "Hello, my name is Antanas." We immediately hit it off and had a great conversation, but little did I know our meeting would °turn into a kinship that I hope will last a lifetime.

He and I have a saying about the Beatrice: "This is Sparta." But *our* Sparta is an alternate universe where we dress in matching leopard-print couture and brainstorm cocktail ideas by day, and fight back-to-back in the trenches of service at night.

Building the bar program at the Beatrice has been our passion. In August 2016, we shut down the restaurant for the entire month to revamp the menu and the space. Two days before we were to open, Antanas was madly dialing our liquor purveyors, trying to find a specific delivery, as he was testing cocktails and writing recipes. "They insist they delivered it, but it's not here!" he wailed. "I've been waiting for two days, I don't understand what happened."

Money was tight for us then, as I had spent most of mine buying the restaurant and what I had left had been used to keep everyone on payroll. I tried to stay calm (not an easy thing for me given that I inherited my father's temper), and somehow concluded that the liquor must have been delivered to the wrong address. So we set about asking the neighboring restaurants if they had accepted our delivery by mistake. We went door to door and sure enough, one of our neighboring restaurants had not only accepted our delivery, but had already stocked their shelves with the booze they hadn't ordered or paid for. I sat outside this restaurant, chain-smoking, peering through the window as my assistant went over a list of missing product and my bartenders pulled our bottles off of their walls. I had made a vow, now that I was a business owner, to try to delegate more. As they packed bottles into cardboard boxes, the tension seemed to grow palpable between the other restaurant owner and my staff. Then I saw my assistant throw her notorious finger full of attitude in the owner's face. . . . She was getting Bronx, meaning, *it was going down*. I rolled my eyes, put out my cigarette, and walked in.

"Is there an issue? We just want our delivery back," I said as coolly as possible. "We're still missing about $5,000 in product, Chef," my assistant said, pointing to the invoice. "You should be grateful we accepted your delivery for you. So what if you're missing a few bottles?" snapped the other owner.

That was the exact point at which I blacked out from sheer and utter rage. Antanas says he and one of the other bartenders dragged me back to the Beatrice for my own protection, as I was on the street screaming about how I'd burn her restaurant to the ground if I didn't get every single bottle back. We've been working on my delegation skills ever since.

(Most) bottles back in hand, we spent the rest of that month developing the narrative of our cocktail menu. It lies somewhere between classic and cutting-edge, with a dose of whimsy thrown in for good measure: Manhattans are smoked with cherrywood and presented under crystal cloches, gin and tonics are remade with a forest of herbs, and a Vesper becomes exotically perfumed through Antanas's creative genius. When I sit at our bar, the sense of history is palpable—the Beatrice Inn was one of New York's first speakeasies, frequented by the likes of Zelda and F. Scott Fitzgerald, Ernest Hemingway, and others. It was a mobbed-up Italian joint for over fifty years, where the greats came to eat veal Milanese, and the famed American dancer Paul Draper tapped on the tables after his meal. It was later owned by downtown nightlife impresario Paul Sevigny, who transformed it into a notorious club and den of sin for A-list celebrities and their hangers-on. We draw from this history daily, most especially at the bar.

Marco Pierre White once said that to make a great restaurant, you need three things: service, ambience, and food—in that order. The bar at the Beatrice has all three in spades. Every night is a new show at our bar. When we first open for the evening, it feels like a cabaret—intimate and sophisticated, with glossy ceilings reflecting the candlelight. As the night progresses, it becomes more like a rock concert. My bartenders are all charismatic and devastatingly charming. At any given moment, magic tricks are performed, ice cubes fly through the air, and women climb up onto the bar—it's truly a sight to behold. Somehow, through all the chaos, the nightly dance at the bar continues to be one of the most beautiful ballets I have ever seen.

ONE OF THE FIRST classic French braises I mastered was Julia Child's beef bourguignon, which I find tremendously soul-satisfying to make in addition to being satisfying to eat. In this recipe, I've taken the idea of classic beef bourguignon and snails cooked Burgundy-style and married them to create something quite delicious. I love to pair rich cuts of beef like oxtail with escargots, which are, by their very nature, a flavor vessel, absorbing whatever they're cooked in. The dish is a lovely and warming one that you can leave simmering on the stovetop all day for a Sunday dinner, though like most braises, it tastes even better when made a day in advance and given time to settle.

OXTAIL AND ESCARGOT BOURGUIGNON *Serves 2 or 3*

2 tablespoons (27 g) extra-virgin olive oil

3 pounds (1.35 kg) oxtail, cut into 3½-inch pieces (ask your butcher)

Kosher salt

¼ cup (30 g) all-purpose flour

1 (750 ml) bottle red wine, such as Cabernet Sauvignon

6 cups (1.3 kg) Beef Stock (page 283)

1 medium onion, halved

1 head garlic, halved horizontally

1 bunch thyme

2 bay leaves

15 escargots, in the shell, cleaned, or 1 cup (151 g) highest quality canned escargots, rinsed and drained

Chopped fresh parsley, for garnish

In a large Dutch oven or heavy-bottomed pot, heat the olive oil over medium-high heat. Generously season the oxtail with salt on all sides. Working in batches as needed, sear the oxtail, turning, until deep golden brown all over, about 10 minutes total. Pour off any drippings and discard.

Sprinkle the flour on the oxtail and shake to coat, then return the pot to medium-high heat and cook, turning occasionally, until the flour has browned slightly, 3 to 4 minutes. Add the wine and allow to simmer for at least 2 minutes to cook off the alcohol and deglaze the pan, scraping up any browned bits from the bottom. Add the beef stock and bring to a simmer.

Wrap the onion, garlic, thyme, and bay leaves in a square of cheesecloth and tie the ends to make a sachet. Add the sachet to the pot, bring the liquid to a boil, then reduce the heat to low. Cover with a cartouche (see page 293) to slow the rate of evaporation, then cover with a lid. Gently simmer

until the oxtail is totally tender and slipping off the bone, about 4 hours. Skim as much fat off the top as possible. (If you choose to make this a day in advance, refrigerate the cooked oxtail overnight at this point and remove the fat that solidifies on top the next day.)

To serve, uncover the oxtail, place the pot over medium heat, and bring it to a simmer. Add the escargots and cook for 10 minutes to heat them through and thicken the sauce slightly. Remove the cheesecloth sachet, sprinkle in chopped parsley, and taste for seasoning. Serve immediately.

SUMMER

WHEN I WAS A CHILD, maybe seven or eight years old, my father had two classic Jaguars, special editions, only one hundred of them made in the world. He loved those cars. We'd go out for a drive and pass the farmers from eastern Washington who had come to set up little fruit stands, with cardboard signs advertising their cherries. They'd have Rainiers, the big beautiful yellow cherries, and Bings, which are my favorite. We'd get big brown paper bags full of cherries, and I'd sit in the passenger seat, eating the fruit and spitting the pits out the window. He would constantly scold me for getting sticky cherry juice all over his burnished red leather seats, but I had fun anyway. This dessert reminds me of those drives—and I think it keeps the cherries true to what they are.

CHERRY CLAFOUTIS WITH HONEYED WHIPPED CREAM *Serves 6*

CLAFOUTIS

2 tablespoons (30 g) unsalted butter

6 tablespoons (95 g) sugar

6 tablespoons (55 g) all-purpose flour

1 teaspoon (3 g) kosher salt

¾ cup (180 g) whole milk

3 large eggs

Seeds of 1 vanilla bean

9 ounces (264 g) Bing cherries (about 2 cups), pitted

HONEYED WHIPPED CREAM

2 cups (450 g) heavy cream

1 tablespoon plus 1 teaspoon (20 g) sugar

2 tablespoons (40 g) Smoked Honey (page 271)

MAKE THE CLAFOUTIS: Preheat the oven to 425°F.

In a small pot, heat the butter over medium-high heat and swirl constantly until the milk solids are toasted and brown, about 4 minutes. Remove the pan from the heat and set aside.

In a large bowl, whisk together the sugar, flour, and salt. Whisk in the milk until fully incorporated. Crack in the eggs, one at a time, whisking after each addition. Add the vanilla seeds and stir to incorporate. When the batter is even and smooth, slowly stream in the browned butter, whisking as you pour, making sure to scrape up and incorporate all the ingredients.

Pour the batter into a deep 9-inch pie dish and dot the cherries evenly over the batter. Bake until puffed and golden brown and the center is set but still slightly wobbly, 35 to 45 minutes. The clafoutis will puff up like a soufflé while it bakes and sink as it comes out of the oven.

MAKE THE HONEY WHIPPED CREAM: In a stand mixer fitted with the whisk attachment, whip together the cream and sugar until stiff peaks form, about 6 minutes. Using a rubber spatula, gently fold in the smoked honey.

Present the clafoutis whole, while still warm, with the whipped cream in a separate bowl alongside, for people to garnish as they wish.

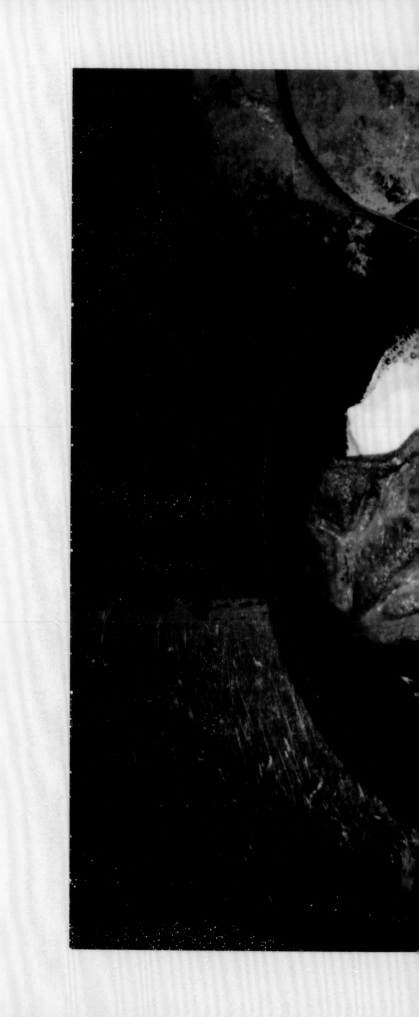

SMOKED PORK SHOULDER STEAK WITH SUMMER HERBS, CHERRY CONSERVA, AND MUSTARD–BONE MARROW BUTTER *(page 160)*

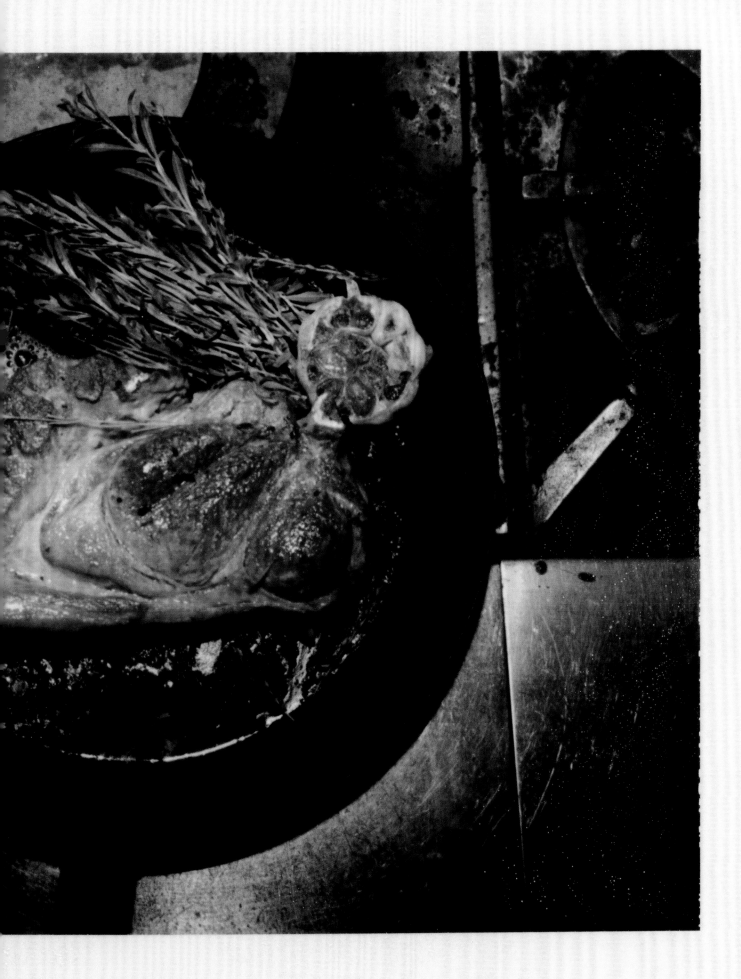

BEFORE I BECAME A CHEF, I left my job in the corporate world, took out all my savings, and traveled around the globe to try to figure out what I wanted to do. I dined alone at the only Michelin-starred restaurant in Seville at the time, where I was served an Ibérico pork shoulder that changed my life in one bite. The pork was dark and marbled with fat, seared, and served rare. It was unlike any pork I'd ever had before—and I realized then and there that I should be cooking.

Because that dish was burned so vividly and exactly in my memory, I resisted cooking pork chops for years. None of the pork I could find in the US had the right flavor or marbling; it usually tasted more like chicken than the full beefy flavor I remembered so fondly. I searched long and hard before finally discovering the pork rib eye, a little-used butcher's cut that's a cross section of the shoulder. (It's not actually a rib eye since it's not from the rib, but that's what some butchers call it because its texture and marbling are so similar to that of a beef rib eye.)

It's incredibly special—you can only get two off each animal, so it's worth calling a butcher you trust in advance to ensure you can experience it yourself. Because this cut is so flavorful, I like to keep the garnishes simple. Everyone associates pork with apples, but I prefer cherries, especially in the summer, when I can't seem to get enough of them. Meaty Bing cherries pair spectacularly with a rich cut of pork. I prefer to use slow-churned French Beurre de Baratte in the mustard–bone marrow butter here, because I like the way its natural funkiness stands up to the meat.

SMOKED PORK SHOULDER STEAK WITH SUMMER HERBS,
CHERRY CONSERVA, AND MUSTARD–BONE MARROW BUTTER   *Serves 2*

NOTES: *You will need a handheld smoking gun (see page 293) for this recipe.*

The conserva should be chilled immediately after making for at least 3 hours and up to overnight to preserve its vibrant color. As it chills, its color should brighten into a jeweled garnet tone.

1 (42-ounce/1.2 kg) bone-in pork shoulder steak

Applewood chips, for smoking

1 head garlic, scalped (see page 293)

1 tablespoon (14 g) extra-virgin olive oil

Kosher salt and freshly ground black pepper

3 tablespoons (44 g) rendered pork fat (see page 286) or olive oil

1 tablespoon (15 g) unsalted butter

½ bunch thyme

2 sprigs rosemary

½ bunch lavender

½ bunch savory

5 tablespoons (70 g) Mustard–Bone Marrow Butter (recipe follows)

½ cup (60 g) Cherry Conserva (page 203)

Cold-smoke (see page 293) the pork with applewood chips for 20 minutes, until the meat has absorbed the smoky flavor.

Preheat the oven to 400°F.

Dress the garlic with the olive oil and salt and pepper to taste. Wrap in foil and roast until the cloves are golden and soft, about 25 minutes.

Meanwhile, in a large ovenproof sauté pan, heat the rendered pork fat over high heat. Season the pork all over with salt. Add to the pan and sear for 1½ minutes on one side, then flip and sear for another 1½ minutes. Continue to sear the pork, flipping every minute, for 8 minutes, until evenly golden brown.

Transfer the pan to the oven with the garlic pouch. Roast the pork for 5 minutes, then flip and roast for another 5 minutes until medium-rare (a thermometer inserted in the center should read 115°F) and a beautiful deep golden color.

Remove the pork from the oven and return it to the stovetop over medium-high heat. Add the butter and all of the herbs. Cook the pork, basting it with its own rendered fat, until the herbs are fragrant, 1 to 2 minutes. Transfer the pork and the herbs to a wire rack to rest for 10 minutes; the internal temperature will rise to about 120°F for medium. Reserve the browned butter and fats in the pan.

To serve, carve the pork off the bone and cut into ½-inch slices. Arrange on a platter and pour any accumulated juices over the pork. Dot the marrow-mustard butter over the meat and dress with a few spoonfuls each of cherry conserva and the reserved browned butter and fats. Arrange the roasted garlic and herbs on top as garnish.

MUSTARD–BONE MARROW BUTTER
Makes 2 cups

8 ounces (235 g) salted butter (ideally Beurre de Baratte), at room temperature

1 cup plus 3 tablespoons (235 g) Rendered Bone Marrow (page 284)

1 teaspoon (3 g) kosher salt

1 tablespoon (25 g) whole-grain mustard

In a food processor, pulse the softened butter, bone marrow, salt, and mustard together until just combined. Alternatively, you can do this by hand in a medium bowl. Mustard–bone marrow butter keeps, refrigerated, for up to 5 days.

PINK FLOYD *Makes 1 cocktail*

—ANTANAS SAMKUS, BAR DIRECTOR

"Rhubarb is one of my favorite summer ingredients, and Chef uses it a lot in the kitchen, so it's nice to have a cocktail that matches. Everything in this drink shouts summer, really—grassy cachaça, flowery St-Germain, fresh strawberries, and of course, the rhubarb. These ingredients come together with a silky pureed texture, and just a hint of bitterness from peppercorns at the end. There's a full bouquet of flavors here, which are altogether very sexy, very light, and very fresh, perfect when it's blazingly hot outside. It's pink in color, and therefore is named after one of my favorite bands."

1½ ounces cachaça

½ ounce St-Germain elderflower liqueur

½ ounce Campari

½ ounce lemon juice

½ ounce simple syrup

1½ ounces Rhubarb Puree (recipe follows)

1 dash of grapefruit bitters

Ice cubes

Freshly ground pink peppercorns, for garnish

Combine the cachaça, St-Germain, Campari, lemon juice, simple syrup, rhubarb puree, and grapefruit bitters in an ice-filled cocktail shaker. Shake hard for 30 seconds. Strain into a coupe glass and garnish with ground pink peppercorns.

RHUBARB PUREE
Makes about 2 cups

5 stalks rhubarb, cut into 2-inch pieces

8 ounces (225 g) strawberries (about 1½ cups), halved

¾ cup (150 g) sugar

½ cup (120 g) lemon juice

2 slices fresh ginger

In a small pot, combine the rhubarb, strawberries, sugar, lemon juice, ginger, and ½ cup water and bring to a boil over high heat. Reduce the heat to low and simmer, stirring frequently, until the rhubarb is soft, 10 to 15 minutes. Transfer the mixture to a blender and puree until smooth, then chill for 1 hour before using. Store in the refrigerator for up to 2 days.

BOUDIN NOIR *(page 166)*

MANY CULTURES have their own version of blood sausage, and I love them all—*morcilla* in Spain, black pudding in the UK, and blood cake in Vietnam, to name just a few. But my very favorite is the French *boudin noir,* which is traditionally made with pork fat and blood, bound with rice.

This recipe pays homage to *boudin noir,* but with my own touches: I like to use not only the pork belly fat cap, but also some of the meat that it lines for texture, as well as jasmine rice, dried overnight and finely chopped, so it becomes almost pearlescent. I like the jasmine rice for its floral notes

as well, which add an unexpected feminine element. Too often, you hear "blood sausage" and think big, iron-y flavors, but here you get notes of cinnamon, nutmeg, brown sugar, and jasmine balancing out the meaty, metallic bass notes. Think Chanel.

BOUDIN NOIR *Makes eight 5-inch links*

NOTES: Boudin noir *takes 2 days to make, so plan accordingly. The jasmine rice must be cooked in advance, spread out on a baking sheet, and chilled overnight, uncovered, in the refrigerator to dry it out.*

Fresh pig's blood can be sourced from a butcher you respect with a few days' notice. Use it within 1 to 2 days, or freeze it. It should be cooked gently to avoid curdling.

Hog casings can also be sourced from a butcher you respect.

Boudin noir *is wonderful served on its own, or as part of the venison cassoulet on page 88.*

8 ounces (220 g) unsalted butter

2 cups (220 g) diced Spanish onion

Kosher salt

2 loosely packed cups (262 g) diced pork fatback

1 cup (189 g) cooked jasmine rice, dried overnight in the refrigerator (see Notes)

3½ cups (850 g) pig's blood

⅓ cup (62 g) brown sugar

½ teaspoon (1 g) ground cinnamon

½ teaspoon (1 g) grated nutmeg

1 cup (225 g) heavy cream

1 teaspoon (3 g) freshly ground black pepper

4½ ounces (130 g) hog casings (two 30-inch lengths)

1 tablespoon (14 g) olive oil

In a large sauté pan, melt the butter over medium-low heat. Add the onion and sweat very slowly until it's just cooked through but hasn't taken on any color, about 20 minutes. Season to taste with salt, then spread out on a parchment-lined baking sheet and set aside.

Bring a medium pot of water to a boil and season until salty like the sea. Add the pork fat and cook until tender, 8 to 10 minutes. Drain and set aside.

Meanwhile, place the dried rice on a cutting board and chop until it becomes pearlescent, or is roughly the texture of coarse grits.

In a medium pot, bring 3 inches water to a boil. In a large metal bowl that can sit over (but not in) the boiling water, whisk together the blood, brown sugar, cinnamon, and nutmeg. Set over the boiling water and whisk until the blood becomes very foamy, 6 to 8 minutes. Once foamy, the blood will change in consistency, beginning to resemble cold maple syrup, and the foam will die down.

When the foam dies down, whisk in the heavy cream. The consistency will first loosen, but continue whisking until the mixture starts to tighten again, 4 to 6 minutes. Use a rubber spatula to scrape down the bottom and sides of the bowl to ensure nothing is stuck and overcooking. (If the mixture is cooking too quickly on the bottom or sides, remove the metal bowl from over the steam and continue whisking off the heat, alternating back and forth between hot steam and no steam to ensure even cooking.) Continue whisking until the mixture turns a dark chocolate color with the consistency of a thick melted chocolate, 2 to 4 minutes more. Remove the metal bowl from the double boiler and whisk in the chopped rice, onions, and pork fat. Season with 1 tablespoon (9 g) kosher salt and the pepper.

Rinse the casings in cold running water, then open them beneath the faucet to ensure there are no holes. Cut the casings into two 30-inch lengths and tie a knot at one end on each length.

Set up a large bowl of ice and water. Bring a large pot of water to just below a simmer (165°F) over medium-low heat.

Divide the blood mixture evenly between two pastry bags. Snip ¼ inch off of the end of the pastry bag and loosely pipe the mixture into the casings, leaving at least 1 inch between the end of the filling and the end of the casing. Tie off one end of the casing in a small knot. Twist each casing as you go into 5-inch links, then tie off the ends.

Gently place the sausages in the barely simmering water and poach until they have firmed up (but are not hard), 30 to 35 minutes. The sausages should be slightly firm but still with a little give when squeezed, and the color should be a deep oxblood. If any of the links rise to the top

of the water, use a cake tester to poke a few holes in the casings so the air can escape.

Plunge the sausages into the ice water bath until completely cool, 6 to 8 minutes. Transfer the sausages to the refrigerator to chill for at least 3 hours and up to overnight to set. As they set, their color will deepen to a shade closer to black.

To serve, add the olive oil and the sausages to a large sauté pan. Turn the heat to medium and warm the sausages very slowly, so the casings brown but remain intact, and the internal temperature rises gradually. Cook on one side without disturbing for 6 to 7 minutes. Flip once and reduce the heat to medium-low, and cook until heated through and browned on all sides, about 5 minutes.

AT THE BEA, we have a fantastic late-night bar scene. I love the contradiction of a fun-yet-elegant dining room against a raucous bar, so naturally I wanted a late-night bar bite that embodied all of that, and as a bonus, is meant to be eaten with your hands. We decided to serve the fried chicken we often make for family meal at the bar, which draws quite a crowd during those late hours. In keeping with the romantic high-low spirit of late-night New York, we pair our fried chicken with a Champagne—as any civilized New Yorker would.

BUTTERMILK FRIED CHICKEN *Serves 3 or 4*

6 bone-in, skin-on chicken thighs

6 chicken drumsticks

Kosher salt

3 cups (705 g) buttermilk

4 cups (480 g) all-purpose flour

¼ cup (24 g) cayenne pepper

About 4 quarts (3.5 kg) canola oil, for deep-frying

6 ounces (174 g) honey

1 tablespoon (12 g) Tapatío hot sauce

1 tablespoon (15 g) Tabasco sauce

Smoked sea salt

NOTE: *The chicken must cure for 3 hours, so plan accordingly.*

Arrange the chicken on a baking sheet and season generously all over with kosher salt. Set aside for 3 hours to cure—1½ hours in the refrigerator, then 1½ hours at room temperature.

Set up a dredging station in 3 medium bowls: Fill one with the buttermilk. Evenly divide the flour and cayenne between 2 bowls. Add 2½ tablespoons (25 g) kosher salt to each bowl of flour and stir together.

Pour 5 inches oil into a countertop fryer, Dutch oven, or large heavy-bottomed pot with a thermometer clipped to the side. Bring the oil to 325°F over medium-high heat.

While the oil heats, dredge the chicken: Working in batches, dip the chicken into one bowl of the flour mixture, turning to coat evenly, and shaking off any excess. Dip the chicken in buttermilk, then dip it into the second flour mixture, ensuring an even coating. Transfer the chicken to a baking sheet with a wire rack set on top.

When the oil reaches 325°F, working in batches, carefully drop in one piece of chicken at a time, shaking the pot ever so slightly so the pieces don't stick together. Cook, turning occasionally with tongs, until golden brown and crispy, 15 to 20 minutes. A thermometer inserted into the thickest part of each piece should reach 160°F, which will rise to about 165°F as it rests. Transfer the chicken to a wire rack to drain and season lightly with kosher salt while hot. Repeat with the remaining chicken. Let the chicken rest somewhere warm for 8 to 10 minutes.

In a small pot over medium heat, combine the honey and both hot sauces and bring to barely a simmer. Remove from the heat.

Transfer the chicken to a serving platter and, using a spoon, lightly drizzle the spicy honey over the top. Season with a pinch of smoked sea salt and serve.

**BUMBLEBERRY CAKE WITH
WHIPPED CRÈME FRAÎCHE**

(page 172)

I BELIEVE one of the greatest processed desserts of all time is the Entenmann's All Butter Loaf Cake. When I was growing up, my mother, who wasn't a huge cook, would buy a Butter Loaf and macerate some berries for it and top it with Cool Whip when she wanted a quick dessert that looked beautiful but didn't require much effort in the kitchen. To this day, I think that if any homemade dessert can even come close to that, you have a winner.

This recipe is about taking that idea, but making a beautiful butter pound cake with all of these amazing berries baked into it. As I've gotten older, I've come to appreciate desserts that are a bit less sweet, so having a whipped crème fraîche adds a tartness and acidity that cuts through the dense pound cake just enough. It's a perfect dessert for the dog days of summer, when berries are at their peak.

Just to be clear, there is no such thing as a bumbleberry; the term "bumbleberries" refers to the Canadian mixed-berry pie that I loved as a child.

BUMBLEBERRY CAKE WITH WHIPPED CRÈME FRAÎCHE *Serves 10*

2 cups (277 g) blueberries

1¼ cups (156 g) raspberries

1⅓ cups (184 g) blackberries

2¼ cups (486 g) sugar

1 pound (453 g) unsalted butter, at room temperature

6 large eggs

3½ cups (414 g) all-purpose flour

2 teaspoons (6 g) kosher salt

½ cup (119 g) heavy cream

2 tablespoons plus 1 teaspoon (25 g) crème fraîche

1 teaspoon (4 g) vanilla extract

WHIPPED CRÈME FRAÎCHE

2 cups (450 g) heavy cream

2 tablespoons (27 g) sugar

1 cup (168 g) crème fraîche

Freshly cracked black pepper, for garnish

Preheat the oven to 325°F. Grease the bottom and sides of a 10-inch cake pan, then line the bottom with a round of parchment paper and grease the parchment as well.

In a large bowl, combine the blueberries, raspberries, blackberries, and ¼ cup of the sugar and set aside to macerate for 15 to 20 minutes.

In a standing mixer fitted with the paddle attachment, beat together the butter and remaining 2 cups sugar on high speed until light and fluffy, 6 to 8 minutes. Reduce the speed to medium and add the eggs, one at a time, beating well after each addition, and scraping down the sides of the bowl every two eggs.

In a large bowl, combine the flour and salt. Reduce the mixer speed to low and add the flour mixture in three additions, alternating with the heavy cream, beginning and ending with the flour. Add the crème fraîche and vanilla and mix until combined.

Pour the berries and their juices into the prepared pan, then top with the cake batter, smoothing the surface and gently tapping the bottom of the pan against the counter to release any air bubbles.

Bake until a tester comes out clean, about 1 hour 20 minutes. Remove the cake from the oven and run a thin knife around the edge of the pan, then invert the cake onto a rack to finish cooling to room temperature. I like to do this as soon as the cake comes out, to keep the berries from caramelizing and sticking to the pan. It should be sturdy enough to hold together.

JUST BEFORE SERVING, MAKE THE WHIPPED CRÈME FRAÎCHE: In a stand mixer fitted with the whisk attachment, combine the heavy cream, sugar, and crème fraîche and whip on high speed until soft peaks form, 6 to 8 minutes.

To serve, cut the cake into wedges and top with a dollop of whipped crème fraîche and a few cracks of black pepper.

APRÈS NOUS, LE DÉLUGE
AFTER US, THE FLOOD

WHEN MY TWO BROTHERS and I were kids, our uncles would regale us with tales of their childhood: growing up in the slums of Seattle's Chinatown, getting into fights at the local pool hall, riding their motorcycles through the window of a bar because someone made a pass at one of their girlfriends. We were enchanted, fully enthralled by the drama of the stories, and frankly, floored that our uncles were so badass. But our father usually sat quietly with a slight smile on his face, and I sensed he was recalling those days himself, with both fondness and pain. My father was the second youngest of ten children, and they grew up in both of these extremes.

In the early 1920s, my grandfather, who had come to the States to work on the railroad, had accumulated a sizable amount of wealth, but by his death had either gambled it or loaned it all away. When my grandmother tried to collect what was owed, she was met with a cold shoulder by the people they had once called friends. So she was left to raise ten children by herself, and when she passed, my father's two older sisters returned to Seattle from New York to take care of him and the other siblings. If they hadn't, the younger children would have been split up into orphanages. Through those years, during the Great Depression, my family suffered extreme poverty. There was never enough food to go around. My father never spoke about that time, but my uncles told us my Auntie Ruby sent them to the back doors of Chinatown restaurants for scraps every day, or fishing so they could eat. Ruby was the eldest of the children and when my grandmother passed, she naturally became the matriarch of the Mar family. She worked tirelessly to provide for her siblings so they could have an education, something she had forgone. In the '40s and '50s she worked to become a celebrated restaurateur, hustling on the floor of her famed Ruby Chow's dining room every night, shaking the hands of politicians and celebrities, and providing jobs for not only her siblings and Seattle's Chinese community, but also for future stars such as Bruce Lee, who washed pots in the kitchen.

The Mar siblings' experiences in the early years taught them something they passed down to our generation, and something that has been the foundation for my chosen family at the restaurant: We stick together. They worked to put each other through school. They went into the navy together. They started businesses together, and employed other members of the family. As they rose, they brought each other up. Because every move they made beginning from the time my grandparents passed was not just for their betterment, but for their survival.

I often reflect on how the three of us kids and our cousins were raised. My father, my uncles, and my aunties always stressed the importance of family. My Uncle Ping, Auntie Ruby's husband, nicknamed my brothers and me "Big, Medium, and Little Horses," because our last name means "horse" in Chinese, and as such he told us always to remain noble, like a trusted warhorse that has seen many battles. Sometimes used to our advantage, albeit not our better judgment, we'd use the "I'm from *that* Mar family" card if pulled over for

AUNTIE RUBY REGULARLY HOSTED SUNDAY SUPPERS, SERVING MY FAVORITE CHINESE DISHES, LIKE COLD NOODLES WITH HAM AND SCALLIONS, OR MY FATHER'S FAVORITE, TOMATO BEEF. UNCLE PING WOULD SING CHINESE OPERA SONGS FOR US.

speeding, or if we'd been caught by the police for partying a little too hard. The elder Mars believed ardently that it takes a village to raise a child, and at least one of them always seemed to be around to pull us back when we were getting out of hand. We'd hide from them for days, but somehow they would always find out.

Auntie Ruby regularly hosted Sunday Suppers, serving my favorite Chinese dishes, like cold noodles with ham and scallions, or my father's favorite, tomato beef. Uncle Ping would sing Chinese opera songs for us. When my father hosted these dinners at our place, we would have roasted racks of lamb glazed with orange marmalade, roast duck, and Ruby's sticky rice. My family never believed in courses—rather, we just believed in one giant meal with all the delicious things set about the table for us to pick at

throughout the evening, bouncing from savory to sweet and back again. The men would retire to the formal living room, sinking into the plush green-silk sofas, smoking cigarettes and reminiscing. The ladies would clean the kitchen and complain about the cigarettes in the house and how the smoke would stain the antiques. Sunday Supper has long been a tradition in our family, and it's one I still hold very dear to this day. Those meals taught us the value of family, staying together, and of self-sacrifice for the betterment of everyone as a whole. They also taught us about success, strategy, compromise, and the art of war, as no family with ten siblings and countless cousins ever comes without a bit of drama.

Every summer, my cousin Melissa, daughter of Auntie Darlene, would get dropped off at my house. We were thick as thieves. We went horseback riding together, blackberry picking together, shopping together, and—much to my father's horror—when we were eight, we got our ears pierced together. Melissa and I now own the Beatrice together—a full realization of her mother and my father's dream: for us to keep any of the businesses we have in the family. Because we could always trust each other, they said, and we could help one another. Knowing that we are blood means our endgame will always be the same, regardless of any disagreements that arise between us from time to time. We protect each other, now and always. And Jordan Luke, our second cousin, is a cook at the Bea. My father would have loved that—Melissa and I grew up running around Jordan's father's restaurant in Seattle, and now he's growing up in our kitchen, just as it should be.

The saying *après nous, le déluge,* or "after us, the flood," comes from the tumultuous love between Madame de Pompadour and King Louis XV. I turn to this phrase time and time again, as it means a great deal to me. When I use it to describe our restaurant, it means that after you experience what we do, the bar is set and everything and everyone else who follows must live up to it. But when I use it in reference to my family, I mean the depth of love, loyalty, and dedication we have built, spanning generations and cementing legacies. This is everything. There can be nothing else.

ONE OF MY FATHER'S SPECIALTIES was rack of lamb glazed with a sticky orange marmalade, which he always made in the summer for backyard barbecues and pool parties. What I loved most about his method was that as it cooked, he continued to glaze it, so all the sugars would start to caramelize and the top wound up crispy, almost like a brûlée. My brothers would snag the meat and then give me the bones when we were kids, which were (and are) my favorite part. I love the little bits of crunchy-tender, savory-sweet meat and fat and sinew closest to the bones, where the marmalade has almost crystallized around the cartilage. This version is very much my homage to my father's dish, with an updated cooking technique. The in-and-out roasting process creates a perfectly even pink color in the lamb, so it almost looks like it's been cooked sous vide, but without any special equipment.

ROAST RACK OF LAMB WITH ORANGE AND SUMMER MINT   *Serves 4*

2 lamb racks (3½ to 4 pounds/ 1.6 to 1.8 kg total)

8 cups (1.7 kg) Chicken Stock (page 283)

2 oranges

¼ cup (47 g) sugar

Kosher salt and freshly ground black pepper

MINT SAUCE

1 cup (55 g) chopped fresh mint

¾ cup (35 g) chopped fresh parsley

2 tablespoons (26 g) chopped salt-cured anchovies

½ cup (110 g) extra-virgin olive oil

Kosher salt

Trim and French the lamb racks, reserving the fat and finger meat and any chine bones.

In a large pot, combine the reserved lamb bones and finger meat and cook over medium-high heat until deep mahogany-hued, 10 to 12 minutes. Pour off the rendered fat, leaving the bones and meat in the pan, and return the pot to medium heat. Add the chicken stock, bring to a simmer, and deglaze the pot, scraping up any browned bits from the bottom. Increase the heat to high and bring to a boil, then reduce the heat to low and simmer until the liquid is reduced by half, 50 to 60 minutes.

Pull off 2 strips of orange zest with a vegetable peeler and juice both oranges. Add the zest strips, orange juice, and sugar to the pot. Cook until the liquid is reduced again by half, 35 to 40 minutes more. The glaze should have a very sticky consistency from all the collagen in the bones, but still be liquid, with a satin finish on the back of a spoon. Strain out the solids, check for seasoning, adjust as necessary, and set the orange glaze aside.

Meanwhile, preheat the oven to 450°F.

Season the lamb racks all over with salt. Place fat-side up on a rack set inside a baking dish and roast for 7 to 8 minutes. Remove from the oven, flip the lamb bone-side up, return to the oven, and roast for 7 to 8 minutes more. Remove the lamb and let rest for 10 minutes. Reduce the oven temperature to 250°F.

Return the lamb to the oven, bone-side up, and roast for 5 minutes. Remove and flip to fat-side up, then baste the meat with the reserved orange glaze using a spoon or pastry brush. Return to the oven for another 2 minutes, then baste again with the glaze, and roast another 3 minutes until medium-rare (a thermometer inserted into the thickest part should read about 115°F). Remove and brush one last time with the glaze, and season with 10 to 15 cracks of freshly ground black pepper on the fat side. Let the meat rest for 10 to 12 minutes.

WHILE THE MEAT TAKES ITS FINAL REST, MAKE THE MINT SAUCE: In a small bowl, combine the mint, parsley, anchovies, and olive oil and whisk to combine. Check for seasoning, adjusting as necessary, and transfer to a serving bowl.

To serve, cut the lamb into double chops and serve with any leftover glaze and mint sauce alongside.

**ROAST RACK OF LAMB WITH
ORANGE AND SUMMER MINT**

(page 178)

THIS CAKE IS RICH, dense, moist, and sweet—in other words, everything a classic chocolate cake should be. It's not on the menu, but I'll make it by special request, and it's the cake I make for my kid brothers when I visit them, as well as send to Pat LaFrieda any time I need to butter him up for a meat favor (quite literally).

I'm not a pastry chef at all, so the intimidating part of this recipe for me has always been getting the extra-thick frosting right, texturally speaking, so that I can spread it evenly. I don't have the patience to smooth the frosting perfectly; I just like to pile it on the top and move it around a bit on the sides with an offset spatula or even the back of a

soup spoon to make it even. You'll probably have more patience, but don't be overly concerned with smoothing the frosting. This is a rustic, grandmother-style cake, perfectly imperfect as it is.

DOUBLE LAYER CHOCOLATE AND ESPRESSO CAKE *Serves 8 to 10*

FROSTING

2 cups plus 1 tablespoon (485 g) heavy cream

5 tablespoons (60 g) sugar

6½ tablespoons (142 g) light corn syrup

2¼ pounds (1 kg) 70% cacao chocolate, roughly chopped

17 ounces (493 g) butter, at room temperature, cut into ½-inch cubes

CAKE

4½ ounces (127 g) 70% cacao Valrhona chocolate, roughly chopped (1 cup)

2 cups plus 2 tablespoons (500 g) hot brewed coffee

5 large eggs

1 cup (217 g) canola oil

1 cup (235 g) buttermilk

1½ teaspoons (6 g) vanilla extract

3¼ cups (383 g) all-purpose flour

3 cups plus 2 tablespoons (249 g) unsweetened cocoa powder

2½ cups (507 g) sugar

1¼ teaspoons (6 g) baking soda

⅜ teaspoon (2 g) baking powder

1 teaspoon (3 g) kosher salt

MAKE THE FROSTING: In a small pot, combine the cream, sugar, and corn syrup and bring to a low simmer over medium heat, stirring frequently. Remove the pan from the heat.

In a heatproof bowl set over (not in) a pan of simmering water, melt the chocolate completely, stirring often, about 10 minutes. Whisk into the cream mixture to combine.

Slowly add the butter, whisking to melt. Transfer to a large shallow bowl to cool. Stir occasionally until cool enough to spread, 30 to 60 minutes.

MEANWHILE, MAKE THE CAKE: Preheat the oven to 350°F. Grease two 10-inch cake pans and line the bottoms with parchment paper.

Place the chocolate in a heatproof medium bowl. Pour the hot coffee over the chocolate and let sit for about 10 minutes to melt. Stir until smooth.

In a stand mixer fitted with the whisk attachment, beat the eggs on high speed until thick and light yellow, 4 to 5 minutes. On medium speed, slowly beat in the oil, buttermilk, vanilla, and chocolate-coffee mixture until fully combined.

In a medium bowl, whisk together the flour, cocoa powder, sugar, baking soda, baking powder, and salt until incorporated.

With the mixer on low speed, slowly add the flour mixture in two batches to the wet ingredients and beat until just combined.

Divide the batter evenly between the prepared pans. Bake until a tester inserted in the centers of the cakes comes out clean, 10 to 15 minutes. Let the cakes cool completely in the pans before unmolding, about 30 minutes.

TO ASSEMBLE THE CAKE: Place one layer on a cake stand or wire rack. Spoon enough frosting on the cake layer to cover, about ½ inch deep (about 2 cups). Place the second cake layer on top and spread the remaining frosting over the top, then spread as evenly as possible across the sides. Serve.

THERE IS a Sophia Loren movie called *La Mortadella* (or, as it was known in America, *Lady Liberty*), in which she plays a woman coming to New York from Italy with a gift of a giant roll of mortadella for her fiancé. She gets detained at customs and then proceeds to feed all of the agents her mortadella, sparking a diplomatic controversy. I love this movie, not only because I love Sophia, but also because it reinforces the idea of food solving problems.

Our mortadella (otherwise known as bologna, and originating from the Italian town of Bologna) isn't traditional at all—we use amaretto liqueur, and add tremendously feminine notes like vanilla and pink peppercorn. I like to think of this mortadella as a beautiful tribute to the actress herself.

BOLOGNA DE BOLOGNA

Makes five 6-inch links

CURED PORK

2 pounds (962 g) pork shoulder, cut into 1-inch cubes (about 5 loose cups)

7¼ ounces (205 g) pork fatback, cut into 1-inch cubes (about 1½ loose cups)

¼ cup (35 g) kosher salt

1½ teaspoons (9 g) pink curing salt (see page 292)

⅜ teaspoon (1 g) grated nutmeg

2 tablespoons (13 g) juniper berries

3 tablespoons (12 g) pink peppercorns

1 vanilla bean, split lengthwise

BOLOGNA

Kosher salt

5 ounces (145 g) pork fatback, cut into ½-inch cubes (1 cup)

1 large egg white

3 tablespoons (22 g) milk powder

3 tablespoons (48 g) amaretto liqueur

½ cup plus 2 tablespoons (135 g) whole milk, frozen flat in a sturdy zip-top bag

2 tablespoons (9 g) black peppercorns

1 cup (120 g) pistachios

NOTE: *Mortadella takes 4 days to cure and 1 day to chill before serving, so plan accordingly.*

CURE THE PORK: In a large bowl, combine the pork shoulder, pork fatback, kosher salt, pink curing salt, nutmeg, juniper berries, and pink peppercorns. Scrape in the vanilla seeds and add the pod, too. Stir well to combine, ensuring that every bit of meat is coated in the seasonings. Cover tightly with plastic wrap and cure in the refrigerator for 4 days.

MAKE THE BOLOGNA: When the meat has cured, bring a small pot of water to a boil over high heat and salt it like the sea. Add the pork fat and boil for 3 minutes to blanch. Drain and set aside.

Discard the vanilla pod from the cured pork mixture. In a food processor, combine the cured pork mixture, egg white, milk powder, amaretto, and frozen milk (break it into small pieces with your

hands) and pulse until chopped. Run the machine until the mixture is whipped and smooth, about 8 minutes. Transfer to a large bowl and stir in the blanched pork fat, black peppercorns, and pistachios.

Divide the meat into 4 equal portions, about 1 pound each. Working with one portion at a time, lay out a sheet of plastic wrap about 2 feet long and place the mixture in the middle. Wrap the plastic around the pork very tightly, like a burrito or sushi roll,

making each tube about 6 inches long and 3 inches wide. Tie the ends of each tube so they can't unwrap, then prick a few holes in each tube with a cake tester or fork. Wrap the tube twice more in plastic.

Set up a large bowl of ice and water. Fill a large pot with water, clip a candy thermometer to the side, and bring to a simmer over low heat. Bring the water as close to 165°F as possible.

Add the bologna to the simmering water and poach until a thermometer inserted in the middle of the links reads 150°F, about 30 minutes. Plunge the bologna into the ice bath to cool, then refrigerate overnight to chill.

To serve, remove the bologna from the plastic and thinly slice. Enjoy as is.

PLAYING WITH FIRE: LONDON-STYLE

ONE OF THE THINGS I look most forward to every year is cooking in London, which I am fortunate enough to do every August with my sous-chef Nicole. London is a departure from how we cook at the Bea every day. We work outside, building an enormous A-frame out of piping and chains. It's about twelve feet tall, with a firepit with grill grates underneath. We start by hanging meat—animals we don't normally have access to in the States—from hooks on the chains very early in the day, at the very top of the frame. We start the fire using vines, and as the day goes on, every hour, slowly, we move the beef down the chain, closer and closer to the fire. This imparts a beautifully smoky flavor, and since the beef is suspended in the air over the fire, slowly cooking for almost ten hours, it picks up a great deal of that flavor. Eventually, we take it off the hooks and the steaks end up on the grill over direct heat to finish.

London is where I really became fascinated with breeds of beef and types of wood and vines to cook over, and where I began to learn about the nuances of terroir when it comes to both. Surely you've heard of terroir in relation to wine, but the concept applies much more widely. Terroir, whether in wine or wood, fruits or beef, is an expression of where the thing we are consuming comes from. How old was it? What did it eat when it was alive? What was it aged in? What is the climate like? How much beta-carotene is in the grass? How many dead Romans were in the soil? All of these factors apply. I found it tremendously eye-opening to be able to spend time with fantastic butchers, cooks, and owners of the London Log Company, who specifically turned me on to the subtleties in the terroir of the wood and vines we cook our animals over.

Owner Mark Parr is as crazy about firewood as I am about beef. I met him the first time I was cooking in London in August 2016. He asked me what type of wood I was looking for, and I answered "cherrywood, please." I could see his heart break just a bit, but I didn't know what I had done to disappoint him. Knowing what I know about Mark now, I had let him down with my incredibly basic request. I would soon learn that not all tinders are created equal. Mark beckoned me to the back of Tobacco Dock, the event space where we were cooking, saying he had something very special to show me. He revealed gnarled and knotted Pinot Meunier vines, hidden in large bags made of blue tarp, that looked like something out of a storybook. They were dirty, whimsical, and stunning all at once; I was transfixed by their curves, knots, and the long strands of bark that peeled back to reveal their inner layers. I knew I wouldn't be cooking with cherrywood that day.

Since then, I have felt a bond with Mark and the gents at London Log Company—they send me all kinds of different vine clippings, including Muscadet, Tempranillo, Grenache, Albariño, Pinot Meunier, and more—all of which burn differently, have different sugar contents, heat, smoke levels, and stories of how they came to be. Mark's adventures in procuring and harvesting all sorts of vines are some of the most romantic tales I've ever heard. He recently told me about a trip to Spain: Shortly after a lunch at Etxebarri, he received a call from a perfect stranger. He was instructed to drive forty-five minutes north of the restaurant to meet a man outside a rundown shack.

"Are you Mark?" the mystery man asked. "Come with me, I have something you'll be interested in." Mark was led behind the shack and through a gate, where he found one of his greatest discoveries to date: an entire valley of ninety-year-old Tempranillo vines that had been lost to the frost. He took the whole lot, dried them out, and now he houses them partially in his mill just outside of London, and partially in the basement cellar of the Beatrice Inn.

Cooking over a fire created from carefully chosen vines is a primal act, concerning only meat, salt, and flame. We are the only restaurant to cook over vines in the United States. I often think about how lucky we were to have met Mark when we did. I had just purchased the Beatrice,

and I believe that meeting him, learning from him, and sourcing from him has changed the course of my cooking—both how I view food and the creation of it.

Live-fire cooking is basic in concept, but complex in execution. At the Bea, we make sauces and accoutrements and all of these things to serve with composed dishes, which we of course love to do, but there is something equally powerful in the act of taking a tremendous piece of beef, accentuating it only with salt, then using interesting woods and the manipulation of fire to impart different flavors. Using this live-fire technique is unlike what we do at the restaurant, but at the same time, it's very much at the core of what we do. And that, to me, is a truly beautiful thing.

ONE OF MY FAVORITE things about dining in London is the British love of game meats. Whether roasted to the perfect medium-rare, confited, or pan-seared, these meats are presented simply and beautifully, often with a fruit compote or jelly. They might be served hot, at room temperature, or refrigerator-chilled. Experiencing this type of dining taught me a great deal. It crystallized in that moment in my head that food isn't just about seasoning, but also about temperature and texture. Every meal should touch every sense.

This hare dish is a perfect example. In the summer, when it's 100 degrees, my cousin and I sip rosé in the garden, surrounded by hydrangeas, and make this. It's lovely to have these summer flavors—savory, lavender, and crispy hare—contrasted with the cold huckleberry conserva.

TEMPRANILLO VINE-SMOKED HARE
WITH HUCKLEBERRY CONSERVA AND VANILLA   *Serves 2*

NOTES: *The hare needs to be salted at least 3 hours in advance or ideally overnight, so plan accordingly.*

You will need a handheld smoking gun (see page 293) for this recipe.

SMOKED HARE CONFIT

1 whole hare (3¾ pounds/1.7 kg), cut into 7 pieces (see Notes, page 91)

Tempranillo vines

Kosher salt

About 4 quarts (3.5 kg) canola oil

HUCKLEBERRY CONSERVA

4 cups (635 g) huckleberries

1 tablespoon (14 g) sugar, plus more to taste

1½ teaspoons (4 g) kosher salt

5 cracks black pepper

FOR FINISHING

1 head Garlic Confit (page 280)

1 bunch savory

1 bunch lavender

1½ vanilla beans, split lengthwise, seeds not scraped

MAKE THE SMOKED HARE CONFIT: Cold-smoke (see page 293) the hare with Tempranillo vines for 20 minutes, until the meat has absorbed the smoky flavor.

Season the hare with salt on all sides and allow it to sit uncovered in the refrigerator, for a minimum of 3 hours, or ideally overnight.

Preheat the oven to 300°F.

Place the hare in a large Dutch oven or heavy-bottomed pot and add enough canola oil to submerge completely. Cover with a cartouche (see page 293) to keep the hare under the oil, then cover the pot and transfer to the oven. Cook the meat until tender and the hind legs (the thickest part)

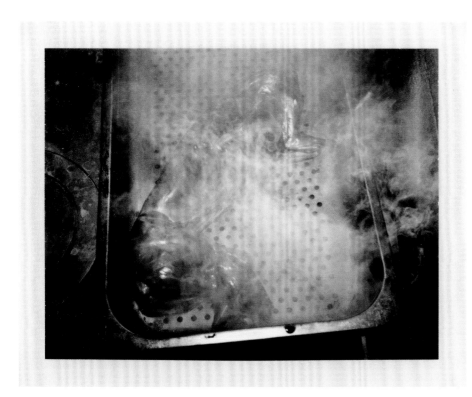

start to pull away from the bone, about 4 hours.

MEANWHILE, MAKE THE HUCKLEBERRY CONSERVA: First, taste the huckleberries, which are notoriously fickle, to see how sweet or tart they are and adjust the sugar amount accordingly. In a small saucepot, combine the huckleberries and desired amount of sugar and bring to a simmer over medium heat. Reduce the heat to medium-low and continue to simmer until the berries soften and release their juices, about 10 minutes. They should break down slightly and release some syrup, but do not crush the berries. Continue reducing until

the conserva evenly coats the back of a spoon, 25 to 30 minutes.

Remove the pan from the heat, season the conserva with salt, pepper, and sugar as needed. Transfer it to a shallow bowl and spread out to cool, then transfer quickly to the refrigerator to chill for 3 hours, to preserve the vibrant color. As the conserva chills, its color should brighten.

Let the hare cool in its oil at room temperature to maintain its juiciness. Remove the meat from the bones, reserving the confit oil.

FINISH THE DISH: In a large sauté pan, heat 5 tablespoons of the reserved hare confit oil over

high heat. Add the hare in a single layer and cook, undisturbed, until browned and crisp, 8 to 10 minutes. Flip and repeat on the other side, 8 to 10 minutes more. The hare will naturally release from the bottom of the pan when it's ready. In the last minute of cooking, add the garlic confit, savory, lavender, and vanilla beans to the pan. Use a spoon to baste the rendered fat up around the meat and herbs to release their aromas, 30 to 45 seconds.

Transfer the hare to a serving platter and garnish with the herbs, vanilla beans, and garlic. Serve with chilled conserva.

IT'S OFTEN SAID around this restaurant that when I die, I want to go with a lot of dead animals and a shit-ton of Mexican food. Lucero Ramales has been my sous-chef since the very beginning—she's been through life at the Bea when we were both just employees here, through my purchase of the Bea, and the revamping of this restaurant. And one of the things I love like a person is her pozole verde. Lucero learned how to make it from her mother, and I'm so grateful she's shared it with me. In a lot of ways, Lucero is like a mom here— she's always making sure things get done and everyone gets fed.

We make this for family meal— it screams soul and community. There's nothing like walking into our downstairs prep area when Lucero has just finished the pozole. All of the cooks are so excited, they take the back of a spoon and crack the boar's head, so all the chicharróns fall apart and into the soup (see the final step of the recipe). There is simply nothing like the joy that this dish brings. That's why I say, when it's time for me to go, I want to be buried with this.

WILD BOAR POZOLE VERDE *Serves 8 to 10*

NOTES: *Boar's head can be special-ordered from a reputable butcher. Or you can use pig's head.*

This recipe requires a very large pot that must be able to fit the boar's head, and also fit inside of the oven and the refrigerator.

This recipe takes 3 days to complete, so plan accordingly.

½ boar's head (about 8 pounds/ 3.5 kg), skin on

Kosher salt

1 (750 ml) bottle white wine, such as Chardonnay

11 cups (2.3 kg) Chicken Stock (page 283)

6 pounds (2.8 kg) tomatillos, husks removed

2 medium jalapeño peppers

1 Spanish onion, halved

1 bunch cilantro

8 garlic cloves, thinly sliced

12 cups (2.8 kg) canned white hominy (from four 29-ounce cans)

3 cups (478 g) crème fraîche

5 limes, cut into wedges

Season the boar's head with salt and wrap tightly in cheesecloth to ensure the skin stays in place. Refrigerate for at least 6 and up to 24 hours.

On the day of cooking, preheat the oven to 210°F.

Place the head into a very large Dutch oven or heavy-bottomed pot. Add the white wine, chicken stock, and enough water to cover. Cover with a cartouche (see page 293), then cover with the lid. Transfer to the oven and cook until the meat is beautifully tender and gelatinous and starting to fall off the bone, and you can pierce the skin easily with a knife, about 17½ hours. Remove the cheesecloth and return the head to the liquid, then cool overnight in the refrigerator.

On the day of serving, position a rack 3 to 4 inches from the heating element and preheat the broiler. Arrange the tomatillos, jalapeños, and onion in an even layer on a baking sheet and broil, turning once, until charred on both sides, 10 to 12 minutes per side. Working in batches in a blender or food processor, puree the charred vegetables together with the cilantro until smooth.

Remove the head from the braising liquid and set aside on a rimmed baking sheet. Spoon 1 to 2 cups of the liquid over the head to keep it moist, then cover the baking sheet tightly with foil.

Bring the braising liquid to a simmer over low heat. Stir in the pureed vegetables, garlic, and hominy and season to taste with salt. Cook on low for 2 hours to meld the flavors.

Shortly before serving, preheat the oven to 500°F.

Place the covered tray with the head in the oven and cook for 20 minutes, then remove the foil and return to the oven to allow the skin to brown, crisp, and puff up (like chicharróns), about 30 minutes.

To serve, transfer the broth to a very large serving bowl and place the hot boar's head on top. Serve with bowls of crème fraîche and lime wedges on the side. Encourage guests to dig in to the head directly, tearing meat from the cheeks and more, and use the chicharróns that fall off as you dig in as garnish.

IN MY FAMILY, Sundays were for prime rib. My father would roast it, carve it in the kitchen, then put it on the lazy Susan in the formal dining room, which we only used when the entire family was over. All of my brothers and cousins and I would fight over the bones. And the next morning we'd race to the refrigerator, still in our pajamas, and grab whatever hadn't been consumed the night before and eat the bones cold for breakfast, standing over the kitchen sink.

I don't believe there is ever not a time for prime rib, and throughout the year I make it constantly—in the winter, I cook it with just a salt crust and add a bordelaise; in autumn, when Périgord truffles are around, I love to make a butter with them and serve the roast with a light beef jus. But in the summer, I feel lighter, and love to take advantage of the availability of fresh lavender. This recipe combines sweet, savory, and salty ingredients that you might not think go together. But they do, dovetailing beautifully into a summer roast that I often make on Sundays or over any long weekend in the Hamptons with my family. And yes, we still bicker over the bones.

DRY-AGED PRIME RIB
WITH ANCHOVY, ROSEMARY, AND LAVENDER   *Serves 10*

NOTE: *This in-and-out roasting method helps ensure that the meat evenly cooks to a perfect medium-rare and stays rosy pink throughout.*

1 prime rib rack with 5 bones, dry-aged for 60 days, trimmed, bones Frenched to 1 inch

Kosher salt

8 ounces (237 g) black anchovy fillets, such as Ortiz, chopped

½ cup plus 3 tablespoons (68 g) chopped fresh rosemary, plus 2 bunches whole sprigs

¾ cup (60 g) chopped fresh lavender, plus 2 bunches whole sprigs

Freshly cracked black pepper

5 tablespoons (68 g) olive oil

3 heads garlic, scalped (see page 293)

Flaky sea salt

Preheat the oven to 275°F.

Season the rib rack generously with kosher salt on all sides. In a small bowl, stir together the chopped anchovy, rosemary, lavender, 20 cracks of black pepper, and 2 tablespoons of the olive oil. Using your hands, coat the fat cap of the prime rib with a ⅛-inch layer of the anchovy mixture.

Lay the bunches of whole rosemary and lavender along the bottom of a roasting pan with a wire rack set on top, then place the rib rack on top, fat-side up.

Drizzle the remaining 3 tablespoons olive oil over the garlic and season with kosher salt and pepper. Wrap in foil.

Place the roasting pan and the foil-wrapped garlic in the oven. Roast together until the herbs are just starting to become fragrant, about 20 minutes. Remove the beef from the oven and let rest for 20 minutes in a warm place, leaving the oven on and the garlic roasting.

Return the beef to the oven and roast until a thermometer inserted in the thickest part of the meat reads 85° to 92°F, 20 minutes more. Remove from the oven and let rest for another 20 minutes. Check the garlic at the same time and remove when golden and soft.

Increase the oven temperature to 475°F.

Return the rack of beef to the oven and cook until dark golden brown and medium-rare (a thermometer inserted in the center should read 115°F). Remove from the oven and let rest for 30 minutes.

To serve, slice the meat off the bone completely, cut into ¼-inch slices, and arrange on a serving platter. Sprinkle with flaky sea salt. Arrange the bones on a separate platter for guests to enjoy.

WHEN I BOUGHT this restaurant from Graydon Carter, I was lucky to retain many of his regular customers (and he had *many*). One of them is a gentleman named Tom Fontana, who comes in at least once a week, always to be seated at the head of Table 17, right under the beautiful tiger painting, with a Bulleit bourbon on the rocks in his hand.

What I love about Tom is that when he walks in, he shakes everyone's hand and says hello. No other customer does that, and it speaks volumes to me, because that's a policy that we have as a team—to say hello and good-bye to everyone, and shake their hands, as a sign of respect.

The week I bought the restaurant, he asked how I was doing, as usual, and I said, "I'm doing really well, Tom, I actually just bought the restaurant." He didn't congratulate me, he didn't wish me well, he just had a look of horror on his face. He said, "Are you keeping the Scotch egg on the menu?" He was immediately very concerned, because he starts every meal here with Scotch eggs. And I said, "Well, I was thinking about taking it off, but even if I do, I will ensure it will always be available to you." A great look of relief washed over him and only then did he congratulate me heartily. He gave me a kiss on the cheek, sent me on my way, and has been supporting me (and receiving his Scotch eggs) ever since.

SCOTCH EGGS *Makes 10 eggs*

3 pounds (1.45 kg) lamb shoulder, cut into 1-inch cubes

14 ounces (400 g) pork fat, cut into 1-inch cubes

10 tablespoons (90 g) kosher salt

1½ teaspoons (8 g) fennel pollen

1 tablespoon (13 g) whole milk

10 duck eggs

3 chicken eggs

1⅓ cups (150 g) fine dried breadcrumbs

About 2 quarts (1.7 kg) canola oil, for deep-frying

Flaky sea salt

In a large bowl, toss together the lamb, pork fat, kosher salt, and fennel pollen. Place the bowl in the freezer for 30 minutes to chill. Pass the meat through a grinder twice—once through a large die, and once through a medium die.

Transfer the ground meat to a stand mixer fitted with the paddle attachment. Add the milk and mix on medium speed until incorporated, 3 to 4 minutes. Refrigerate the sausage mixture to firm it up while you cook the duck eggs.

Set up a bowl of ice and water. Place the duck eggs in a medium pot and add water to cover by 1 inch. Bring to a simmer over medium-high heat and cook for 8 minutes. Drain the eggs, then plunge them into the ice water bath. When the eggs are cool enough to handle, carefully peel, then rinse them to remove any shell fragments.

Cut ten 14-inch squares of plastic wrap. Divide the sausage into 10 equal portions, using your hands to round each one into a disk about ¼ inch thick and 6 to 7 inches across. Working with one at a time, place a portion of sausage on a square of plastic wrap and place an egg in the center. Wrap the sausage around the egg, using the plastic like a sushi roller to wrap it tightly. Remove the plastic and use your fingers to smooth the seams, ensuring that there are no gaps and the egg is completely covered.

In a small bowl, beat the chicken eggs. Place the breadcrumbs in a medium bowl. Roll each of the Scotch eggs through the beaten egg, then through the breadcrumbs. Place the coated Scotch eggs on a parchment-lined baking sheet.

Pour 5 inches oil into a countertop fryer, Dutch oven, or large heavy-bottomed pot with a thermometer clipped to the side. Bring the oil to 350°F over medium-high heat. Working in batches, add the eggs and fry until golden brown, about 9 minutes. Set aside to drain on a wire rack set on a baking sheet. When cool enough to handle, cut each egg in half, season the inside with flaky sea salt, and serve.

IN NEW YORK in the 1970s, haute French cuisine was having a moment. Chefs like André Soltner at Lutèce and Alain Sailhac at Le Cirque were introducing diners to incredible techniques. One of the dishes wildly popular at the time was Tournedos Rossini: filet mignon placed on a crostini with a lobe of foie gras and a few slices of truffles on top, a rich Madeira sauce spooned over it all. When we were developing new summer meat dishes, I had visions of truffles, specifically Australian winter truffles, which are in season during the summer in New York. We became obsessed with the idea of doing a take on Rossini with clover-fed lamb and Australian truffles and, much to my delight, it worked out beautifully.

LAMB ROSSINI *Serves 2*

2 (8-ounce/237 g) pieces lamb tenderloin

Kosher salt

1½ tablespoons (20 g) extra-virgin olive oil

2½ ounces (68 g) morels (1 loosely packed cup), halved if large

¼ cup (50 g) brandy

2 cups (420 g) Beef Stock (page 283)

½ cup (108 g) Madeira

½ ounce (14 g) Australian winter truffles

4½ tablespoons (64 g) unsalted butter

2 tablespoons (6 g) chopped fresh tarragon

Freshly cracked black pepper

4 (1½-ounce) pieces foie gras (6 ounces/170 g total)

Preheat the oven to 375°F.

Season the lamb on all sides with salt. In an ovenproof medium sauté pan, heat the olive oil over high heat. Add the lamb and sear, turning, until golden brown on all sides, about 8 minutes total. Transfer the lamb to a baking sheet and place in the oven for about 5 minutes to finish cooking to medium-rare (a thermometer inserted in the center should read 110°F). Set aside to rest.

Return the same pan to medium-high heat. Add the morels and sauté until tender, about 6 minutes. Add the brandy and ignite the fumes with a barbecue lighter. Flambé until the alcohol cooks off, about 30 seconds. Add the beef stock and Madeira, bring to a boil, then cook until the sauce has reduced by half; it should be sticky and coat the back of a spoon, about 10 minutes. Remove the pan from the heat and shave in the winter truffles. Swirl in the butter until melted and the sauce has a sheen, then stir in the tarragon and season with 6 cracks pepper.

Season each piece of foie gras on both sides with salt. Heat a small sauté pan over medium-high heat. Add the foie and quickly sear until golden, about 30 seconds per side.

To serve, slice each lamb tenderloin on the bias into 3 thick pieces. Arrange on a platter, alternating with the seared foie gras, starting and ending with lamb (save the final slice of lamb as a cook's snack). Drizzle the sauce over the top.

THE BEATRICE: LA FAMILLE

THERE IS, IN LIFE, the family you are born into, and then there is the family you choose. The family we are born into can be complicated, but I was taught that we always stick together, because we are blood.

The family we choose can be even more complicated. Friendships come and go, so deciphering the real from the fake, knowing when to let go, and knowing to whom you should give yourself, your loyalty, and your vulnerability is confounding. These relationships come with twists, turns, perils, and fantastic surprises around every corner. Who deserves it? Will they return it? Will they be down for me, as I am for them? I've learned the hard way, but in that education I've earned more of a return on investment than I could have ever hoped for.

It's no secret that over the years I've gone

through more managers and captains than I care to count. I'm a tough person to work with because I expect perfection. I am stubborn, bullish, and always tormented by my desires. I firmly believe that arriving at one goal is simply the jumping-off point on a quest to the next. So regardless of successes, I am always hustling the next idea and working the bigger game—and I expect everyone to keep up.

Early on, before I had any kind of track record, my entire kitchen was filled with what the late Anthony Bourdain described as "mercenaries"—cooks who were in it for the money, not for the love of the business or the accolades that some of us aspire to. They were talented and smart, but they didn't give a fuck about me or whether the Bea was successful, so long as they were getting paid, and paid well. They had nasty habits of putting powder up their nose, and drinking smuggled booze any time my back was turned. But I kept them around because I needed people to execute a highly complicated level of cooking and, despite their flaws, they always said "Yes, Chef."

One day the "Yes, Chefs" lost the respect they'd once had, and my food appeared absent of passion and love. I looked across my pass in the middle of a busy service, and I realized their ambivalence had gone too far. They thought I owed them. They had taken for granted that the "thank-you" was the fact that I still cut them a paycheck every week. I left my sous-chef Nicole in charge of the kitchen and took a walk around the corner to Chef Andrew Whitney's Dell'anima. I sat at the chef's counter, sipping Champagne and eating carbonara, contemplating my next move. It was a Friday night, in the middle of our busy season. We had 250 covers on the books for the next day. But I didn't give a fuck. Nicole, my daytime chef Lucero, and I would cook everything ourselves. I refused to take anyone's bullshit, or settle for people less than worthy of my money or my time—that's just how I was raised. At 12:30 a.m., I finished my glass of Champagne and called Nicole. "Fire them ALL."

That night, and the subsequent months, defined the culture of what my kitchen (and later, my front of house) would become. A clean slate for the three of us to build a team that in my heart of hearts, I hope will one day be better than me. We focus on cultivating the next generation of industry professionals. We have beginning-of- and end-of-night meetings that are powerful, inspirational, and push my team members to grow not only as cooks, but also as people. We are selective about whom we hire, and work hard to bring them into the family. Getting through what we did took away all of the fear, and reminded me what my father taught me long ago: Never accept that which is less than worthy.

This is my work ethic because I've clawed my way up, and as Jay-Z says, "It's easy to make it to the top, but staying there is the struggle." My team acknowledges that we have been through hell and back, and we are all the better for it. As a matter of fact, we revel in it. We have a saying in our house: "This is Sparta." Only the strong. Only the hard. And if you are strong enough, and if you are hard enough, you will not only prosper, but you will gain a family, and you will thrive.

It took time to build that culture within my team. We survived multiple wars together, fighting back to back, in the trenches, which forced us to come together for a common goal. When we bought the restaurant, my core team and I decided on a code of conduct:

PAY IT FORWARD TO THOSE WE TAKE UNDER OUR WINGS. PAY IT BACK TO THE PEOPLE RESPONSIBLE FOR PUTTING US WHERE WE ARE. NEVER TALK SHIT. KEEP YOUR MOUTH SHUT. AND IF YOU ARE GOING TO OPEN YOUR MOUTH, OPEN IT ONLY TO CELEBRATE OTHERS AND THEIR SUCCESSES WHEN RIGHTFULLY DESERVED. COOK WITH INTEGRITY. SERVE WITH HUMILITY. RISE ABOVE OPPOSITION. BRING YOUR ENTIRE FAMILY UP WITH YOU. NEVER ACCEPT ANYTHING OR ANYONE LESS THAN WORTHY. AND NEVER FORGET WHERE WE COME FROM.

My chosen family is essential to understanding how I got to where I am today. It takes a village to raise a child, and so, too, does it take one to raise a restaurant.

LEFT TO RIGHT: SEBASTIAN MORALES, AARON CHANG, ADAMA ZORNE, LUCERO RAMALES, ANGIE MAR

LEFT TO RIGHT: ANGIE MAR, MEGAN HIGGINS, JESSICA KOTULA, CELIO TAMANIS, NICOLE AVERKIOU, DUNCAN BURGIN, DYKOTA ROBINSON

MY MOTHER GREW UP going back and forth from Taipei to Oxford, and one of the things she picked up from her time in the UK was a love of the Sunday roast. This version is a bit unconventional because instead of doing roast prime rib, I like to make a leg of mutton. I think this dish is perfect for summer, when cherries are in season. The sweet cherry conserva, spicy mustard, and rich, clean broth are lovely together. You can eat this dish a variety of ways—as meat with accompaniments followed by the broth to cleanse your palate, or as meat with broth ladled over it to incorporate everything into each bite. Either way, it's perfect for those nights when you've been out all day, enjoying the sun, then return to your chilly, air-conditioned home and crave something just a little bit warming.

ROAST LEG OF MUTTON
WITH YORKSHIRE PUDDING, CHERRY CONSERVA, AND MUSTARD   *Serves 6*

YORKSHIRE PUDDING BATTER

4 large eggs

1 cup (140 g) all-purpose flour

1 cup (232 g) whole milk

½ tablespoon (4 g) kosher salt

MUTTON BROTH

5 pounds (2.3 kg) mutton neck bones

1 head garlic, halved crosswise

½ Spanish onion

1 bay leaf

Kosher salt and freshly ground black pepper

ROAST MUTTON

1 (10- to 12-pound/4.5 to 5.4 kg) mutton leg

15 garlic cloves

Kosher salt

3 bunches thyme

2 bunches rosemary

FOR SERVING

1 cup (286 g) Cherry Conserva

½ cup (200 g) Dijon mustard

NOTE: *The Yorkshire pudding batter must rest for 24 hours before cooking and the broth can be made 1 to 2 days in advance, so plan accordingly.*

PREPARE THE YORKSHIRE PUDDING BATTER: In a large bowl, combine the eggs, flour, milk, 1 tablespoon plus 2 teaspoons water, and the salt. Cover and refrigerate for 24 hours. Remove the batter from the refrigerator just before baking the pudding.

THE NEXT DAY, MAKE THE MUTTON BROTH: In a large stockpot, working in batches to avoid overcrowding, brown the mutton neck bones over medium-high heat on all sides, 10 to 15 minutes, removing them to a plate as they are finished. Return all the bones and their accumulated juices to the pot and add cold water to cover by 2 inches. Tie the garlic, onion, and bay leaf in a square of cheesecloth to make a sachet. Add the sachet to the pot.

Bring to a simmer over medium heat and cook, occasionally skimming the fat and impurities off the top, until the stock is a beautiful deep clear brown with a silken texture, 6 to 8 hours. Strain out the bones and sachet, return the liquid to the pot, and cook the broth until reduced by one-third, about 30 minutes. Season to taste with salt and pepper and set aside.

ON THE DAY OF THE SERVING, ROAST THE MUTTON: Preheat the oven to 475°F.

Using a paring knife, make 15 small incisions all over the mutton leg. Stuff a garlic clove into each incision and season generously all over with salt. Arrange the thyme and rosemary in the bottom of a roasting pan and place the leg on top of the herbs. Transfer to the oven and roast for 20 minutes. Remove the lamb from the oven and let rest for 20 minutes in a warm place. Reduce the oven temperature to 275°F.

Return the mutton to the oven and roast for another 20 minutes. Remove it from the oven and let rest for 20 minutes, leaving the oven on. Repeat the 20 minutes in/20 minutes out cooking process until the thickest part of the mutton reaches an internal temperature of 120°F (3 to 4 times total). Take the mutton out, but leave the oven on and increase the temperature to 425°F.

TO FINISH THE PUDDING: Measure out 6 tablespoons of the drippings from the roasting pan. Evenly divide the mutton drippings among six 8-ounce ramekins. Place the ramekins on a baking sheet and place in the oven for 10 minutes to warm up the drippings. Remove the ramekins and ladle the batter into them, dividing evenly. Bake until puffed and golden brown, about 15 minutes.

Cut the mutton into ¼-inch-thick slices and arrange on a platter. Serve family-style, with a big, beautiful bowl of broth alongside, as well as smaller bowls of cherry conserva and Dijon mustard. The Yorkshire pudding can be eaten directly from its cooking vessel.

CHERRY CONSERVA
Makes 2 cups

- 1¼ pounds (555 g) Bing cherries (about 4 cups), pitted
- ⅓ cup (65 g) sugar
- 2 teaspoons (4 g) white wine vinegar
- 1 teaspoon (3 g) kosher salt
- 1 teaspoon (3 g) freshly ground black pepper

In a small saucepan, combine the cherries, sugar, and white wine vinegar and bring to a boil over medium-high heat. Cook, stirring constantly, until the cherries are slightly candied but still intact and the mixture reaches a compote-like consistency, 20 to 25 minutes. Remove the pan from the heat, season the mixture with the salt and pepper, then transfer it to a large shallow bowl and spread it out to cool and lock in its color. Transfer to the refrigerator to chill for 3 hours or up to overnight. Cherry conserva keeps, refrigerated, for up to 3 days.

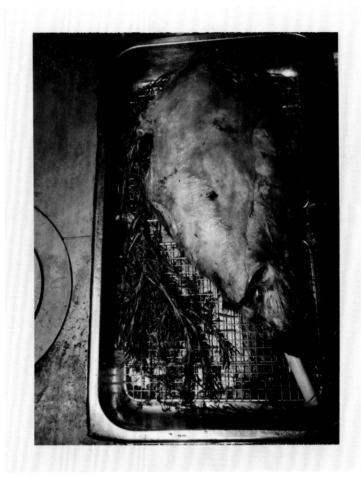

AFTER A MEAL, large or small, I always like to finish with cheese—but I think it's very nice to have a bit of bitter chocolate to offset the richness. These truffles offer that perfect hit. I like to keep them, lush and luxurious, in my refrigerator for a bit of a late-night nibble before I turn in for bed. Serve them with Champagne, or a bottle of red wine.

CHAMPAGNE AND CHOCOLATE TRUFFLES *Makes 26 truffles*

1¼ pounds (566 g) 70% cacao chocolate, roughly chopped (4½ cups)

1 cup plus 1 tablespoon (238 g) heavy cream

⅜ teaspoon (1 g) kosher salt

6 tablespoons (75 g) Champagne

Boiling water, for dipping

1 cup (88 g) unsweetened cocoa powder, for dusting

Flaky sea salt

Grease a 9-inch square baking dish and line it with parchment paper, leaving a 1-inch overhang on two sides.

Bring 1½ to 2 inches of water to a simmer in a medium pot. Place the chocolate and heavy cream in a large heatproof bowl that can sit over (not in) the pot. Place the bowl over the simmering water (the bowl should not touch the water), reduce the heat to low, and stir constantly until the chocolate is melted and the cream is fully incorporated, 5 to 7 minutes. Add the salt and remove the bowl from the heat. Whisk in the Champagne until smooth.

Pour the chocolate mixture into the prepared baking dish and refrigerate until set and well chilled, at least 4 hours.

Lift the chocolate out of the baking dish to a clean cutting board. Dip a sharp knife into the boiling water, then wipe it dry with a clean kitchen towel. Trim the edges of the chocolate so the square is even, then cut it into 1-inch squares, dipping and wiping the knife between cuts.

Place the cocoa powder in a medium bowl. Gently toss each truffle in the powder to lightly coat, and sprinkle with sea salt to finish. Serve or store in an airtight container for 3 to 4 days.

AUTUMN

GAME SEASON is one of my favorite times of the year, and one of the greatest things about autumn is when Pat LaFrieda drops off venison for me at the Bea. I love to have a whole animal in the restaurant to skin, butcher, and break down—the process is very primal and very satisfying.

Venison is generally quite lean, so we incorporate trotters into this pie to give it more richness and depth, and beef fat in the crust, along with a healthy bit of butter for richness. There's a bit of a Noah's Ark thing going on in here, with four animals cooked different ways: beef fat in the suet dough; pork trotters in the duck stock for extra gelatin and fat, and meat and skin in the pie itself; and, of course, the venison. Somehow, though, the pie still ends up feeling very light—although there is a beautiful velvety mouthfeel from the collagen in the trotters, it doesn't sit heavily on the stomach.

VENISON AND TROTTER PIE *Serves 6*

5 cups (1 kg) Duck Stock (page 283)

1 pork trotter, split

3 tablespoons (42 g) extra-virgin olive oil

1½ pounds (700 g) venison shoulder or leg, cut into 2-inch cubes

1½ tablespoons (12 g) kosher salt

¼ cup (30 g) all-purpose flour

½ bottle (375 ml) white wine, such as Chardonnay

1 medium onion, halved

1 head garlic, halved horizontally

2 bay leaves

1 bunch thyme

12 fingerling potatoes, cut into obliques

50/50 Dough (page 277)

1 egg, beaten

NOTES: *The filling should cool completely before going into the shell. Ideally you will make the filling ahead and refrigerate it overnight so the flavors can meld.*

You will need two large Dutch ovens for this recipe.

In a large Dutch oven or heavy-bottomed pot, combine the stock and trotter and bring to a boil over high heat. Reduce the heat to medium, cover, and simmer until the meat is tender, about 3 hours. Remove the trotter and set aside to cool. Strain the braising liquid (discard the solids) and set the liquid aside. When the trotter is cool enough to handle, pick all of the meat, tendons, and skin from the bones. Roughly chop the skin and tendons into 1-inch pieces. Set the meat, tendons, and skin aside.

Meanwhile, preheat the oven to 325°F.

In a separate large Dutch oven, heat the olive oil over high heat. Season the venison shoulder all over with the salt. Working in batches, sear the venison on all sides until golden brown and beautifully crusty, about 15 minutes total. Reduce the heat to medium-high, return all the seared venison to the pot, and sprinkle with the flour. Cook, turning it ever so slightly, until browned, 4 to 5 minutes. Add the wine, bring to a simmer, and deglaze the pan, scraping up the browned bits from the bottom.

Add enough of the reserved braising liquid to cover the venison by 1 inch. Tie the onion, garlic, bay leaves, and thyme in a square of cheesecloth to make a sachet. Increase the heat to high and bring to a boil, then add the sachet. Cover with a cartouche (see page 293), then cover the pot tightly with the lid. Transfer to the oven to braise until tender, about 3 hours. Add the potatoes and the reserved trotter meat, tendons, and skin to the venison and mix well to incorporate. Taste the gravy and adjust the seasoning as necessary. Let cool completely in the refrigerator, ideally overnight.

On the day of assembly, preheat the oven to 350°F.

Divide the dough roughly in half. Roll one portion into an 11-inch round and the other into a 13-inch round, both ¼ inch thick. Place the larger round of dough into the bottom and up the sides of a deep 9-inch pie dish and press in with your fingers, leaving a 1-inch overhang.

Add the cooled venison mixture, then drape the smaller round of dough over the top. Fold the edge of the bottom crust over the top and pinch the edges together. Trim any excess dough. Using a fork, crimp the edges of the crust. Make 3 slits on the top using a knife or pastry cutter. Brush heavily with the beaten egg.

Bake until the crust is shiny and deep golden brown, like a new penny, and the filling is bubbling hot, about 1 hour 30 minutes.

Remove from the oven and let rest for 10 minutes before serving.

CREATIVITY AND MADNESS
THE MAKING OF A MENU

MY CREATIVE PROCESS is one of the hardest things for me to explain to other people. Most cooks I know go to the farmers' market every morning at the crack of dawn, pillaging through piles, pushing each other out of the way, and finally settling on the perfect Kyoto Red carrot or tangle of lamb's-quarter, accepting whatever they've found as inspiration.

That is not me. I'm not a morning person and I don't believe in seasonality, except as related to how best to cook meats (confit in the spring, braises in the winter, and so on, as I've demonstrated throughout this book). But I love to eat chilled cherries when there's two feet of snow on the ground, and meat pies when it's swelteringly hot. My dream is to live blissfully in an eternal winter, wrapped in fur and snuggled near either of the two always-on fireplaces at the Bea.

WHEN I CREATE, I LOCK MYSELF AWAY IN A HIGHLY AIR-CONDITIONED ROOM, AND BRING ALL MY SNOWBOUND ASPIRATIONS TOP OF MIND. I SLIP INTO MY OWN WORLD AND CAN WORK FOR HOURS, UNABLE TO HEAR ANYONE, MY TEMPER EXPLODING LIKE A BEAR BEING AWOKEN FROM HIBERNATION IF DISTURBED. I CAN WRITE AN ENTIRE SEASON'S MENU IN ONE SITTING.

My creative process starts on a piece of paper. Instead of basing a dish or a menu around a single ingredient, I begin with an idea, which might be a word, an emotion, a piece of art, or a fashion collection. My inspiration has nothing to do with actual ingredients or Mother Nature's willingness to make them available at a certain time of year. Instead, I write down the central idea in the middle of a piece of paper, and build out adjectives and descriptors around it, creating a web of words all loosely related to that core notion. If you look closely, you will see these word webs in a form that has spiraled out of control, their inceptions concepts like "madness," "New York," "back to basics," "McQueen," or "Dalí." For me, the ingredients are a vessel to translate that concept to the plate. This process is precious and personal to me; it evokes where I am and how I feel in my life at the time.

Every year, I close the Bea during the last week of August. My staff all goes on holiday, but I use the time to reset creatively, and write the Autumn/Winter menu for the upcoming season. I do the same thing during the first week in January, when the restaurant is quietest, to write the menu for Spring/Summer. It's an odd time for everyone usually around me, as I disappear into my own world, living mainly at the Met's exhibits, flipping through art books, exclusively eating sushi, and watching on repeat runway shows from Galliano, Dior, Yves Saint Laurent, or whomever I happen to be interested in at the time. By the end of the week, I emerge physically exhausted, yet mentally exhilarated, often running on fumes and craving red meat or liver, with an entire season's menu scribbled on the backs of old paper, indecipherable to anyone but me. The food, of course, has yet to actually be cooked, but the components themselves will only require small edits.

I strictly and notoriously do not allow anyone to run specials or put their own dishes on my menu, as I like to have exclusive control. I never give other chefs my recipes or techniques—until now, at least. I rarely go out to eat, for fear that I will subconsciously be influenced by what other people are cooking; and when I do, it's only for sushi or pasta, both of which are absent from my menus. I am irate when I see other cooks ripping off our dishes, especially those unique to our menu, such as the whisky-aged beef (page 33) and bone marrow crème brûlée (page 64). Some people say imitation is a form of flattery, but I find that "flattery" happens more often than you'd think. But I suppose that's the price of hustling hard and gaining success: Someone will always try to cop your ideas to make a few bucks, or worse, *gain fame*, off of your hard work and ingenuity. You'd be hard-pressed to find a successful chef out there who hasn't fallen victim to this kind of thievery. Although it's maddening, I find peace knowing that I will constantly come up with something new. If our ideas and techniques are being replicated, clearly it's a sign we're onto something smart.

It took about a year for me to get into my own head once I took the reins as the executive chef at the Bea, and about another year while I was in the process of purchasing the restaurant to dream about what I had to say about food and who I wanted to become. When I first started here, I believed everything should be seasoned with lemon juice, olive oil, sea salt, and Aleppo pepper—that was the kitchen world I had come from. When I finally emerged from that mindset and began to develop my own palate, I felt creatively liberated. I believe that reinvention should happen constantly and is the foundation for progress, but there is never a replacement for when you finally come into your own creativity.

When I was writing the original opening menu for the Beatrice in August 2016, everyone was in my ear with their opinions: *You should have multiple fish options available. Why are the steaks so large? Add a few more salads for the ladies. That plum tart should be a dessert, not an appetizer.* Noise, noise, noise—and noise from people who had zero clue who I was, what I was about, or what my vision was for the restaurant. I fell victim to the vast array of opinions for a short time, until I was so blocked that I was unable to come up with any ideas that I truly loved. So I threw it all out the window. I started from scratch, with a pile of blank papers, and began with a word web around the sentiment *WHO I AM*. I started filling the page with words like *rebel, impertinent, disruptive, vamp, artist, craftsman, caution to the wind, fuck their opinions, fuck convention, fuck 'em if they can't take a joke, masculine, feminine, dark, maddening, controversy, polarizing, integrity, bold, drama, soul*—and from this dark and beautiful place, the opening menu of the Beatrice was born.

I often refer back to that first word web and reflect on how far we've come. I ask myself *Have I changed? Have we changed? Where do we go from here?* The truth is that I desperately need that dose of reality sometimes—something to bring me back to the basics, the core of who I am. My team and I have poured our blood, sweat, and tears into building the Beatrice, and we've experienced great success. But in the times I begin to lose myself, or feel I am being pulled in a million directions, or feel lost or creatively blocked, I turn back to those tattered papers that started it all. At the end of the day, despite the awards, the reviews, and the noise of other people's opinions that constantly surround me, I am at my creative best when I am cooking for me and my interests alone—and telling everyone else to fuck off.

I FIRST VISITED PARIS with my parents when I was seven. My father, an adventurous eater, encouraged me to try veal kidneys at a local bistro, which horrified my more restrained mother—so of course I had to order them. I loved their snappy, toothsome bite, and immediately declared to my parents that in an effort to avoid the terrible food at school, I would not be returning to the United States with them. That attempt at a coup was ended immediately, but my love of kidneys was cemented from that point forward.

If kidneys intimidate you or your guests, this dish is a great introduction because it's so multifaceted—the meat is rich and earthy, but sweet, too, from the prunes and Madeira. There are unexpected floral elements from the lavender and tarragon, and parsley for freshness.

VEAL KIDNEYS WITH PRUNES, MADEIRA, AND CREAM *Serves 2 to 4*

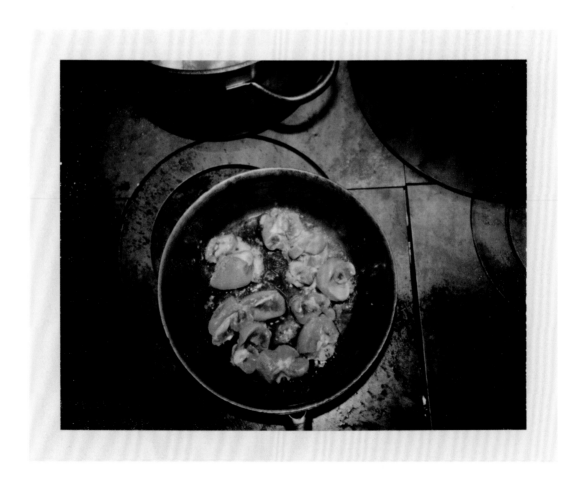

1 pound (455 g) cleaned veal kidneys, thawed if frozen

About 4 cups (928 g) whole milk

6 pitted prunes

⅔ cup (143 g) Madeira

2 tablespoons (27 g) extra-virgin olive oil

3 large cipollini onions, quartered

Kosher salt

1½ teaspoons (3 g) chopped fresh lavender

1 tablespoon (3 g) chopped fresh marjoram

¼ cup (49 g) Cognac

½ cup (119 g) heavy cream

2½ tablespoons (34 g) unsalted butter

5 tablespoons (50 g) crème fraîche

1 tablespoon (3 g) chopped fresh tarragon

1 tablespoon (5 g) chopped fresh parsley

NOTES: *The kidneys need to soak for 3 hours or ideally overnight, so plan accordingly.*

Veal kidneys are available at butcher shops in 1- to 2-pound packages, typically frozen. Ask for them cleaned, meaning free from the outer membrane and a large vein.

Cut the kidney lobes apart into separate pieces. Place them in a medium bowl and pour in enough milk to cover them completely. Cover with plastic wrap and refrigerate for at least 3 hours or up to overnight, then drain and pat dry.

In a small saucepan, combine the prunes and Madeira and cook over low heat until the prunes plump up a bit, about 10 minutes. Remove the pan from the heat and set aside.

In a medium sauté pan, heat the olive oil over medium heat. Add the onions and toss to coat evenly in the oil. Cook, shaking the pan several times, until the onions are soft and golden, about 8 minutes. Season lightly with salt.

Season the kidneys generously with salt. Push the onions to one side of the pan, increase the heat to medium-high, and sear the kidneys, turning until medium-rare (a thermometer inserted in the center should read 145°F), 2 to 3 minutes total. The onions will be browning and crisping during this time, so keep them moving around a bit, too.

Add the lavender and marjoram to the pan, letting them crackle in the oil. Turn off the heat. Add the Cognac, letting it sizzle in the residual heat of the pan, reducing by about one-quarter to a slightly syrupy consistency, about 1 minute.

Return the pan to medium-high heat and add the cream. When it starts to simmer, stir in the butter until it melts to form a sauce that lightly coats the back of a spoon, about 2 minutes. Add the plump prunes and the Madeira they soaked in. When the mixture begins to simmer again, cook just until the sauce is reduced and thick enough to coat the back of a spoon, about 4 minutes.

Remove the pan from the heat. Add the crème fraîche and swirl the pan to incorporate it. Add the tarragon and parsley at the last minute, then divide onto plates and serve immediately.

THIS DISH perfectly encapsulates the mixed bag of cultures and foods I grew up with in a Chinese American family that included a mother who spent a lot of time in the UK. It blends Asian ingredients like shiitakes and *lap cheong* with oysters, bacon, and fresh herbs, in a recipe my father picked up from his sister-in-law, Auntie May, the matriarch of my cousin Melissa's family. My father would start making this dressing days in advance. The one shortcut he allowed himself was buying Stove Top stuffing mix, just for the dried bread, which we'd snack on for days leading up to the holiday. Of course, there are several versions of this recipe in the family, which means our Thanksgiving somehow becomes reason for The Great Dressing Competition. But regardless of whose reigns, the finished result intertwines sweet, savory, and herbaceous flavors all at once, with textural contrast from the golden-toasted top and soft, pillowy bread within. These contrasts form the fundamentals of my food philosophy; and for all I know, this dressing may have been where it all began. My version today replaces the bread with a tender and sweet brioche, and adds mountains of herbs to the mix.

Turkey has never been my family's thing, as we instead opt for a prime rib Thanksgiving, so we've always done dressing as its own dish, though it certainly works as stuffing inside of a holiday bird. Either way, the leftovers are worth fighting over.

OYSTER, BACON, AND SAGE DRESSING   *Serves 6*

1 (2½-pound/1.125 kg) brioche loaf, cut into 2-inch cubes (with crust)

1 pound (453 g) bacon, sliced into ½-inch strips (2¼ cups)

12 ounces (340 g) Chinese sausage (lap cheong), thinly sliced into rounds (2¼ cups)

1 medium Spanish onion, finely diced

2 cups (14 ounces/411 g) diced celery

¼ cup (37 g) thinly sliced garlic (about 1 head)

2 tablespoons (12 g) roughly chopped fresh rosemary

10 sprigs thyme, leaves picked

9½ ounces (273 g) unsalted butter

3 cups sliced shiitake mushroom caps (8 ounces/225 g)

2 tablespoons (12 g) roughly chopped fresh sage

Kosher salt and freshly ground black pepper

5 cups (1 kg) Chicken Stock (page 283)

8 ounces (235 g) shucked raw oysters with their liquor, roughly chopped

Preheat the oven to 400°F.

Arrange the brioche cubes on a baking sheet and toast until light golden brown, 6 to 8 minutes, tossing them halfway through to ensure even coloring. Transfer the toasted bread to a large baking dish or Dutch oven.

In a large sauté pan, cook the bacon over medium heat for 5 minutes, stirring often, until as much fat as possible is rendered—don't worry as much about crisping the bacon.

Add the lap cheong and cook until the bacon is starting to brown and the sausage is glistening, 5 to 7 minutes more. Add the onion and celery and sweat until softened but still retaining a bit of bite, 8 to 10 minutes. Stir in the garlic, rosemary, and thyme and cook until very fragrant, 2 to 3 minutes more.

Add the onion mixture to the dish with the bread and toss to combine. Don't rinse the sauté pan—return it to the stovetop over medium heat and melt the butter. Add the shiitake mushrooms and cook until just softened, 8 to 10 minutes. Add the mushrooms and butter to the bread mixture. Add the sage and

salt and black pepper to taste and toss to combine.

In a small saucepot, bring the chicken stock to just below a simmer over medium heat. One ladleful at a time, scoop the stock into the bread mixture, tossing after each addition until it's evenly absorbed. I encourage you to use your hands, tossing and tearing to aid in the absorption of liquid. After all the stock has been incorporated, add the chopped oysters and their liquor, and gently fold the dressing one last time.

Cover with foil and bake until heated through and a knife inserted into the center comes out hot, about 30 minutes. Remove the baking dish from the oven, uncover, stir, and reduce the oven temperature to 200°F. Return the dish to the oven for another 15 minutes until the dressing is golden brown on top and deliciously moist and pillowy below.

Serve straight out of the oven in the baking dish with a giant spoon.

STONE FRUITS are at their best in the early autumn, but for some reason, I can never seem to find a perfect peach in New York. It has become a lifelong search for me here—that, and an apartment with a dishwasher. I set out to develop this dish with peaches on my mind.

After days and days of searching markets and grocery stores, calling purveyors and angrily sending unripe and unflavorful peaches back, it dawned on me that maybe I was thinking about it all wrong. Perhaps, I thought, I should refocus to what we *did* have, which

was a surplus of beautiful white nectarines. I love the contrast of the sweetness of the nectarine, the floral notes of the tea, and the cold, thick unsweetened cream in this recipe. It's so simple, but when you eat it, it feels cerebral and thought provoking.

JASMINE-SCENTED NECTARINES
WITH SMOKED HONEYCOMB AND CHILLED CREAM *Serves 2*

½ cup plus 1 tablespoon (110 g) sugar

4 bags jasmine tea

¾ teaspoon (2 g) kosher salt

3 large ripe nectarines

1 cup plus 2 tablespoons (255 g) heavy cream

2 ounces (60 g) Smoked Honeycomb (page 271)

In a wide, shallow pan, bring 6½ cups water to a simmer over medium-high heat. Add the sugar, tea bags, and salt and cook for 15 minutes to brew the tea, then remove the tea bags and discard.

Meanwhile, set up a large bowl of ice and water. Bring a large pot of water to a boil. With a paring knife, cut a very shallow X on the top of each nectarine, where the stem was, just piercing the skin. One by one, plunge the nectarines into the boiling water. Cook for 1 minute, then immediately transfer the nectarines to the ice bath. At this point, their skins should slip off easily; work any remaining skin with your fingers to fully remove.

Halve and pit the nectarines and place them in the tea/simple syrup mixture. Place over medium heat

and simmer until the fruit is just cooked through but still gives a bit of resistance when pressed, about 15 minutes. Remove the nectarines from the syrup and set aside to drain. Chill the nectarines in the refrigerator for 30 minutes to 1 hour.

In a small pot, cook the heavy cream over medium-high heat until reduced by half, about 15 minutes. While the cream cooks, fill a large bowl with ice and nestle a medium bowl into the ice. When the cream has reduced, pour it into the medium bowl and stir to quickly chill.

To serve, divide the chilled cream between two dessert bowls. Place 3 nectarine halves on each portion and garnish with shards of smoked honeycomb that you can break into smaller pieces with a spoon.

ROAST DUCK FLAMBÉ *(page 223)*

WHEN I WAS YOUNG, my family would walk through Seattle's Chinatown on weekends after eating dim sum. The Peking ducks hanging in the windows, lustrous, shining, and the color of burnished mahogany, were the most beautiful things I'd ever seen. But my absolute favorite—and really the only duck dish cooked in our house—was my father's cured, cold-smoked duck, which he only indulged us with for Christmas. I knew I wanted to create something on the menu at the Bea that paid homage to my father's recipe, but I wanted to make something that looked like the ducks in Chinatown. Marrying those two ideas led to the creation of this dish, which we flambé tableside for dramatic effect.

During the grand reopening weekend of the Beatrice, legendary fashion designer Diane von Fürstenberg hosted an amazing Fashion Week party in the restaurant. She has always been a regular and has become one of our most gracious supporters, often walking straight into the kitchen, standing at the pass with me to decide what to eat that night. Her party was a big deal; news of it was splashed across the pages of *Vogue*, *Women's Wear Daily*, Page Six, *Harper's Bazaar*, and the like.

On that particular night, Valentino Garavani was also in attendance. He looked dashing as ever in his emerald-hued tuxedo; his Bentley purred softly out on West 12th Street, driver patiently waiting inside. I had just sent out entrées, and left the kitchen to check on their table. When I rounded the corner to the dining room, I saw Diane and Valentino, exuding glamour and eating duck wings with their hands. I knew an iconic Beatrice dish had been born.

I've never fully committed this recipe to the page, often skirting sheepishly around "how-to" questions when asked. This duck even graced the December 2018 cover of *Food & Wine*, yet I've managed to avoid giving anyone the true recipe—until now.

This dish has been cooed over by critics and our clientele alike, but what it means to me personally is more important than any of that: It represents my family, both past and present. And in my mind, it's proof that this iconic dish will transcend generations as part of my legacy, and continue bringing everyone to the table.

ROAST DUCK FLAMBÉ *Serves 4*

NOTES: *The duck cures for 4 days, so plan accordingly.*

You will need a handheld smoking gun (see page 293) for this recipe.

Pekin ducks, which have a nice fat cap, are ideal for this slow-roasted recipe, yielding a bird with golden-crisp skin and about ⅛ inch of juicy fat below. (I prefer to have a little fat left on the meat, as opposed to rendering it all out into a dry, crispy shell.)

Save the duck carcass after serving—it makes an amazing soup base for future recipes, my favorite being a hearty split pea soup.

DUCK CURE

¼ cup plus 2 teaspoons (59 g) granulated sugar

2 tablespoons plus 2 teaspoons (41 g) dark brown sugar

3 tablespoons plus 1 teaspoon (28 g) kosher salt

3 tablespoons (60 g) smoked sea salt

1½ teaspoons (9 g) pink curing salt (see page 292)

DUCK

1 whole duck (5 to 6 pounds/ 2.25 to 2.7 kg), preferably Pekin

Cherrywood chips, for smoking

1 bunch thyme

¼ cup (49 g) Cognac or brandy

CHERRY JUS

6 cups (1.3 kg) Duck Stock (page 283)

10 ounces (280 g) dried cherries (2 cups)

Kosher salt and freshly ground black pepper

Recipe continues »

ROAST DUCK FLAMBÉ *(continued)*

MAKE THE DUCK CURE: In a large bowl, combine the granulated sugar, brown sugar, kosher salt, smoked salt, and pink curing salt.

CURE THE DUCK: Remove the neck from the duck and set aside for the sauce (discard the giblets). Add the duck to the bowl of cure. With gloved hands, rub every inch of the duck, inside and out, with the cure mix. Use all of it. Cover the bowl with plastic wrap and cure in the refrigerator for 4 days, turning once for evenness.

Remove the duck from the refrigerator. Cold-smoke (see page 293) with the cherrywood chips for 20 minutes, until the duck has absorbed the smoky flavor.

On the day of cooking, place the duck on a roasting rack set over a rimmed baking sheet. Do not rinse the duck. Stuff the duck's cavity with the thyme and truss it.

Position a rack in the center and lower third of the oven and preheat the oven to 325°F. Place a baking dish with 2 inches of water on the lower rack as the oven preheats.

Roast the duck until the fat has rendered slightly and the skin begins to turn a deep golden, about 20 minutes. Remove it from the oven and also remove the water bath. (Increase the oven temperature to 425°F.) Allow the duck to rest for 20 minutes somewhere warm.

Return the duck to the oven (without the water bath) and continue cooking until the skin begins to crisp and it reaches a deep mahogany brown, about 15 minutes. Remove the duck from the oven and let rest for 10 minutes.

MEANWHILE, MAKE THE CHERRY JUS: In a medium saucepan over medium heat, sear the reserved duck neck until very dark, about 10 minutes. Pour off any fat that has rendered, but leave the neck in the pan. Add the duck stock, bring to a simmer, and deglaze the pan, scraping up any browned bits from the bottom. Increase the heat to high and bring to a boil, then reduce the heat to medium-low and simmer, skimming off any impurities, until the liquid is reduced by half, 15 to 20 minutes. Strain the stock, discarding the solids, and return the liquid to the pot.

Reduce the heat to medium-low, add the dried cherries, and simmer until the liquid is reduced by half again and the cherries are rehydrated, about 15 minutes. Season with salt and pepper to taste. Hold the sauce over very low heat.

FLAMBÉ THE DUCK—IN FRONT OF AN AUDIENCE IF POSSIBLE: Remove the trussing twine and transfer the roasted duck to a clean flameproof dish or serving platter. Pour the Cognac into a small saucepan over medium heat and ignite the fumes with a barbecue lighter. Pour the flaming alcohol evenly over the duck; it should burn for about 10 seconds before the flame dissipates.

Transfer the flambéed duck to a cutting board and break it down: Slice off the legs and wings (they will be pink from the curing salt—don't be alarmed), and then the breasts, which you can slice into individual pieces, about ½ inch thick. Stir any leftover juices from the flambé into the cherry jus. Arrange the sliced duck on a serving platter and spoon the sauce around it.

LONG BEFORE I started cooking professionally, I had dinner parties at my house, so I've been serving these tarts on my table for the better part of fifteen years. I love how it offers all these different textures, flavors, and temperatures. The mix is fun and almost refreshing—it wakes up the palate, in a way. The all-suet crust bakes up beautifully flaky and crispy, but without feeling too heavy. Paired with cool, crisp arugula, nutty Parmesan, and juicy-sweet plums, this tart is an exercise in balance, and one of my favorite autumn recipes.

SAVORY PLUM TARTS WITH BEEF SUET CRUST, ARUGULA, AND PARMESAN *Makes 6 tarts*

FILLING

12 Italian plums, halved and pitted, or 8 black plums, pitted and sliced into wedges (about 6 cups)

¼ cup (47 g) sugar

2 tablespoons (15 g) all-purpose flour

2 teaspoons (5 g) ground cinnamon

¼ nutmeg, freshly grated

10 cracks pink peppercorn

½ bunch thyme, leaves picked

2 teaspoons (6 g) kosher salt

ASSEMBLY

Beef Suet Dough (page 276)

1 egg, beaten

GARNISH

1 pound (450 g) wild arugula

2 large handfuls parsley leaves

½ cup (50 g) shaved Parmesan cheese

Juice of 1 lemon

Olive oil

Flaky sea salt

NOTE: *Italian plums are best for this dish and available in early fall; black plums are an acceptable substitute.*

MAKE THE FILLING: In a medium bowl, toss the plums with the sugar, flour, cinnamon, nutmeg, pink peppercorn, thyme, and salt and allow the mixture to sit so the plums release some juices, about 30 minutes.

ASSEMBLE THE TARTS: Preheat the oven to 375°F.

Divide the dough evenly into 6 portions. Using a rolling pin, roll out each piece of dough into an 8-inch round about ¼ inch thick. Transfer the dough rounds to baking sheets.

Place about 1 cup plums in the center of each round, leaving a 2-inch border all around. Fold the border of dough up and very slightly over the plums, leaving the center open, and gently crimp the edges with your fingers, then brush the dough with the beaten egg. Bake until the crust is golden brown, about 25 minutes.

Just before serving, in a large bowl, toss together the arugula, parsley, and Parmesan. Add the lemon juice and olive oil and sea salt to taste, tossing again.

Serve the tarts hot with the cool arugula cascading from the top to amplify the contrast.

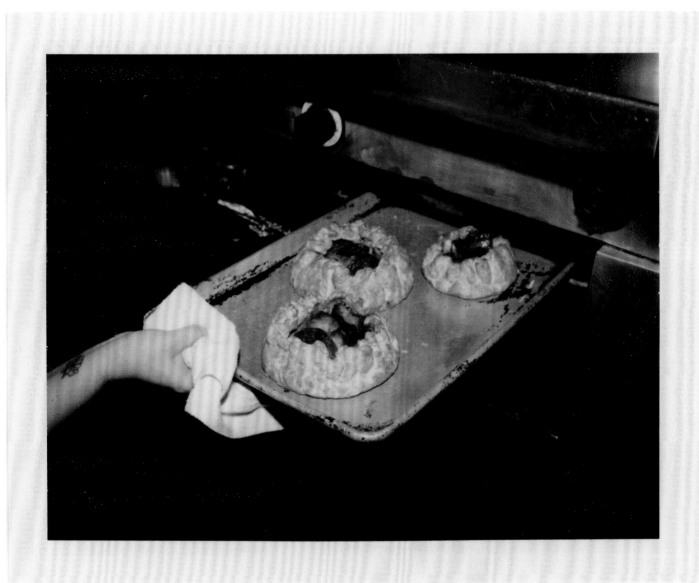

I DON'T THINK there's any dessert as classic New York as a cheesecake, which immediately makes me nostalgic for old-school diners with their towering dessert displays in glass cases. At the Bea, we've taken that idea and put it on a grandiose dessert cart, along with our signature bone marrow crème brûlée (page 64) and apple and sage pie (page 248). It felt only right, given that we run a nouveau chophouse, to have a nouveau dessert display, with this cheesecake as its centerpiece.

One of the reasons I love it is because we've taken traditional cheese course accompaniments (honey and black pepper) and put them into the cake itself. So you have a tremendously beautiful and simple dessert with these immense flavors incorporated into it. This cake is intended to taste very light and fluffy, so it's important to whip the sugar, goat cheese, and cream cheese well. The crème fraîche adds a final ethereal element, so light that each bite almost disappears on the palate.

CHÈVRE CHEESECAKE *Serves 8 to 10*

FILLING

1½ pounds (694 g) goat cheese, at room temperature

1½ pounds (680 g) cream cheese, at room temperature

9 tablespoons (110 g) sugar

1½ teaspoons (4 g) kosher salt

2½ cups (426 g) crème fraîche

6 ounces (174 g) honey

8 large eggs, at room temperature

CRUST

13½ ounces (384 g) graham crackers (about 25 cracker sheets), broken into pieces

1 teaspoon (3 g) kosher salt

15 cracks black pepper

1 heaping teaspoon (6 g) sugar

8 ounces (226 g) unsalted butter, melted

Preheat the oven to 325°F. Grease the bottom and sides of a 10-inch springform pan.

MAKE THE FILLING: In a stand mixer fitted with the paddle attachment, beat the goat cheese and cream cheese on high speed until combined, about 1 minute. Add the sugar and salt and continue to beat on high until the mixture becomes very fluffy, about 5 minutes. Scrape down the sides of the bowl occasionally to ensure everything is incorporated.

Still on high speed, beat in the crème fraîche and honey until incorporated. Reduce the speed to medium and add the eggs, one at a time, beating until fully incorporated, scraping down the sides of the bowl once.

MAKE THE CRUST: In a food processor, combine the graham crackers, salt, pepper, and sugar and pulse into fine crumbs. Drizzle in the melted butter and pulse to combine. Transfer the mixture to the prepared springform and press it into a crust all along the bottom and only about ¼ inch up the sides.

Pour the filling into the pan and bake until golden brown on top and set in the middle, 60 to 70 minutes.

Remove the pan from the oven and allow the cheesecake to cool to room temperature, about 1 hour. Transfer it to the refrigerator to set, still in the pan, for 3 to 4 hours.

To serve, remove the cheesecake from the springform and slice into wedges.

THIS DISH, in my way, is a take on French onion soup, the cold-weather standby whose contrasting flavors and textures I've always found seductive. I wanted to create something that carried the experience of French onion soup without the broth, and to highlight not only onions but several alliums, each with its own sweetness and aroma, all melting into one another. I swap the traditional Gruyère for a sharper and nuttier Comté, and, in the name of decadence, top the whole thing with a lobe of seared foie gras. In order to incorporate the full beefy flavor into the alliums without any liquid, I like to cook them in a mixture of foie gras fat and rendered bone marrow, along with duck stock and beef stock. It's a way of packing a lot of pure, clean animal flavor into humble onions, and it's worth the effort (you can substitute high-quality chicken fat for the duck if need be). Don't be afraid of getting color on the onions—dark is desirable so long as it's not burning, as it helps develop flavor and caramelize the natural sugars.

ROASTED ALLIUMS WITH FOIE GRAS *Serves 4 to 6*

1 (1¼-pound/562 g) lobe foie gras

ALLIUMS

¾ cup (157 g) Beef Stock (page 283)

¾ cup (157 g) Duck Stock (page 283)

5 tablespoons (60 g) Rendered Bone Marrow (page 284)

1½ tablespoons (22 g) unsalted butter

14 pearl onions, peeled and trimmed

11 shallots, peeled and trimmed

6 cipollini onions, peeled and trimmed

1 tablespoon (14 g) sugar

2½ teaspoons (9 g) kosher salt, plus more to taste

3 heads Garlic Confit (page 280)

2 tablespoons (16 g) thyme leaves

Freshly ground black pepper

MORNAY SAUCE

1½ tablespoons (22 g) unsalted butter

2½ tablespoons (22 g) all-purpose flour

¼ cup (60 g) milk

5½ tablespoons (70 g) heavy cream

¼ cup (24 g) shredded Comté cheese

Kosher salt and freshly ground black pepper

FOR ASSEMBLY

8 cups (429 g) torn stale boule or country bread, from a 1-pound boule

½ cup (50 g) shredded Comté cheese

Slice the foie gras into 3 evenly sized steaks and return to the refrigerator, covered, until ready to cook. Reserve the end cuts and trimmings to use in the allium sauce.

PREPARE THE ALLIUMS: In a small saucepan, heat the beef and duck stocks over low heat. Keep warm, stirring occasionally.

In a large sauté pan, cook the reserved foie gras trimmings over low heat until they have almost completely melted into liquid, 8 to 10 minutes. Remove any solids and add the bone marrow and butter to the pan. Increase the heat to medium-high and add the pearl onions. Cook until lightly browned, about 5 minutes. Add the shallots and cipollinis and cook, stirring occasionally until evenly colored, about 5 minutes more. Sprinkle in the sugar and salt and cook until beginning to caramelize, about 2 minutes.

Ladle ½ cup of the warm stock mixture into the onions and cook, scraping up any browned bits from the bottom of the pan, until the liquid has completely evaporated, about 3 minutes. The onions should be a slightly deeper shade of copper now. Add another ½ cup stock and reduce all the way down again, scraping as necessary, 2 to 3 minutes. The onions should be almost cooked through and a deeper shade of brown at this point.

Add a third ½ cup stock, but this time, don't reduce it all the way down—cook it for 1 to 2 minutes so it creates a sticky, deep brown sauce that coats the back of a spoon. Pop the garlic confit out of its skin and fold it into the onion mixture, along with the thyme.

Move the alliums aside in the pan and transfer as much of the sauce as you can to a small bowl—it will likely only be a few spoonfuls. Season the alliums with salt and pepper to taste and remove the pan from the heat.

Preheat the oven to 400°F. Take the foie gras steaks out of the refrigerator to come to room temperature.

MAKE THE MORNAY SAUCE: In a small saucepan, melt the butter over medium heat. Add the flour, whisking until it just comes together to create a blond roux (it should have no color), about 2 minutes. Whisking constantly, slowly stream in the milk, and then the cream. Simmer the mixture for 10 minutes to cook out the raw flour taste. Stir in the Comté to melt, then remove the pan from the heat. Season the sauce with salt and pepper.

ASSEMBLE THE DISH: In a large soufflé dish, arrange half the bread covering the bottom. Spoon all of the allium sauce over the bread, then top with the remaining bread. Spoon the reserved onion sauce

over the bread, then spoon all the mornay over it as well. Sprinkle the shredded Comté over the top and bake until bubbling and golden, about 20 minutes.

About 5 minutes before the roasted alliums are done, heat a large sauté pan over high heat. Season the foie gras with salt and add to the pan. Sear on one side for 1½ minutes, then flip and sear on the other side for another 1½ minutes, basting it in its own rendered fat. Turn off the heat and allow the foie gras to sit in the hot pan for 4 to 5 minutes to cook through. The finished foie gras should have some give when touched, and feel squishy and silken, but warm all the way through when a tester is inserted into their centers.

When the dish come out of the oven, stack the foie gras steaks over the top, holding them in place with a steak knife for presentation. Serve immediately.

ROASTED ALLIUMS WITH FOIE GRAS *(page 230)*

I LOVE THE START OF AUTUMN. Everyone is over summer in New York and longing for warm sweaters and chilly nights, and for me, game meat and chestnut season is when I'm at my happiest. This recipe is perfect to mark the transition of seasons. It's soul satisfying and warming, but still requires a cer- tain level of skill to execute. The technical aspect is in cooking the rabbit, but I love to serve it with this homey, rustic dressing made of brioche and chestnuts with herbs. The perfect bite is a bit of meat, a bit of chestnut, and a bit of bread with this rich, beautiful brandy sauce.

MUSCADET VINE–SMOKED RABBIT WITH CHESTNUT STUFFING, PRUNES, AND BRANDY *Serves 4*

RABBIT CONFIT

1 whole rabbit (3¾ pounds/ 1.7 kg), cut into 7 pieces (see Notes, page 91)

Muscadet vines, for smoking

Kosher salt

About 4 quarts (3.5 kg) canola oil

CHESTNUT STUFFING

1¼ pounds (582 g) brioche, cut into 1½-inch cubes

1 (7.8-ounce/222 g) piece foie gras, sliced into ½-inch cubes

1 teaspoon (3 g) kosher salt

7 tablespoons (102 g) unsalted butter

1 medium onion, finely chopped

11 ounces (314 g) peeled chestnuts (2 loosely packed cups), halved

5 sprigs savory, roughly chopped

6 sprigs rosemary, roughly chopped

Freshly cracked black pepper

1¾ cups (367 g) Duck Stock (page 283)

FOR FINISHING

⅓ cup (64 g) brandy

12 pitted prunes

2 cups (420 g) Duck Stock (page 283)

2½ tablespoons (34 g) unsalted butter

5 sprigs savory, for garnish

NOTES: *The rabbit can be confited up to 3 days in advance.*

You will need a handheld smoking gun (see page 293) for this recipe.

Seek out frozen shelled chestnuts.

Recipe continues »

MAKE THE RABBIT CONFIT: Cold-smoke (see page 293) the rabbit with the Muscadet vines for 20 minutes, until the meat has absorbed the smoky flavor.

Season the rabbit with salt on all sides, and allow to sit uncovered in the refrigerator, for a minimum of 3 hours, or ideally overnight.

Preheat the oven to 300°F.

Place the rabbit in a large Dutch oven or heavy-bottomed pot and add enough canola oil to submerge completely. Cover with a cartouche (see page 293) to keep the rabbit under the oil, then cover the pot and transfer to the oven. Cook the meat until tender and the hind legs (the thickest part) start to pull away from the bone, about 4 hours.

Let the rabbit cool in its oil at room temperature to maintain its juiciness. Remove the meat and set aside. Reserve 5 tablespoons of confit oil (discarding or saving the remainder for another use, such as cooking potatoes). Rabbit can be confited up to 3 days in advance.

MAKE THE CHESTNUT STUFFING: Preheat the oven to 350°F.

Spread the brioche in an even layer on a baking sheet. Toast in the oven until golden brown,

10 to 12 minutes, removing the pan halfway through cooking and gently tossing the bread for even toasting. Transfer the toasted brioche to a large bowl. Leave the oven on.

Meanwhile, season the foie gras with the salt. Heat a large sauté pan over medium-high heat. Add the foie gras and sear, flipping once, about 45 seconds per side. Remove the foie to a plate, leaving the rendered fat in the pan.

Reduce the heat under the pan to medium and add the butter to melt. Add the onion and sauté, stirring, until translucent and starting to brown, 6 to 8 minutes. Add the chestnuts and toss to combine, 2 to 3 minutes. In the last minute of cooking, add the savory and rosemary and season with salt and pepper to taste.

Transfer the mixture to the bowl with the brioche and toss to combine. Roughly chop the cooked foie gras, add to the brioche, and toss to combine.

In a small saucepot, warm the duck stock over medium-low heat. Ladle by ladle, pour it into the brioche-onion mixture, allowing the liquid to absorb between each ladle.

Transfer the chestnut stuffing to a large shallow casserole dish, cover, and bake for 15 minutes to warm it through. Reduce the oven temperature to 225°F, uncover the brioche, stir, then continue to bake until most of the liquid has evaporated and you are left with a beautiful, chewy, but still slightly moist mixture, about 20 minutes. Remove from the oven but leave the oven on and increase the temperature to 350°F. Check for seasoning and adjust if necessary. Tent the stuffing with foil to keep warm.

MEANWHILE, TO FINISH: In a small pot, combine the brandy and prunes and warm over low heat so the prunes warm through, soak up the brandy, and rehydrate.

In a large ovenproof sauté pan, heat the reserved 5 tablespoons rabbit confit oil over medium-high heat. Add the rabbit in a single layer, working in batches and replenishing the oil if necessary, and cook, undisturbed, until browned and crisp, 8 to 10 minutes. Flip and cook another 8 to 10 minutes on the other side; the rabbit will naturally release from the pan when it's ready.

Remove the pan from the heat and fit as much stuffing as possible into the rib cage of the rabbit. Place any remaining stuffing in a baking dish to serve alongside the rabbit (there's no such thing as too much stuffing). Place all of the pieces of rabbit (including the stuffed rib cage) back into the sauté pan, and place the pan, along with the baking dish of stuffing, in the oven for 6 to 8 minutes to heat through. Transfer the rabbit to a serving platter to rest and tent with foil.

Pour off any fat from the sauté pan and return to medium-high heat. Add the prunes and brandy to the pan. Ignite the brandy fumes with a grill lighter and flambé for 30 seconds, until the alcohol cooks off. Add the duck stock to deglaze the pan, scraping up any browned bits from the bottom. Increase the heat to high and bring to a boil, then reduce the heat to medium and cook until the sauce is reduced by one-quarter and thickens enough to coat the back of a spoon, about 10 minutes. Reduce the heat to medium and whisk in the butter to melt. Check for seasoning, adjust as necessary, and remove the sauce from the heat.

To serve, spoon the prunes and sauce over the rabbit, and garnish with savory.

MADEIRA

"AT THE HEART of the Beatrice Inn is food that tells a story—dishes that have personal meaning to Angie's life, dishes she cooked with her family, or dishes that have historical significance. There's a great deal of romance behind the stories that go into many of Angie's dishes, so we wanted the restaurant's wine program to reflect that. And there's no wine with a better story than Madeira.

I fell in love with Madeira when I was a sommelier at Per Se many years ago. As I learned more about it, I started referring to Madeira as 'vampire wine'—you can't kill it because it's already dead, so to speak. Its origins go way back to the 1600s, when the British navy was shipping wine from the islands of Madeira to the New World, where it 'cooked' in the sun-drenched hulls of the boats as they made the journey. After being exposed to heat and losing its freshness, the wine was effectively dead. Early Americans actually liked the flavor of Madeira in that state, but they wanted a way to make it last, so they fortified it with some sort of spirit. Once you fortify a wine, whether it's Madeira or port or sherry, it's immortal.

Madeira was what our Founding Fathers drank—it's what they toasted with at the signing of the Declaration of Independence. George Washington had it at his inauguration. In the Civil War era, it was the single most popular drink among Americans. It was on every dinner table, at every celebration. Ladies perfumed their handkerchiefs with it and used it to dab their necks. Madeira may have been introduced to the New World in the eighteenth and nineteenth centuries by the British Empire, but it was America's love of it that helped take it to the next level.

Thanks to this rich history, we at the Bea have the ability to build a collection that goes way back—right now, no one in New York has a selection as extensive or as old as ours, especially by the glass. Our oldest vintage is 1908. That bottle isn't just drinkable—it's fantastic. Madeira might be the only wine you can take pleasure in two hundred years later.

I put together our collection at the Bea thoughtfully, nodding to Angie's personal stories, classic New York stories, and stories with historical interest. Many people think of Madeira as an after-dinner drink, but you can enjoy it alongside an entire meal from start to finish, based on the specific grape. There are lighter, more acid-driven styles, and there are richer, more unctuous ones as well. Madeira as a dessert wine is a misperception. You can have it as an aperitif, make cocktails with it, or pair different varieties with all kinds of different dishes. That's part of why our collection is so vast.

Once you understand that, you become what I like to think of as a true believer. People who get it really get into it, and we have customers come back time and again to try different styles and vintages because it's so versatile. I often pour Madeira for guests, on me, because I just want them to try it. A single sip can be an entirely eye-opening experience. It's a pleasure to have the opportunity to help people discover something new that's not new at all."

—NATHAN WOODEN, BEVERAGE DIRECTOR

ONCE A QUARTER, my best friends in the food world and I get together in my apartment, and no matter what season it is or what else we're eating, we always start our meal off with this seafood roast. We throw all caution to the wind and eat like the savages we are, with our hands, shells flying every which way. I am lucky enough to have acquired two of the greatest wine minds in the city, Eric Asimov and Jason Smith, as friends, so there is always some beautiful Oloroso sherry and various white wines spread out as well, some of which are older than I am. Everyone is excited to be there, but I feel the most fortunate of them all, able to sit among such wonderful company and truly go wild.

SUNDAY ROAST OF SHELLFISH AND POTATOES *Serves 6*

POTATOES

1 pound (453 g) small Yukon Gold potatoes

1 bunch thyme

Kosher salt

¾ cup plus 1 tablespoon (180 g) rendered duck fat (see page 286)

SHELLFISH

15 langoustines

3 (1½-pound/680 g) lobsters

½ bottle (325 ml) white wine such as Chardonnay

1 pound (453 g) fresh seaweed (see Note)

1 bunch thyme

3 lemons, halved

3 Dungeness crabs

½ pound (227 g) mussels, scrubbed and beards removed

15 head-on tiger prawns

36 large oysters

FOR SERVING

1 cup Roasted Garlic Aioli (page 280)

1 cup Drawn Langoustine Butter (page 274)

1 cup Juniper Mignonette (page 281)

1 cup Yuzu Cocktail Sauce (page 281)

NOTE: *Fresh seaweed often comes with live lobsters and crabs.*

COOK THE POTATOES: In a large pot, combine the potatoes and thyme and add water to cover. Season with salt and bring to a boil. Cook until tender, about 20 minutes. Drain and when cool enough to handle, smash the potatoes slightly.

In a medium sauté pan, melt the duck fat over medium-high heat. Add the smashed potatoes and cook, flipping occasionally, until browned on both sides, 12 to 15 minutes. Season with salt and set aside somewhere warm.

PREPARE THE SHELLFISH: Set up a large bowl of ice and water. Bring a large pot of water to a boil over high heat. Add the langoustines and boil until opaque, about 3½ minutes, then plunge them into the ice bath to stop the cooking. Boil the lobsters until opaque, about 8½ minutes, then plunge them into the ice bath. Drain the shellfish and chill in the refrigerator.

Rinse out the pot and in it combine the wine, seaweed, thyme, 2 of the lemon halves, and about 12 cups water. Bring to a boil over medium-high heat. Add the crabs and cook, covered, until opaque, about 8 minutes. Add the mussels and prawns, cooking until the mussels open and the prawns are opaque, giving the pot a shake, another 4 minutes.

Meanwhile, shuck the oysters and arrange on a serving platter over crushed ice and any extra seaweed.

To serve, cover your table with butcher paper and dump everything onto it, along with the remaining lemon halves. Arrange bowls of aioli, drawn butter, mignonette, and cocktail sauce for dipping. Also put out the oysters, empty bowls for shells, crab crackers, forks . . . and a great many napkins.

**CHAMPVALLON DE TÊTE
WITH PORCINI, CHANTERELLES,
AND HEIRLOOM POTATOES**

(page 244)

I LOVE DISHES with a rich history and a romantic story, and this one is stunning. King Louis XIV was known to have many mistresses, including Madame de Champvallon. Legend has it that one of her rival mistresses cooked a dish of lamb en papillote for the king. Determined to prove her superiority, Madame de Champvallon cooked him lamb encrusted in thinly sliced potatoes, thereby winning the king's heart—and creating the dish that still bears her name. The moral of the story: At the Beatrice we only cook the food of champions.

At the restaurant, we use meat entirely from the veal's head to create one of the most elegant dishes on our menu, but at home, it's a bit more sensible to use beef cheek and veal shoulder. This dish offers a velvety texture on your palate, which comes from all of the collagen hidden within the bones. The braise is light and ethereal, and the herbaceousness from the lavender and thyme adds a sensual femininity that I like to think Madame de Champvallon would have appreciated.

CHAMPVALLON DE TÊTE
WITH PORCINI, CHANTERELLES, AND HEIRLOOM POTATOES *Serves 6*

2½ pounds (1.13 kg) oxtail

Kosher salt

4 tablespoons (54 g) extra-virgin olive oil

½ bunch lavender

½ bunch thyme

½ medium Spanish onion

1 bay leaf

½ head garlic, unpeeled, halved horizontally

2 pounds (900 g) beef cheek, cleaned and cut into 2-inch pieces

1½ pounds (675 g) veal shoulder, cut into 2-inch pieces

12 ounces (350 g) porcini mushrooms (5 cups), cleaned and halved

13 ounces (375 g) chanterelle mushrooms (6 cups), cleaned and halved

½ bottle (375 ml) white wine, such as Chardonnay

1 pound 5 ounces (600 g) Yukon Gold potatoes (3 medium), unpeeled, sliced ⅛ inch thick

Bâtard and rich European-style butter, for serving

NOTE: *The point of constantly basting the potatoes in stock is to continue to keep liquid on top of them so they cook as though being simmered, but as the stock evaporates, it leaves behind a beautiful sticky collagen, without crisping the potatoes.*

Season the oxtail all over with salt. In a large heavy-bottomed pot, heat 2 tablespoons of the olive oil over medium-high heat. Sear the oxtail, turning on all sides until golden brown, 8 to 10 minutes total.

Fill the pot with enough cold water to cover the oxtail by 3½ inches. Tie the lavender, thyme, onion, bay leaf, and garlic in a square of cheesecloth to make a sachet. Add the sachet to the pot.

Increase the heat to high and bring the liquid to a simmer, then reduce the heat to low. Cover with a cartouche (see page 293) and then a lid. Braise until you can pull the meat from the bone, but the meat is not completely cooked, 2 to 2½ hours.

While the oxtail braises, season the beef cheeks and veal shoulder with salt. In a large 4-quart Dutch oven, heat the remaining 2 tablespoons olive oil over medium-high heat. Working in batches, sear all the meat until golden brown, 6 to 8 minutes total. Set the meat aside in a large bowl.

In the same Dutch oven over medium heat, sauté the porcini and chanterelle mushrooms until beginning to soften, 6 to 8 minutes. Add the mushrooms to the beef cheeks and veal shoulder.

Pour off any fat from the Dutch oven and place it over high heat. Add the white wine to deglaze the pan, scraping up any browned bits from the bottom. Let the liquid reduce by about one-quarter, 10 to 15 minutes. Transfer the reduced wine to a bowl and set aside. Do not rinse the Dutch oven.

When the oxtail is ready, remove it from the braising liquid and place in a bowl. Spoon some of the braising liquid over the oxtails while they rest to keep them from drying out. (Reserve the remaining braising liquid.) Loosely cover the oxtail with foil and let cool to room temperature, about 15 minutes.

Pull the oxtail meat off the bones. (Transfer the bones to the Dutch oven and set aside.) Return the meat to the bit of braising liquid it cooled in. Mix the picked oxtail meat with the beef cheek, veal shoulder, and mushrooms.

Pour the reserved braising liquid over the oxtail bones in the Dutch oven. Bring to a boil over high heat to pull as much collagen out of the bones as possible. Cook until reduced by about one-quarter, 15 to 20 minutes. Strain the oxtail stock—it should be velvety and smooth, and you should have 4 to 5 cups (discard the solids).

Preheat the oven to 325°F.

ASSEMBLE THE CHAMPVALLON: In the bottom of the 4-quart Dutch oven used to sear the meat, arrange half of the potatoes in concentric circles, just to cover the bottom. Spread the meat and mushroom mixture on top of the potatoes, gently pressing down to even out the top (but without packing it too tightly).

Add all of the reduced wine, then just enough of the oxtail stock to submerge the meat evenly. Layer the remaining potatoes on top of the meat in concentric circles, so the entire surface is covered. Spoon about 1 more cup of the oxtail stock on top of the potatoes, or enough to just cover. Cover with a cartouche (see page 293), then cover with the lid and transfer to the oven.

Braise, covered, for 2 hours. Remove the lid and cartouche, ladle some more oxtail stock on top, and continue to braise, uncovered and ladling in more stock every 30 minutes, until the potatoes are deep amber and sticky, about 3 hours. The dish is done when if you press down on the potatoes with the back of a spoon, the liquid comes up over the edge without ruining the top.

To serve, bring the Dutch oven to the table and ladle into individual bowls. Serve with a beautiful crusty bâtard on the side slathered with the richest butter you can find.

I'VE ALWAYS LOVED LIVER. When I was a teenager in Seattle, I became so smitten with one particular chicken liver pâté recipe that I found in one of my father's old cookbooks that I began to make it constantly—I toyed with it and adjusted the ingredients and technique until I found something just right for me. I swapped the thyme out for sage, increased the onion ratio, and added Champagne. I continue to make my version in the restaurant to this day. It's very simple to execute, but I consider it essential; and the reason I love this recipe so ardently is because the pâté is a mousse style, so it feels light, while still maintaining the integrity of the sumptuous, irony liver taste that I love. It's a perfect entry-level pâté for charcuterie enthusiasts.

I've never been one to pair my pâté with pickles or cornichons because I don't like that vinegar-enhanced acidic taste—I prefer the pairing of a juicy-sweet blackberry conserva and grainy mustard instead. Serve straight out of the ramekin with a crusty baguette alongside.

CHICKEN LIVER PÂTÉ
WITH BLACKBERRY CONSERVA AND MUSTARD *Serves 6*

CHICKEN LIVER PÂTÉ

14 ounces (390 g) chicken livers

Kosher salt

13½ ounces (380 g) unsalted butter

1 medium Spanish onion, thinly sliced

2 sprigs sage, leaves picked

¼ cup (60 g) Champagne

¼ cup (53 g) duck fat

BLACKBERRY CONSERVA

2 pounds (884 g) blackberries (about 7 cups)

5 tablespoons (79 g) sugar

4 sprigs thyme

3 whole cloves

¼ teaspoon (1 g) salt

5 cracks black pepper

Crusty grilled bread, for serving

Whole-grain mustard, for serving

NOTES: *If possible, make this a day in advance so the flavors have time to settle overnight.*

When you are pureeing the liver, it will most likely be hot, so season with salt slightly more aggressively than you might think, as the chilling process will dull the seasoning.

MAKE THE CHICKEN LIVER PÂTÉ: In a large bowl, season the livers well all over with salt.

In a sauté pan, melt the butter over medium heat. Add the onion and cook, stirring frequently, until soft and translucent, but without any color, 8 to 10 minutes. Season with salt. Increase the heat to high and add the chicken livers. Sear on each side, turning until medium-rare (they should be a vibrant pink all the way through), 2 to 3 minutes total.

Add the sage and let its essential oils release, about 30 seconds. Turn off the heat and stir in the Champagne. Let the mixture rest in the pan for 5 minutes for the flavors to meld.

Meanwhile, in a small pan, melt the duck fat over medium heat.

In a blender, working in batches, puree the liver mixture and its liquid until smooth and silky, 2 to 3 minutes. Season with salt to taste.

Transfer the pureed liver to a large (15- to 18-ounce) terrine or multiple smaller (8- to 10-ounce) ramekins and tap the bottom(s) squarely against the counter a few times to remove any air. Cover the mixture with the melted duck fat and place in the refrigerator to set for at least 3 hours or ideally overnight.

WHILE THE PÂTÉ SETS, MAKE
THE BLACKBERRY CONSERVA:
In a small saucepot, combine
the blackberries, sugar, and
2½ tablespoons water. Tie the
thyme and cloves in a square of
cheesecloth to make a sachet.
Add the sachet to the pot and let it
steep for 2 to 3 minutes.

Increase the heat to high and
bring to a boil. Reduce the heat to
medium-low and cook, stirring
constantly so the blackberries

start to break down and release
their juices into a beautiful syrupy
liquid, 15 to 20 minutes. Increase
the heat to medium and bring
the mixture back to a boil, then
let the liquid reduce into a thick,
compote-like consistency, 10 to
12 minutes.

Remove the pan from the heat
and stir in the salt and pepper.
Transfer to a shallow bowl and
spread out to cool, then quickly
transfer to the refrigerator to chill

for 2 to 3 hours, to preserve the
vibrant color. As the conserva
chills, its color should brighten
into a beautiful jewel tone.

Serve the finished pâté with
crusty grilled bread, blackberry
conserva, and whole-grain
mustard.

When I was growing up, my family made all-American apple pie at our beach house on the Washington coast and, without fail, my proper, Oxford, England–raised mother would melt a piece of decidedly déclassé American cheese over the top before serving it à la mode. As strange as it sounds, I loved the interplay of the sweet-tart-molten-frozen elements, and it inspires me to this day.

Over the years, my palate has evolved and has become less drawn to sweet flavors. Now, I bake sage into my apple pie for herbaceousness and brown butter for nuttiness. The savory, cream cheese–infused crust is incredibly easy to make; it was the first crust I, a dedicated nonbaker, ever mastered at home, thanks to a *Bon Appétit* recipe for chicken potpie. And my palate has also moved on from Kraft Singles to Winnimere, a rich, lightly funky triple-crème beauty that tastes like butter and cheese in one, with a smoothness that reminds me of ice cream when it melts softly into the warm pie.

APPLE, BROWN BUTTER, AND SAGE PIE
WITH WINNIMERE CHEESE AND BLACK PEPPER *Makes one 10-inch deep-dish pie*

PIE DOUGH

3 cups (345 g) all-purpose flour

2 tablespoons plus 2 teaspoons (25 g) sugar

1 teaspoon (4 g) kosher salt

1 teaspoon (3 g) freshly ground black pepper

8 ounces (226 g) cream cheese, at room temperature, cut into 1-inch cubes

8 ounces (226 g) unsalted butter, at room temperature, cut into 1-inch cubes

---

NOTES: *You may wish to adjust the level of sugar depending on the tartness of your apples.*

If Winnimere is unavailable, use another rich triple-crème cheese such as Brillat-Savarin.

FILLING

1 pound (453 g) unsalted butter

13 cups (2.5 kg) peeled ½-inch slices Granny Smith apple (12 to 14 apples)

1¾ cups (349 g) sugar

1 tablespoon (8 g) kosher salt

2½ tablespoons (20 g) ground cinnamon

½ teaspoon (1 g) grated nutmeg

½ cup plus 1 tablespoon (70 g) all-purpose flour, plus more for dusting

½ cup (17 g) chopped fresh sage

2 eggs, beaten

1 (8-ounce) piece Winnimere cheese, at room temperature

Freshly cracked black pepper

MAKE THE PIE DOUGH: In a food processor, combine the flour, sugar, salt, and pepper. Add the cream cheese and butter, pulsing until the dough comes together, about 1 minute. Turn the dough out onto a floured surface and press it into a large, smooth ball. Divide the dough into 2 balls, flattening each into a 1-inch-thick disk. Wrap each disk of dough in plastic wrap and refrigerate for 1 hour.

MAKE THE FILLING: In a large sauté pan, melt ½ pound of the butter over medium heat. Add the apples, half of the sugar, and the salt and stir to coat. Cook until the apples release their juices, about 6 minutes. Add the remaining half of sugar, the cinnamon, and nutmeg and stir gently to coat and incorporate. When the apples are just barely cooked through, sprinkle the flour over them to thicken the juices, about 10 minutes.

In a large saucepan, melt the remaining ½ pound butter over medium-high heat, swirling the pan as it cooks and letting the milk solids brown, until the butter takes on a nutty, deep aroma, about 5 minutes. When the butter stops crackling and singing, remove the pan from the heat and add the sage, cooking until toasted and fragrant, about 1 minute. Stir into the apple mixture. Spread in an even layer on a baking sheet and allow to cool completely, about 1 hour.

On a lightly floured surface, roll out one dough disk into a round about 16 inches in diameter and ⅛ thick, enough to line a large (10-inch), deep (4-inch) pie dish. Roll out the second dough disk into a round about 12 inches in diameter and ⅛ inch thick. Fill the pie dish with the cooled apple mixture and top with the second crust. Trim the edges to a ½-inch overhang. Crimp the edges using your thumb and forefinger to pinch together and seal, and make three slits in the top to vent. Chill the pie for at least 30 minutes

before baking, placing a damp kitchen towel over the top so the crust doesn't dry out.

Meanwhile, preheat the oven to 350°F.

Brush the crust liberally with the beaten eggs. Bake until golden brown and fragrant, 35 to 40 minutes.

Let the pie cool for 30 to 40 minutes. Serve the pie whole, with the Winnimere and a peppermill at the table to add a good crack of heat to each piece.

THE PERFECT CHEESE CART

Serves 4 to 6

CHEESE IS a tremendously important part of the dining experience at the Bea. When it comes to dining courses, I ardently believe that if you are going to have a salad, it should be eaten after the meat course to cleanse your palate, and that a cheese course should come between the main course and dessert—it's just the civilized thing to do.

You'll notice that this recipe isn't really a recipe—it's an explanation of how we went about building our cheese cart. We chose five cheeses from around the world, with three varietals of honey, all of which pair with each cheese individually for different reasons. At the Bea, where more is always more, we believe that there should be multiple cheeses in multiple quantities—we serve some, like the Hudson Flower, Blanc Bleu Tambour, and Blu di Bufala in large wedges, and some, like the Colombier and Cremont, whole, in all their beauty. There is no such thing as too much cheese.

One 3-ounce piece each of **BLANC BLEU TAMBOUR, HUDSON FLOWER,** *and* **BLU DI BUFALA**

1 whole 5-ounce piece of **CREMONT**

1 whole 12-ounce piece of **COLOMBIER**

3 ounces each of **JAPANESE KNOTWEED HONEY** *(page 272),* **CHRYSANTHEMUM HONEY** *(page 272), and* **SMOKED HONEYCOMB** *(page 271)*

To serve, arrange a platter (preferably a vintage silver one) containing all of the cheeses and set small bowls of honey next to each piece, matching as specified below.

JAPANESE KNOTWEED HONEY: Pair with **COLOMBIER** and **CREMONT.** The Japanese honey has a deep brown butter flavor that balances against the natural brightness and tanginess of Colombier, an amazing goat cheese. Cremont is low on the acid, but it has beautiful light flavors of ice cream, butter, and mochi, which are enhanced by the Japanese honey, providing notes of both freshly churned butter and deeply caramelized brown butter to great effect.

CHRYSANTHEMUM HONEY: Pair with **BLANC BLEU TAMBOUR** and **HUDSON FLOWER.** A sheep's milk cheese, Hudson Flower's rind is covered with herbs and blossoms like thyme, rosemary, hops flowers, marjoram, and elderberry. It's tremendously feminine and very beautiful. Blanc Bleu Tambour is a fairly young goat cheese that's very tart with grassy notes, so the natural pairing to me is something both sweet and floral to accentuate those qualities. The chrysanthemum honey adds another layer of floral flavor to both these cheeses yet remains a bit understated.

SMOKED HONEYCOMB: Pair with **BLU DI BUFALA.** The world has many blue cheeses to offer, but I've always been drawn to Blu di Bufala, not only because it's insanely delicious, but also because I love the story of how it came to be: This cheese is made by two brothers in Lombardy, Italy, who inherited a water buffalo farm from their father, who had made buffalo mozzarella for generations. When they took over, they basically said *fuck you to convention, we're going to make traditional cheese with a nontraditional milk.* And that's exactly what they did. The buffalo milk gives this cheese a light, tangy flavor; it's overall not as deeply blue as a Roquefort or Stilton. The smoked honeycomb provides both the perfect textural contrast and a lovely sweet/savory effect.

WHEN I WAS A KID, one of my favorite dishes my father made was chicken and dumplings. He used an exceptionally simple recipe that called for cooking a whole chicken in water to make stock, pulling the meat, and making dumplings out of Bisquick mix. It was humble, to be sure, but so soul-satisfying. It gave me one of my fondest memories, curling up on the sofa with my brothers and eating our father's stew.

This recipe is my homage to that memory. The dumplings are a little lighter, the soup becomes velvety from the cornmeal, and the rabbit is a bit more full-flavored than chicken, but the idea is the same, and the result just as comforting.

STEWED RABBIT WITH DUMPLINGS
AND HEIRLOOM POTATOES *Serves 6 to 7*

6 tablespoons (84 g) extra-virgin olive oil

1 whole rabbit (3¾ pounds/ 1.7 kg), cut into 7 pieces (see Notes, page 91)

Kosher salt

8 ounces (226 g) pearl onions (about 1½ cups), peeled and trimmed

½ pound (236 g) carrots, cut into 1-inch obliques (about 2 cups)

5 garlic cloves, thinly sliced

2 bay leaves

1 bunch thyme

1¼ cups (240 g) white wine such as Chardonnay

4¼ cups (900 g) Chicken Stock (page 283)

14 ounces (394 g) heirloom fingerling potatoes (such as Pink Fir Apple) or baby red creamers, cut into 1-inch obliques (about 3 cups)

3 sprigs tarragon, roughly chopped

DUMPLINGS

2 cups (238 g) cornmeal

1¼ cups (162 g) all-purpose flour

3 tablespoons (38 g) sugar

2 tablespoons (18 g) kosher salt

1 teaspoon (4 g) baking powder

1 tablespoon (6 g) chopped chives

2¼ cups (510 g) heavy cream

NOTE: *If necessary, due to pot size, remove the cooked rabbit before cooking the dumplings, then gently reheat everything together just before serving.*

In a large heavy-bottomed pot, heat the olive oil over high heat. Season the rabbit all over with salt. Working in batches, add the rabbit to the pot and sear, turning on all sides, until golden brown, 6 to 8 minutes total. Remove to a plate, leaving any fat in the pan.

Add the pearl onions, carrots, and garlic and sauté over medium heat until the onions are light golden brown, 6 to 8 minutes. Add the bay leaves and thyme and stir until crackling and fragrant, about 30 seconds. Pour off excess fat, leaving the herbs in the pan.

Add the wine, bring to a simmer, and deglaze the pan, scraping up any browned bits from the bottom. Return the rabbit and any accumulated juices to the pan, add the chicken stock and potatoes, and stir to combine. Increase the

heat to high to bring the mixture to a boil, then reduce the heat to medium-low, cover, and simmer until the rabbit meat is very tender and starting to pull at the bone, but still holds its shape, about 45 minutes.

WHILE THE RABBIT SIMMERS, MAKE THE DUMPLINGS: In a medium bowl, whisk together the cornmeal, flour, sugar, salt, baking powder, and chives until combined. Slowly stream in the heavy cream, whisking continuously, until the mixture forms a dough.

When the rabbit is tender, uncover, increase the heat to high and bring the liquid back to a boil. Working swiftly, drop large spoonfuls of the dough into the liquid. Reduce the heat to medium and simmer until the dumplings puff and rise to the top, 5 to 10 minutes. The broth will begin to thicken.

Reduce the heat to low and stir in the tarragon. Cook until the dumplings are fully set and the broth coats the back of a spoon, leaving a silky texture on your palate, 8 to 10 minutes more. Taste for seasoning, adjust if necessary, and serve immediately, ladled into bowls, with one whole piece of rabbit per bowl.

BIG POPPA *Makes 1 cocktail*

"This legendary Beatrice drink is a bestseller. And how could it not be, with the combination of truffle-infused gin and edible gold dust? It's big, notorious, and undeniably over the top, just like the rapper for whom it's named. It makes perfect sense here, where we like to put truffles on everything. The technique is to fat-wash gin with white truffle oil (which actually doesn't bombard your palate—it's more subtle than you might think) and combine it with fragrant yuzu juice and herbaceous Chartreuse. Egg whites provide frothiness and a silky texture, and gold dust is the finishing touch, making for one seriously luxurious drink that everyone should try before they die."

—ANTANAS SAMKUS, BAR DIRECTOR

Lemon wedge
Edible gold dust, for garnish
1½ ounces Truffle Gin (recipe follows)
½ ounce yuzu juice
½ ounce lemon juice
¾ ounce yellow Chartreuse
½ ounce simple syrup
1 egg white

Run the lemon wedge around the rim of a coupe glass and dip the rim into edible gold dust. Combine the truffle gin, yuzu juice, lemon juice, Chartreuse, simple syrup, and egg white in a cocktail shaker and shake until the egg whites are foamy. Add ice to the shaker and shake once more, then strain the mixture into the coupe glass.

TRUFFLE GIN
Makes 8 ounces

8 ounces ESP Noho gin
1 ounce truffle oil

Combine the gin and truffle oil in a plastic container and store in the freezer for 8 to 12 hours. As it freezes, the oil will solidify and separate from the gin, which will remain liquid. Separate the frozen oil from the gin and discard the oil, then strain the gin into a clean container or bottle. Store the truffle gin refrigerated in its container for up to 4 weeks.

I OFTEN TURN TO THE PAST when I'm searching for inspiration, which is how I discovered sea pie, which has a rich backstory. Contrary to its namesake, it is a seafood-free meat pie that was served to eighteenth-century British sailors making the crossing to the American colonies. The early recipes were truly the Noah's Ark of meat, using any number of wild game animals, each separated by a layer of suet-infused crust. It is also a traditional Québécois dish, hence the French name *cipaille* (a soundalike of "sea pie").

I love to make this dish in autumn, when temperatures drop and game meats are at their finest. My version doesn't have six layers, as the traditional versions do, but it does have all different meats, stewed with cannellini beans and encased in an expanse of richly intoxicating golden crust. Making this multitiered pie is admittedly not a casual undertaking, but then again, nothing worth having ever is.

FALL GAME CIPAILLE (SEA PIE) *Serves 8 to 10*

1 (13-ounce/385 g) duck leg

1 pound (447 g) venison shoulder, left whole

1 pound 6 ounces (612 g) mutton shank, left whole

1 pound (481 g) wild boar shoulder, left whole

1 whole rabbit (3¾ pounds/ 1.7 kg), cut into 7 pieces (see Notes, page 91)

Kosher salt

Extra-virgin olive oil

5 garlic cloves, thinly sliced

5 tablespoons (37 g) all-purpose flour, plus more for dusting

1 (750 ml) bottle white wine

10 cups (2.1 kg) Chicken Stock (page 283)

About 13 cups (2.7 kg) canola oil

2 cups (356 g) dried cannellini beans, soaked in 6 cups water for 4 hours in 2 changes of water (reserve the last batch of soaking liquid)

½ bunch thyme

7½ tablespoons (108 g) unsalted butter

1 pound (448 g) cipollini onions (about 15 large)

1 whole squab (15 ounces/427 g)

15 sprigs savory

50/50 Dough (page 277)

2 eggs, beaten

1 pound (461 g) fingerling potatoes (3 loosely packed cups), boiled and chilled

1 tablespoon (6 g) finely chopped fresh rosemary

2 tablespoons (6 g) finely chopped fresh tarragon

2 tablespoons (6 g) finely chopped fresh savory

1 (7-ounce/286 g) piece foie gras

NOTE: *This recipe takes 2 days to complete, so plan accordingly.*

Season the duck, venison, mutton, wild boar, and rabbit with salt on all sides and refrigerate overnight.

Preheat the oven to 300°F.

Set a large Dutch oven or heavy-bottomed pot over low heat. Add the duck leg, skin-side down, and cook until most of its fat has rendered and the meat is light golden brown, about 20 minutes. Increase the heat to medium-high, flip the duck so that it's meat-side down, and briefly sear until golden, about 2 minutes. Set the duck aside, leaving its rendered fat in the pot.

In the same Dutch oven over medium-high heat, working in batches, sear the venison, mutton, wild boar, rabbit shoulder, and rabbit legs, turning, until golden, 8 to 10 minutes per batch. Add olive oil as needed between batches, though there should be enough rendered fat in the pot. Remove the seared meats to a plate. Add the garlic to the pan and briefly sauté until blistered and golden, 1 to 2 minutes, then remove and set aside.

Turn off the heat and carefully pour off any residual fat. Return the duck, rabbit legs and shoulder, and venison to the pot and place over medium heat. Sprinkle in the flour and toss to coat the meats. Cook until the flour begins to brown, 5 to 6 minutes. Add the white wine to deglaze the pot, scraping up any browned bits from the bottom. Bring the liquid to a simmer and cook until reduced by three-quarters, 20 to 25 minutes.

Add 5 cups chicken stock and the blistered garlic to the pot and bring to a simmer. Cover with a cartouche (see page 293) and then the lid. This is the "braising pot."

In a separate large Dutch oven or heavy-bottomed pot, place the mutton shank, wild boar, and rabbit saddle and add enough canola oil to cover completely. Cover the pot with a cartouche and then the lid. This is the "confit pot." Transfer both pots to the oven.

After 1½ hours, remove the rabbit legs from the "braising pot" and set aside in a container with ½ to ¾ cup of the braising liquid ladled over the top to keep the meat moist. Cover and place in the refrigerator.

After 2 hours, remove the rabbit saddle from the "confit pot" and set aside in a container with ½ to ¾ cup of the confit oil ladled over the top to keep the meat moist. Cover and place in the refrigerator.

Recipe continues »

After 3 hours, remove the duck leg from the "braising pot" and add it to the container with the rabbit legs, plus another ½ to ¾ cup of the braising liquid, and return to the refrigerator.

After 5 hours, remove the "braising pot" completely from the oven and return the rabbit and duck legs to it, along with their liquid, then cover and chill overnight. Remove the "confit pot" from the oven and return the rabbit saddle and its oil back to it, then cover and refrigerate overnight.

WHILE THE MEATS COOK, PREPARE THE REST OF THE FILLING INGREDIENTS: In a medium pot, combine the remaining 5 cups chicken stock, the beans and their soaking water, and the thyme. Bring to a simmer over medium heat, then cover with a cartouche and a lid, then reduce the heat to low and simmer until the beans are tender and creamy, and most of the liquid has been absorbed, about 2 hours. Set aside to cool, then transfer to a container, cover, and refrigerate overnight.

In a small sauté pan, melt half of the butter over medium-high heat. Add the cipollinis and sauté, stirring, until golden brown, about 20 minutes. Set aside to

cool, then transfer to a container, cover, and refrigerate overnight.

Season the squab inside and out with salt and stuff it with the savory, then tie the legs together with butcher's twine. In a medium sauté pan, melt the remaining butter over medium-high heat. Add the squab and sear, basting it with the butter, until light golden brown and cooked to 125°F for rare, about 10 minutes (it will finish cooking in the pie). Set aside to cool, then transfer to a container, cover, and refrigerate overnight.

On the day of serving, preheat the oven to 350°F. Line a baking sheet with parchment paper.

Divide the dough in half, then divide one half in half again. You should have 3 pieces: one around 400 g, and two around 200 g each.

On a floured work surface, roll out the larger piece of dough to a 10-inch round about ¼ inch thick. Place on the prepared baking sheet and brush with some of the beaten eggs. Bake until cooked through and golden brown, about 15 minutes. Remove and let cool. (Leave the oven on.)

Remove the meats, beans, and onions from the refrigerator. Remove the meats from their

liquids, reserving the braising liquid and discarding the confit oil or reserving for another use.

In a small saucepot, bring the braising liquid to a boil over medium-high heat. Cook until it is reduced by half and coats the back of a spoon, about 30 minutes. Remove the pot from the heat and let the gravy cool to room temperature.

Arrange the beans in an even layer on the bottom of an 8-quart Dutch oven. Add the venison shoulder, rabbit saddle, rabbit shoulder, and 2 of the rabbit legs. Arrange half the potatoes and half the onions around the meat.

Break off a large piece of the baked crust to form an even "top" for this layer in the pot and place it on top. Cover the crust with the wild boar shoulder, mutton shank, duck leg, 2 rabbit legs, the whole squab, and the remaining potatoes and onions. Pour half of the gravy over this layer and check for seasoning.

Roll out one of the smaller pieces of dough into a round to cover the top of the pie and overlap the rim of the Dutch oven. Place it over the meats, cutting slits in the dough for the mutton shank and duck leg to stick up through. Brush all over with the beaten eggs.

Roll out the remaining smaller piece of dough into a 24 × 3-inch rectangle, cut it lengthwise into 3 even strips, and braid the pieces together. Brush the outside edges of the top dough layer with egg wash and gently press the braid around the rim of the Dutch oven to adorn.

Brush the entire crust once more with egg wash and bake until golden brown and heated through, 20 to 25 minutes. Set aside to rest for 10 minutes.

While the pie rests, return the remaining gravy to a small pot over medium heat and bring to a simmer. Stir in the chopped rosemary, tarragon, and savory and taste for seasoning, adjusting as necessary.

Season the foie gras on all sides with salt. In a small dry sauté pan, sear the foie gras over high heat until rare, 1½ to 2 minutes per side.

Place the seared foie on top of the pie, pour the gravy over it, and serve.

I'M PARTIAL TO PASTAS that are thick, toothsome, and incredibly rich; tagliatelle satisfies that craving for me, and warms my soul through and through. I'm also fond of tagliatelle's backstory: It is said to have been invented in the fifteenth century in Bologna (a city nicknamed "The Fat" for its rich cuisine) on the occasion of Lucrezia Borgia's wedding, to honor her long, golden hair. It's a tender pasta, and the one most often associated with being eaten with white truffles—which, if you happen to have some on hand, are a welcome addition to this dish.

I start craving pasta when temperatures drop, especially with this heady braised ragu. This is one of those deeply comforting dishes, one I just want to curl up with on a Sunday night with my friends and a big glass of Barolo. I love adding the Winnimere cheese to finish, which accentuates the beautiful wild game flavor from the boar, and the richness from the pasta itself.

WILD BOAR TAGLIATELLE
WITH CHILE AND WINNIMERE CHEESE *Serves 4*

1 tablespoon (14 g) extra-virgin olive oil

1½ pounds (675 g) wild boar, cut into 2-inch cubes

Kosher salt

¾ cup (145 g) white wine, such as Chardonnay

About 3 cups (630 g) Duck Stock (page 283)

½ head garlic, halved horizontally

½ medium onion, halved

1 bay leaf

½ bunch thyme

2 tablespoons (30 g) unsalted butter

2½ tablespoons (15 g) grated Parmesan cheese

½ teaspoon (1 g) chile flakes

Juice of ½ lemon

Handful of chopped fresh parsley

Duck Egg Yolk Pasta (page 279), cut into tagliatelle

1 (14-ounce) wheel Winnimere cheese, at room temperature

Freshly ground black pepper

NOTES: *Like many great sauces, this ragu of boar is at its best when made a day in advance, so plan accordingly.*

I recommend preparing the pasta while the sauce simmers, and leaving it, uncooked, in loose bundles until just before serving.

If Winnimere is unavailable, use another triple-crème cheese such as Brillat-Savarin.

In a large heavy-bottomed pot or Dutch oven, heat the olive oil over high heat. Season the boar all over with salt. Working in batches as needed, add the boar and sear, turning, until deeply browned, about 15 minutes. Remove the boar to a plate as you cook it.

Pour off the excess fat and return all of the meat and its collected juices to the pot over medium heat. Add the white wine to deglaze the pot, scraping up any browned bits from the bottom, and cook until reduced by half, about 10 minutes. Add enough duck stock just to cover the meat.

Tie the garlic, onion, bay leaf, and thyme in a square of cheesecloth to make a sachet. Add the sachet to the pot. Increase the heat to high and bring to a boil. Reduce the heat to low, cover, and simmer until the meat is very tender and begins to pull apart with a fork, about 3 hours.

Uncover the pot and remove it from the heat. Using two forks, shred the meat into larger chunks, working directly in the pot. Return the pot to medium-high heat and bring to a boil. Allow the sauce to reduce by about one-quarter, until it has reached a beautifully thick consistency, 12 to 15 minutes. In the last minute of

the sauce boiling, stir in the butter to melt. Remove the pot from the heat and stir in the Parmesan, chile flakes, lemon juice, and parsley. Taste for seasoning, adjusting as necessary.

While the sauce reduces, bring a large pot of water seasoned like the sea to a boil over high heat. Add the pasta and stir briefly to separate the strands. Cook until al dente, 15 to 20 seconds. Drain the pasta. As soon as the sauce is finished reducing, add the drained pasta and toss together to coat. Serve immediately, topping each bowl of pasta with large dollops of the Winnimere and freshly ground black pepper.

I HAVE BEEN BEGGING Pat LaFrieda to take me duck hunting for forever, so much so that I might have created this recipe for him as further incentive. Originally, I imagined this meal would be very comforting after sitting in the marshes in a duck blind all day, though it's equally welcome on a cold New York night in the comfort of my own apartment. He finally took me to Arkansas to go hunting for mallards as I was writing this book, and it turns out that I was completely right. I made us this stew the day we returned to the lodge from our early morning kill. Whenever you choose to serve it, do so with buttery garlic toast alongside, as directed.

HUNTER'S STEW *Serves 4*

2 cups (356 g) dried cannellini beans

4 duck legs

Kosher salt

12 garlic cloves, smashed, plus 2 whole cloves

2 bay leaves

1 bunch thyme

½ bottle (375 ml) white wine, such as Chardonnay

4 cups (840 g) Duck Stock (page 283)

10 ounces (293 g) Yukon Gold potatoes, sliced into obliques (2 cups)

4 tablespoons (60 g) unsalted butter

8 ounces (250 g) baguette, halved crosswise on the bias and then halved horizontally (4 pieces total)

2½ cups (90 g) Tuscan (lacinato) kale, center ribs removed, cut into ribbons

———

NOTE: *Like many soups and stews, this one tastes better the second day, after the beans have broken down a bit and made the broth even creamier. I often make a double batch of it and freeze one for later.*

Place the beans in a large bowl and add hot water to cover by 2 inches.

Season the duck legs all over with salt. Set a large Dutch oven or heavy-bottomed pot over medium-low heat. Add the duck legs, skin-side down, and cook slowly, without disturbing, until all the fat has rendered and the duck has turned a deep golden brown, 25 to 30 minutes. Flip the duck using tongs and gently sear on the meat side until golden, about 2 minutes. Remove the meat to a plate. Leaving about 1 tablespoon of the rendered duck fat in the pan, pour out the rest and strain the salt from it. Set the fat aside for toasting the baguette.

Return the pot to medium heat. Add the smashed garlic, bay leaves, and thyme. Sauté until the garlic blisters and turns a light golden and the herbs become fragrant, 3 to 4 minutes. Return the duck legs to the pot, along with any accumulated juices. Add the white wine and deglaze the pan, scraping up any browned bits from the bottom.

Add the duck stock, the cannellini beans and their soaking water, and the potatoes. Bring to a boil over high heat. Cover the ingredients with a cartouche (see page 293) and then the lid. Reduce the heat to low and simmer until the duck legs are tender, with the meat starting to pull away from the bone, and the beans are plump and completely softened, about 2 hours. Taste for seasoning, adjusting as necessary.

Just before the 2 hours are up, in a large sauté pan, melt the butter and 2 tablespoons of the reserved duck fat over medium heat. Place the baguette slices, cut-side down, in the fat and fry until golden brown on both sides, flipping occasionally, 10 to 12 minutes.

When the bread is toasted, slice the whole garlic cloves in half and rub them over the warm bread, allowing them to melt.

Bring the stew to a gentle boil over medium heat, uncovered, and add the kale, stirring until just barely wilted and tender, about 2 minutes.

Ladle the stew into four bowls, with one duck leg each, and serve the toasted, garlic-spiked bread alongside.

I FIND AUTUMN IN NEW YORK incredibly romantic; there's no place I'd rather be than curled up next to the fireplace at the Bea sharing a steak for two. A porterhouse is the perfect cut for that, since it's really two steaks in one: a sirloin and a filet. On one of my summer visits to LaFrieda Meats, walking through their dry-aging room and picking out meat to age in the restaurant, I came across a really stunning short loin with the biggest, most beautiful fat cap I'd ever seen. I looked at Pat and said, "Mine." He sent it over the next day and we spent all fall aging the meat, waiting to make this steak for two.

I got in a lot of trouble with our beverage director when I made this sauce. Some Châteauneuf-du-Pape had been left unattended near the kitchen, which I promptly commandeered unbeknownst to him. I reduced two bottles to almost nothing while braising the trotter, but when he tasted the insanely rich, silky sauce, he couldn't stay mad for very long. And it just so happened that Périgord truffles were in season while we were tasting it, so I figured, what could possibly be better with a dry-aged porterhouse than a Châteauneuf-du-Pape reduction, escargots, and truffle butter? It's an undeniably sensual combination, warming right through to the bone.

PORTERHOUSE WITH ESCARGOTS, TROTTER, AND RED WINE   *Serves 2*

NOTES: *The methodology for flipping multiple times is to allow the internal juices to continually baste the inside of the steaks, slowly building a dark golden brown crust. Because a porterhouse is really two different steaks attached by one bone (a lean filet and a fattier sirloin), the goal is to get the sirloin medium-rare without overcooking the filet. While searing, baste the sirloin side (and only the sirloin side) with its own fat to encourage browning and a cook temperature comparable to the filet's.*

When resting the steak, the bottom of the T should be on the cutting board; a 52-ounce steak will be thick enough to stand up on its own and this method helps the rarest parts get more carryover cooking.

WINE REDUCTION AND DEMI-GLACE

1 (2¼-pound/995 g) pork trotter, split

2 (750 ml) bottles red wine, preferably Châteauneuf-du-Pape

1 star anise

2 bay leaves

½ bunch thyme

1 medium Spanish onion, unpeeled, halved

4 cups (840 g) Beef Stock (page 283)

STEAK

3 tablespoons (42 g) extra-virgin olive oil

1 (52-ounce) beef porterhouse, dry-aged for 90 days

Kosher salt

FOR FINISHING

6 ounces (172 g) highest quality canned escargots, rinsed and drained, roughly chopped

1 tablespoon (15 g) unsalted butter

3 tablespoons (15 g) chopped fresh parsley

Kosher salt and freshly ground black pepper

½ cup (113 g) Truffle Butter (page 273)

MAKE THE WINE REDUCTION
AND DEMI-GLACE: In a large
pot, combine the trotter and wine
and bring to a boil over high heat.
Add the star anise, bay leaves,
thyme, and onion. Reduce the
heat to medium-low and simmer,
uncovered, until the liquid is
reduced to about 1½ cups and is
very sticky, about 2 hours.

While the liquid reduces, make
the demi-glace. In a small
saucepot, cook the beef stock over
medium heat until reduced to
about ¼ cup, 50 to 60 minutes.

Strain the red wine reduction,
discarding the solids. Set both the
red wine reduction and the demi-
glace aside at room temperature
while cooking the steak.

COOK THE STEAK: Preheat the
oven to 375°F.

In a large cast-iron skillet, heat the
olive oil over high heat. Season
the steak generously all over with
salt. Add the steak to the skillet
and sear on one side for 2 minutes,
then flip and sear for 2 minutes
more. Continue to slowly sear the
steak, flipping every minute, for
15 minutes total, until the steak is
crusted and deep golden.

Transfer the skillet to the oven
and continue to cook the steak
to medium-rare (a thermometer
inserted in the center should
read 115°F), about 5 minutes.
Remove the steak from the pan

and let rest, propped up on the
T-bone, for about 12 minutes; the
internal temperature will rise to
about 120°F.

WHILE THE MEAT RESTS, FINISH
THE SAUCE: Pour the fat out of
the cast-iron skillet and return it
to high heat. Add the red wine
reduction and deglaze the pan,
scraping up any browned bits
from the bottom. Cook for about
1 minute, until shimmering, then
add the demi-glace and reduce the
heat to medium-high.

Add the escargots and stir just
to heat through, about 1 minute.
Swirl in the butter for gloss and
remove the skillet from the heat.
Finish with parsley and season to

taste with salt and pepper, but note
that there should be a fair amount
of salt in the fond scraped up from
the steak.

To serve, cut both steaks off the
bone, so you have a filet and a
sirloin. Cut the sirloin into ¼-inch
slices and the filet into ½-inch
pieces.

Dab the truffle butter on the meat
and spoon the sauce on it and
around it, reserving any leftover
sauce for a small bowl on the
side. If you're feeling particularly
decadent, which I am always,
shave any truffles (left over from
making the truffle butter) over the
sauce before serving.

PORTERHOUSE WITH ESCARGOTS, TROTTER, AND RED WINE *(page 264)*

THE LARDER

This section contains the recipes that form the backbone of my cooking. You don't need to make all of them at once, but having a steady supply of things like stocks and compound butters will make your prep time shorter and easier when working your way through my recipes. Plus, they will help you master the fundamental cooking techniques I rely on as a chef to build complex and beautiful finished dishes.

HONEYS

HONEY IS a tremendous representation of terroir, similar to wine. I find the variety afforded by honeys endlessly interesting and quite beautiful. Many we use are seasonal, and from specific regions. Japanese knotweed honey, for example, is completely different from orange blossom honey, because the bees that make it have only picked up pollen from the knotweed plant and bamboo, which yields a completely different flavor than the orange blossom. Honey is truly so diverse and wide-ranging, and when you start going down the rabbit hole, or rather, deep into the hive, you'll find that no two honeys are alike. These are a few of my favorites.

SMOKED HONEYCOMB

Makes 8 ounces

I believe honeycomb can be important whether you're cooking something sweet or savory. It absorbs other flavors—it's like fat in that sense—and it picks up smoke particularly well. At the restaurant, we use Muscadet vine clippings, which make for a very light, elegant, and feminine smoke; you can substitute cherrywood or applewood chips.

NOTE: *You will need a handheld smoking gun (see page 293) for this recipe.*

8 ounces (232 g) honeycomb
2 cups (5 ounces) vine clippings, such as
    Muscadet, or light, sweet wood chips
    such as cherry or apple

Cold-smoke (see page 293) the honeycomb with vine clippings or wood chips for 20 minutes, until it has absorbed the smoky flavor. Transfer to an airtight container and store at room temperature for up to 4 weeks.

SMOKED HONEY

Makes 16 ounces

Smoked honey adds a lovely and unexpected depth to the whipped cream served with the cherry clafoutis on page 156; it's also welcome with many cheeses.

NOTE: *You will need a handheld smoking gun (see page 293) for this recipe.*

16 ounces (464 g) clover honey
2 cups (5 ounces) cherrywood chips

Cold-smoke (see page 293) the honey with cherrywood chips for 20 minutes, until it has absorbed the smoky flavor. Transfer to an airtight container and store at room temperature for up to 8 weeks.

TRUFFLE HONEY

Makes 8 ounces

We have truffle honey in our larder year-round—the flavor changes by season. It's a great way to use up all the extra shavings left over from tableside truffle service. Truffles are such an expensive ingredient that it's nice to use every bit.

8 ounces (232 g) Japanese knotwood honey
1 ounce truffle shavings
½ teaspoon (3 g) truffle salt

In a small saucepot, combine the honey and truffle shavings. Cook over medium heat until the honey just barely starts to bubble, about 7 minutes. Immediately remove the pan from the heat and allow the truffles to steep for 10 minutes before using, until the honey is very fragrant, then stir in the truffle salt. Do not strain the truffle shavings. Transfer to an airtight container and store at room temperature for up to 2 weeks.

SAFFRON HONEY

Makes 8 ounces

I love the pairing here—there's something almost savory about saffron, which plays off the sweetness of the honey itself. I like to leave the beautiful red threads in the honey to give it a deep golden hue. Serve this with cheese, roasted fruit, or desserts like the cheesecake on page 229.

8 ounces (232 g) clover honey
½ ounce saffron

In a small saucepot, combine the honey and saffron. Cook over medium heat until the honey just barely starts to bubble, about 7 minutes. Immediately remove the pan from the heat and allow the saffron to steep for 10 minutes before using, until the honey is very fragrant and stained a deep golden color. Transfer to an airtight container and store at room temperature for up to 4 weeks.

CHRYSANTHEMUM HONEY

Makes 8 ounces

Chrysanthemum is one of my favorite things in life; I love to incorporate the flowers into honey and use it as a garnish to add a bit of that floral essence to any dish. As an added benefit, this honey is also beautiful in appearance, with unfurled tea blossoms suspended in amber.

8 ounces (232 g) clover honey
1½ ounces chrysanthemum tea blossoms

In a small saucepot, combine the honey and tea blossoms. Cook over medium heat until the honey just barely starts to bubble, about 7 minutes. Immediately remove the pan from the heat and allow the tea to steep for 10 minutes before using, until the honey is very fragrant. Transfer to an airtight container and store at room temperature for up to 4 weeks.

JAPANESE KNOTWEED HONEY

This is not a recipe but rather a product we love from Tremblay Apiaries in upstate New York. It's deep and complex, with notes of molasses, brown butter, and caramel—similar to buckwheat honey, but darker and richer. It's a seasonal product, available in the winter and spring, and I like to stock up so it's always in my pantry.

COMPOUND BUTTERS

IN THE KITCHEN at the Bea, though we tend to favor cooking with animal fats rather than butter, we do use it as a condiment. And instead of basting with straight butter, we infuse it to provide contrasting flavors, textures, and depths. All of the compound butters here are made with unsalted butter, which allows the flavors to shine through uninhibited.

TRUFFLE BUTTER

Makes about 2 cups

15 ounces (437 g) unsalted butter, at room temperature
1 ounce Périgord truffles, grated on a Microplane rasp grater
1 teaspoon (6 g) truffle salt
5 tablespoons (70 g) truffle oil

In a food processor, combine all the ingredients and pulse until just combined. Transfer to an airtight container and store, refrigerated, for up to 1 week.

ANCHOVY BUTTER

Makes about 2 cups

NOTE: *If making anchovy butter for the lavender-aged beef recipe on page 46, use Don Bocartes, as they have a naturally rounder, more buttery flavor that pairs well with the meat.*

15 ounces (437 g) unsalted butter, at room temperature
8 ounces (237 g) Ortiz or Don Bocarte anchovies (see Note)

In a food processor, combine both ingredients and pulse until just combined. Transfer to an airtight container and store, refrigerated, for up to 1 week.

SNAIL BUTTER

Makes about 3 cups

15 ounces (437 g) unsalted butter, at room temperature
18 ounces (500 g) highest quality canned escargots, rinsed and drained, roughly chopped
¼ cup (50 g) roughly chopped garlic
2 teaspoons (5 g) kosher salt

In a medium skillet, melt 2 tablespoons of the butter over medium-high heat. Add the snails and garlic and sauté until fragrant and the garlic begins to soften, about 5 minutes. Season with the salt. Transfer to a medium bowl to cool to room temperature.

In a food processor, pulse the remaining butter and the snail mixture together until combined. Transfer to an airtight container and store, refrigerated, for up to 1 week.

HERBES DE PROVENCE BUTTER

Makes about 2 cups

15 ounces (437 g) unsalted butter
⅔ cup (73 g) diced shallots (about 2 shallots)
10 sprigs fresh rosemary, leaves picked, roughly chopped
14 sprigs savory, picked and chopped
2 tablespoons (30 g) white wine vinegar
12 sprigs marjoram, picked and chopped
2 teaspoons (5 g) kosher salt
½ teaspoon (1 g) freshly ground black pepper

In a food processor, combine all the ingredients and pulse until just combined. Transfer to an airtight container and store, refrigerated, for up to 3 days.

VANILLA BUTTER

Makes about 2 cups

12 ounces (330 g) unsalted butter, at room temperature
Seeds of 9 vanilla beans
2 teaspoons (5 g) kosher salt

In a food processor, combine all the ingredients and pulse until just combined. Transfer to an airtight container and store, refrigerated, for up to 1 week.

SMOKED VANILLA BUTTER

NOTE: *You will need a handheld smoking gun (see page 293) for this recipe.*

Make the Vanilla Butter, then cold-smoke (see page 293) with cherrywood chips for 20 minutes, until it has absorbed the smoky flavor. Blend the ingredients and store the butter as directed above.

LANGOUSTINE BUTTER

Makes about 1 cup

1 head-on langoustine (82 g)
8 ounces (226 g) unsalted butter, at room temperature
Seeds of 1 vanilla bean
1 teaspoon (5 g) sea salt
15 cracks black pepper

Set up a small bowl with ice and water. Bring a small pot of water to a simmer over medium-low heat. Add the langoustine and poach until cooked through and opaque, 1 to 2 minutes, then transfer to the ice water to stop the cooking.

When the langoustine is cool enough to handle, peel it. Roughly chop the head and tail meat and combine both with the butter, vanilla seeds, salt, and pepper in a food processor. Pulse until just combined. Transfer to an airtight container and store, refrigerated, for up to 3 days.

CHARRED PRAWN BUTTER

Makes about 2 cups

3 tablespoons (42 g) olive oil
6 head-on tiger prawns (188 g)
12 ounces (330) unsalted butter, at room temperature
Seeds of 9 vanilla beans
2 teaspoons (5 g) kosher salt

In a small sauté pan, heat the olive oil over medium-high heat. Add the prawns and cook until deep brown and caramelized, about 5 minutes. Remove the pan from the heat and set aside to cool slightly.

Roughly chop the prawns and add them to a food processor along with the butter, vanilla seeds, and salt. Pulse until just combined. Transfer to an airtight container and store, refrigerated, for up to 3 days.

DRAWN LANGOUSTINE BUTTER

Makes about 3 cups

½ cup (101 g) langoustine shells (from about 5 langoustines)
14 ounces (419 g) unsalted butter, at room temperature
1 cup (211 g) Charred Prawn Butter (above)
Seeds of ½ vanilla bean

In a small dry saucepot, gently heat the langoustine shells over medium heat until they are roasted, fragrant, and golden, about 5 minutes. Add the butter, charred prawn butter, and vanilla seeds, reduce the heat to low, and cook the butter for 20 minutes. To clarify the butter, scoop off the milk solids as they rise to the top and discard. Strain out any remaining solids and discard. Transfer to an airtight container and store, refrigerated, for up to 3 days.

DOUGHS

FOR ME, crust is a very intimate and sensual thing. I view it as a vessel, a garnish, and moreover, a crowning jewel for an array of dishes—all at once. I only use two crusts in my cooking. One is made using solely beef suet, which gives a heartier feel to the dishes it envelops, and one is made with 50 percent beef suet and 50 percent butter, both ground to a fine meal, giving the crust a silken, flaky touch. Either way, beef suet is the magic ingredient here, and I'd urge you to try out both, as each is completely seductive in its own way.

BEEF SUET DOUGH

Makes enough for two 12-inch pie crusts

I use this all-suet dough in the savory plum tarts on page 226, as well as in the short rib and beef cheek pie on page 94. It makes a beautifully flaky, crunchy crust that's rich without feeling heavy.

1¾ cups (210 g) all-purpose flour, plus more for kneading
4½ teaspoons (18 g) sugar
1 teaspoon (3 g) kosher salt
¼ teaspoon (1 g) baking powder
8 ounces (225 g) beef suet, finely chopped or ground through a medium die (2½ cups), well chilled

In a food processor, combine the flour, sugar, salt, baking powder, and beef suet and process until the mixture looks like rough ground cornmeal. With the machine running, slowly stream ½ cup cold water into the processor until the dough forms a ball.

Turn the dough out onto a floured surface and knead, rotating the dough and adding flour as necessary to avoid sticking, until it has a sticky, silky texture, about 50 turns.

Form the dough into a disk and wrap it tightly in plastic wrap. Refrigerate for at least 30 minutes to chill before rolling out as directed in any given recipe. Store the dough, wrapped in plastic, in the refrigerator, for up to 1 week.

50/50 DOUGH

Makes enough for two 12-inch pie crusts

I originally developed this recipe (which is made with half butter and half animal fat) as a lighter alternative to the all-beef suet dough. I use it in pies with lighter meats, such as the duck and foie gras pies on page 143 and the venison and trotter pie on page 208, whose refined flavors call for a different pastry.

2½ cups (332 g) all-purpose flour, plus more for kneading

2 tablespoons (27 g) sugar

1 tablespoon plus 1 teaspoon (11 g) kosher salt

¼ teaspoon (1 g) baking powder

4¾ ounces (133 g) cold unsalted butter, finely chopped

5¼ ounces (150 g) beef suet, finely chopped or ground through a medium die (1⅓ cups), well chilled

In a food processor, combine the flour, sugar, salt, and baking powder and pulse just to mix. Add the butter and suet and pulse until the mixture takes on a cornmeal texture. With the machine running, slowly stream in ¾ cup cold water and continue pulsing until the dough just comes together.

Turn the dough out onto a floured surface and knead, rotating the dough and adding flour as necessary to avoid sticking, until it has a silky texture, 50 to 60 turns. Do not be concerned about overkneading, as this dough is like pasta dough, and you want it to feel silky.

Form the dough into a disk and wrap it tightly in plastic wrap. Refrigerate for at least 30 minutes to chill before rolling out as directed in any given recipe. Store the dough, wrapped in plastic, in the refrigerator, for up to 1 week.

DUCK EGG YOLK PASTA

Serves 4

I LIKE THINGS that are rich, silky, and velvety on my palate. By their very nature, duck eggs are all of those things, and they bring those qualities to this pasta dough, which is made with only the yolks, lending a dark yellow hue and a supple texture that can't be duplicated.

Consider this a master recipe for all pastas—it's the only recipe I use at the restaurant, and I roll it out to different thicknesses on a pasta machine depending on its use. Tagliatelle should be 2 millimeters thick and ⅜ inch wide; pappardelle is 3 millimeters thick and 1 inch wide, though I do like to make them extra-wide (2 to 2½ inches) for the veal stroganoff on page 124. If you're feeling particularly inclined, you can add squid ink to the dough to make it black.

4 cups (435 g) "00" flour, plus more for dusting
2 teaspoons (5 g) kosher salt
23 duck egg yolks
2 tablespoons (27 g) extra-virgin olive oil

In a food processor, combine the flour and salt and pulse until just combined. In a small bowl, whisk together the egg yolks and olive oil until smooth. With the food processor running, slowly stream the yolk mixture into the flour until a dough just comes together.

Turn the dough out onto a lightly floured surface and divide into 4 even balls. Knead each ball 50 to 60 times, adding more flour as necessary to prevent sticking. The end result should be a beautiful silky smooth texture that feels elastic when you pull it apart, but without breaking too much.

Using your hands, shape each ball into an oval, wrap in plastic, and allow to rest for 30 minutes at room temperature before rolling out. Working with one oval at a time, use a rolling pin to roll the dough out to a sheet ¼ inch thick, turning it and adding a little more flour with each turn to keep it dry and smooth and avoid sticking. From here, you can transfer each sheet to a pasta machine, rolling it out to the desired thickness and then finally cutting to your desired width. As you roll out the pasta, the sheets will become very long—you can cut them in half and stack them on a baking sheet to make them easier to manage.

When the pasta is cut, arrange it in loose, neat bundles on a baking sheet lined with parchment paper and floured.

To cook the pasta, bring a large pot of water seasoned like the sea to a boil over high heat. Add the pasta—it will sink to the bottom, then rise to the surface in 15 to 20 seconds. Drain the pasta and serve immediately with sauce as directed in any given recipe.

GARLIC CONFIT

Makes 4 cups

Slowly confiting garlic brings out its sweet, mellow side, as opposed to the sharp bite it has when raw. I always have some in my refrigerator and use it to cook with, to blend into sauces and dressings, or to simply spoon across warm toast. When we cook with the cloves, we love to keep them in their papery skins, as it lends a beautifully rustic presentation. Because the cloves are scalped at one end, you can easily pop them out of their skins before use or eating if you so choose.

8 heads garlic
4 cups (868 g) extra-virgin olive oil

Preheat the oven to 210°F.

Trim the garlic heads slightly at the top (opposite the root end), just enough to expose a little bit of the clove, then break apart all the cloves with your hands, discarding the root ends.

Place the cloves in a roasting pan or an ovenproof saucepot large enough to fit the garlic in a single layer, but small enough that the oil will fully cover it. Add the oil, then cover with a cartouche (see page 293) and cover the pan with foil. Transfer to the oven and bake until the garlic is very soft, sweet, and fragrant, about 3½ hours.

Remove the pan from the oven and allow the garlic to cool, then pack it into an airtight container, ensuring the garlic cloves are fully submerged in oil (add a bit more if necessary). Store the garlic covered in oil in the refrigerator for up to 3 weeks.

ROASTED GARLIC AIOLI

Makes 2 cups

One of my favorite memories of Paris is sitting outside at a sidewalk cafe in the early spring and dipping the most beautiful chilled prawns into fresh mayonnaise. My version includes roasted garlic for added flavor.

3 large egg yolks
1 tablespoon plus 1 teaspoon (11 g) kosher salt
½ teaspoon (5 g) Dijon mustard
2 loosely packed cups (382 g) Garlic Confit (opposite), skins removed, plus 1 tablespoon confit oil
½ cup plus 3 tablespoons (152 g) canola oil

In a food processor, combine the egg yolks, salt, mustard, and garlic confit and process until a paste forms. With the machine running, slowly stream in the garlic confit oil and canola oil, alternating with a few drops of water as needed to thin out the mixture to a mayonnaise-like consistency. Transfer to an airtight container and store in the refrigerator for up to 1 day.

MARINATED ANCHOVIES

Makes about 1 cup

Anchovies are a polarizing ingredient—people either love them or hate them . . . or they're like me and only love certain kinds. I don't enjoy white anchovies or those cured in vinegar, but the black salt-cured ones, with their round, buttery flavor, are something very special. We use Don Bocarte brand anchovies, which are tremendously luxurious and buttery, and worth the extra expense. Marinating them is a way to impart more herbal flavors to a beautiful fish. (For more on anchovies, see page 291.)

1 (48 g) tin Don Bocarte anchovies

1 sprig rosemary, leaves picked

10 cloves Garlic Confit (page 280), plus confit oil to cover

In a small bowl, combine the anchovies, rosemary leaves, and garlic confit. Transfer to an airtight container and add enough garlic confit oil to cover. Marinate in the refrigerator for 1 day before using. Store in the refrigerator for up to 1 week.

YUZU COCKTAIL SAUCE

Makes 2 cups

When we were creating a cocktail sauce for the Bea, I wanted to put my own spin on the classic condiment. I like flavors that are deeply spicy yet flavorful—not the kind of heat that burns your palate, but the kind that has depth. Fresh horseradish and red *yuzu kosho* give this cocktail sauce those qualities.

NOTE: *Red* yuzu kosho *paste is a fermented Japanese citrus infused with chiles, available online and at many Asian grocers.*

1 cup plus 2 tablespoons (300 g) ketchup

½ cup (70 g) prepared horseradish

1 teaspoon (13 g) Tabasco sauce

1 teaspoon (10 g) Worcestershire sauce

¼ teaspoon (4 g) red yuzu kosho paste

Kosher salt

In a small bowl, whisk together the ketchup, horseradish, Tabasco, Worcestershire, yuzu kosho, and salt to taste until combined. Transfer to an airtight container and store in the refrigerator for up to 1 week.

JUNIPER MIGNONETTE

Makes 2 cups

One of my favorite combinations is a gin martini and fresh oysters—since gin is infused with juniper berries, it's a natural accompaniment to the mignonette you would serve with oysters. This version has a depth of flavor and different dimensions that contrast beautifully with the acidity of the vinegar.

6½ tablespoons (97 g) champagne vinegar

¾ cup (194 g) red wine vinegar

3 tablespoons plus 1 teaspoon (60 g) yuzu juice

¼ teaspoon (2 g) ground juniper

½ tablespoon (7 g) sugar

½ tablespoon (5 g) kosher salt

Freshly ground black pepper

½ cup (120 g) diced shallots (about 2 shallots)

In a small saucepot, combine the champagne and red wine vinegars and bring to a simmer over medium-high heat. Remove the pot from the heat and add the yuzu juice, juniper, sugar, salt, pepper to taste, and shallots. Let steep at room temperature for 10 minutes, then transfer to the refrigerator to chill until cool. Transfer to an airtight container and store in the refrigerator for up to 1 week.

STOCKS: BEEF, CHICKEN, DUCK

Makes 4½ quarts

STOCKS ARE tremendously important, and there are many philosophies on how best to make them. Classic French stocks start with a mirepoix, but over the years I've become a purist—I like a very concentrated, very dark stock that tastes intensely like the animal it comes from. I might add herbs or a mirepoix later during a braising process or while making a soup; however, this is the master recipe for the deep, dark, pure stock I crave and cook with.

NOTES: *For duck or beef stock, get neck bones; for chicken, backbones are preferable.*

If absolutely necessary, you may use store-bought stock as a substitution when stock is called for in a recipe, but I highly advise against it.

5 pounds bones (see Notes)

Preheat the oven to 425°F.

Spread the bones out across a baking sheet in an even layer. Roast until deep, deep brown, flipping once halfway through. For beef it should take about 40 minutes total; for chicken and duck it will be 25 to 30 minutes.

Transfer the bones to a large stockpot and scrape any browned bits and juices from the baking sheet into the pot as well. Cover with 10 quarts cold water. Bring to a boil over medium-high heat, then reduce the heat to low and simmer slowly, occasionally skimming impurities off the top. For beef, simmer 6 hours; for chicken or duck, simmer 4. The stock should be very dark.

Strain the meat and bones out and discard. Transfer the liquid to a clean container and chill in the refrigerator overnight. Skim the fat that solidifies and rises to the top the next day, then use as directed in any given recipe. Stock keeps in the refrigerator for up to 1 week and freezes well.

RENDERED BONE MARROW

Makes about 1 cup

RENDERED BONE MARROW adds a silken quality
to whatever it touches. Note that some butchers
and specialty grocers carry prerendered marrow,
but I prefer to make my own.

NOTE: *Ask your butcher to cut the marrow bones for you.*

6 beef marrow bones, cut into 3½-inch pipes

Put the bones in a large bowl with enough
cold water to cover and let them soak in the
refrigerator. Drain and re-cover with cold water
every hour for 3 hours to purge them of any
blood. Preheat the oven to 425°F.

Arrange the marrow bones in a single layer on
a rimmed baking sheet. Roast until deep brown
in color and the marrow is no longer pink, 20 to
25 minutes. Remove the bones from the oven.
Pour any of the marrow that has rendered into
liquid form out of the pan into a bowl. When the
bones are cool enough to handle, scoop out any
solid pieces of marrow into a small saucepan.

Place the saucepan over low heat and slowly melt
the marrow solids in the pan until liquid, then
add them to the bowl with the other rendered
marrow.

Pour the liquid marrow through a fine-mesh
strainer to remove any solid particles or bone
fragments. Transfer to an airtight container and
store in the refrigerator for up to 2 weeks.

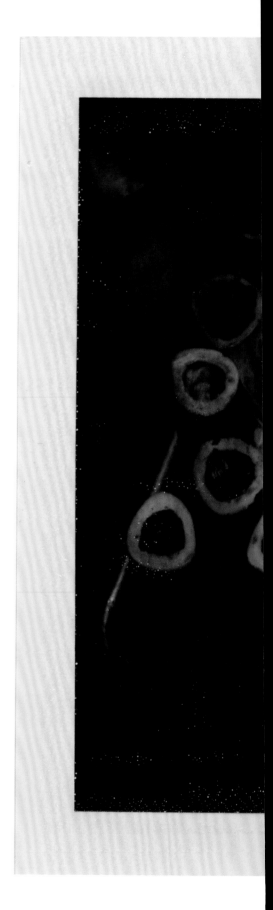

RENDERED FATS

I CANNOT OVERSTATE the importance of animal fats in my kitchen. I cook meats in their own fat, as a way both to honor the whole animal and to avoid the heavy feeling butter or cream leaves you with. You can render the fat from any animal using the technique that follows.

At the restaurant we often end up rendering fat when we have an accumulation of trimmings. We might only get a few tablespoons of fat off an individual piece of meat, so we freeze it, and when we have enough amassed, we cook it down. But sometimes we call our butcher and ask him to send over *his* trim, because we need more—you can always do that. Some specialty butchers will render their duck fat in-house and sell it, but most fat is thrown away, so they will be happy to give it to you.

1 pound (453 g) animal fat, cut into 1-inch pieces

Place the fat and 2 tablespoons water in a large saucepan over low heat. Cook, stirring occasionally, until the fat has melted as much as possible (it may still contain some small solid particles), about 2 hours. Strain out any solids and discard. Let the rendered fat cool to room temperature, then transfer to an airtight container and store, refrigerated, for up to 1 month.

BEEF: Beef is king for me, and it's my favorite fat to cook with. It's so versatile—I use everything from ground suet (kidney fat) in my pie doughs to rendered meat trimmings (including dry-aged trimmings, which are on a whole other level) for cooking our steaks in. I find that beef fat is flavorful and velvety in texture, and it adds a level of depth and dimension to everything it touches. To take it to another level, try the rendered beef bone marrow on page 284.

LAMB: I adore lamb tallow, but definitely have to be in the mood for it. I tend to cook things in lamb tallow in the winter because lamb fat is noticeably sweet and gamey—a bigger flavor than a lot of other fats—but I love its ability to absorb other flavors. One of my favorite things to do when aging lamb is to take the trimmings from the herb-aged meat, render them down, and use the fat to cook the meat itself or some sides for the dish, like potatoes and onions. I highly encourage you to utilize lamb fat, especially if you're going to play with dry-aging.

PORK: Pork fat is also very versatile and quite light in the world of animal fats. I love cooking with lard, which has a medium-to-high smoke point (similar to canola oil, as opposed to olive oil, which has a low smoke point), so it creates a tremendous sear. We like to pan-sear pork steaks in rendered pork fat—it gives the meat so much more flavor, and ensures a beautifully crusty, golden outside.

DUCK: Duck fat is incredibly rich and palate-coating, so I use it only in certain instances, such as when sealing a pâté or terrine. Duck fat is smooth when cold and spreads beautifully on bread as it melts; it adds a silkiness and a luxurious element, so you still want to keep eating it through every stage. It also has a high smoke point, which makes it ideal for searing duck or other poultry. While I love cooking with straight rendered duck fat, I do find that the rendered fat from the smoked bird in Roast Duck Flambé (page 223) makes for more interesting flavors.

VENISON: Every autumn, I receive an obscene amount of deer, and when we break the whole deer down into primal cuts, there's a lot of trim of fat as well as a small trim of meat. In the spirit of nothing going to waste, the meat will be browned and put into stocks, but it's tremendously special to render venison fat to use to cook the venison itself. Venison fat is sweet, and has a slight bit of gaminess. It helps the meat taste like its best self.

INGREDIENTS, EQUIPMENT, AND TECHNIQUES

MY STYLE is over the top. The atmosphere, the decor, and the portion size at the Bea are intentionally extravagant, in a "let them eat cake" kind of way. The recipes in this book are representations of how I do things within the Bea's walls, but the following information will help set you up to achieve similar results at home.

SOURCING: Almost every recipe in this book involves meat. At the restaurant, we get most of ours from Pat LaFrieda, and occasionally from D'Artagnan, for specialty game birds and rabbit. You can order from Pat online, but there also is something to be said for having a relationship with your butcher, or even the people at your neighborhood butcher counter. The truth is, even though I have access to the best meat in the country via Pat, I still have a relationship with the butchers at Whole Foods a block away from my apartment, with Shatzi in Harlem, with Ottomanelli's down the street from my restaurant, and with the gentlemen at the Latin supermarket. The restaurant is the restaurant, but when I don't feel like leaving my neighborhood, I know I can still get great meat. Have a conversation with the people selling your meat, get to know them and their product, and you'll become a better meat cook.

TEMPERING MEAT: Note that all meats should be removed from the refrigerator and brought to room temperature for about 1 hour before being cooked, unless otherwise noted.

ANIMAL FATS: Animal fats are tremendously important to me. I truly began to understand their value when I started working for other chefs in restaurants. I found that a lot of dishes I was executing in restaurants were laden with obscene amounts of butter. Now, I love butter just as much as the next girl—it's delicious, but it makes me feel so heavy afterward. That's when I started playing around with animal fats instead. The more I experimented, the more excited I became. When I ate meat cooked in its own fat, I felt the same richness on my palate, but without the heaviness in my stomach. One of my goals at the Bea is for people to come here, to this incredibly seductive space, and eat our incredibly seductive food, then go home and be able to get laid afterward. Cooking with animal fats helps with that. For more on individual fats and cooking techniques (see Rendered Fats, page 286).

FRESH HERBS: I've never met an herb I didn't like—and in fact they might be the only green things I enjoy. Herbs are very much a centerpiece and focal point in my kitchen. They add a beautiful depth and dimension, whether it's a few sprigs in a braise, chopped leaves for sauces, or basting a whole bunch in a hot pan to release their essential oils. The trifecta for me is thyme, rosemary, and lavender. I use thyme and rosemary year-round, lavender during its peak in the summer and early autumn. When cooking with herbs, don't be too concerned with exact measurements (unless they are finely chopped and incorporated into sauces). I like to err on the side of abundance when using bunches for braises, bastes, and garnishes.

TRUFFLES: Truffles are one of those ingredients that I can never get enough of. I buy them in obscene quantities every season—I bribe our purveyors in cash to ensure I have the first pick, always get the biggest and best, and hoard them like jewels. The layer of umami and richness they add is magical, and in the name of all things extra, we put them on everything. The Bea is all about luxe, and how much more luxe can you get?

Périgords, which are named for the region of France from which they come, are among my favorites. They have deep tones of chocolate and earth, smell intoxicatingly fragrant, and pair well with meats, stone fruits, and vanilla. Harvested in the autumn and winter, the same varietals are available in the summer from Australia.

The most prized truffles, however, come from Italy's Alba and Piedmont regions, where white truffles reign supreme. Their flavor is light and heady, delicate yet deep. In the colder months I shave them into consommé and over our *tartiflette* (page 93) as it oozes with cheese. They are stunning over our wild boar tagliatelle, but the child in me loves them the most over vanilla ice cream with truffle fries to dip into it when I eat alone at the bar.

ANCHOVIES: I am very finicky about anchovies. I will never eat white anchovies that have been cured in vinegar (unless I'm in Spain), but what I will eat all day long is black salt-cured anchovies. My love for anchovies comes from a time in my life when I didn't have a lot of money—I would revert back to my childhood snack of tinned fish on Triscuits. The anchovies we get now are about a dollar a fillet instead of a dollar a tin, but they still bring back warm memories for me.

We have many uses for anchovies in our kitchen—some are finely chopped and used as seasoning to add layers of salinity and umami in dressings and butters; some are used as whole marinated fillets in dishes like carpaccio or pastas. We even have some so beautiful we serve them as is in our seafood towers. The two most commonly used anchovy brands in our kitchen are

ORTIZ: We use these as seasoning. In our kitchen, they are chopped by hand quite finely, and added to garlic to be sautéed with potatoes, carrots, or green beans. These are also what we use in the crust of the prime rib on page 192. Ortiz anchovies have a higher salinity than Don Bocarte (see below) and taste a bit sharper; their meats are a bit rougher, like velvet (as opposed to Don Bocarte's silk). They're fished from the Mediterranean and cured for six months in rock salt, then trimmed by hand with a knife (not scissors), to maintain their integrity, and hand-packed in olive oil. Ortiz is a bit of a heavier anchovy, which is why I like to pair it with meats as a seasoning rather than as a garnish.

DON BOCARTE: These are a relatively recent discovery for me, and I'm smitten with them. They are like no other anchovy I've ever tasted—silky, buttery, round, and light, Don Bocarte anchovies are special. They are also wildly expensive, and make no financial sense for us to use in the restaurant, but I don't care, because they're worth it. The fish themselves are purchased by Bocarte from Cantabria in northern Spain only in April, May, and June, when they are at their best, then they are hand-packed in olive oil and take eight months to cure in salt. We use these to garnish the veal carpaccio on page 120, but I would be happy to sit at home and eat these out of the tin with nothing more than crusty bread and beautiful butter from Normandy.

SALT: In our kitchen, we use Diamond Crystal kosher salt for almost everything. I love that the grains are medium in size and uniform, which allows for better control when I'm seasoning. Because the brand is so consistent, over the years I've been able to hone my own internal measurement skills to the point where I know that my three-finger pinch will be exactly 1 gram of salt. Anything that gets additional seasoning after being cooked and sliced is finished with Maldon sea salt. Maldon has a bigger flake than many other sea salts, and I love the flavor it imparts. The salinity level has a softness and roundness that adds a wonderful depth to any dish.

Pink curing salt, also called Prague Powder, is table salt with sodium nitrite in it to inhibit the growth of anaerobic bacteria. I call for it in some cured meat recipes; look for the curing salt labeled Cure #1.

BLACK PEPPER: It is always freshly ground.

FLOUR: Almost all the flour called for in this book is all-purpose.

OLIVE OIL: It is always extra-virgin, unless otherwise noted.

BUTTER: All butter called for in this book is unsalted unless otherwise noted. See page 273 to read about compound butters.

SHIRODASHI: Shirodashi is a liquid soup base made from bonito, kombu, white soy sauce, mirin, and sugar. It adds a rounded flavor to sauces without any additional color, and creates a velvety, creamy texture that's still quite light on the mouth. You can find it in many Asian markets or online.

PIG'S BLOOD: Fresh pig's blood can be sourced from a reputable butcher with a few days' notice. Use it within 1 to 2 days, or freeze for up to 4 weeks. Blood should be cooked gently to avoid curdling. Hog casings can also be sourced from a butcher you respect.

MEASUREMENTS: For traditional US volume measures, such as cups and tablespoons, I have included their equivalents in grams for all recipes. In restaurants, we do everything by the gram because the recipes need to be exact. I urge everybody to operate in grams, especially when it comes to things like pasta, pastry, and charcuterie, because those recipes call for more specifics than what cups and tablespoons can really capture. (Stews and braises are slightly more forgiving.) All you need is a digital scale—after a while, you may find that you prefer this method.

DRY-AGING: Through a lot of trial and error and education (thanks, Pat LaFrieda) I have learned that our perfect dry-aging conditions at the Bea are 38°F with 40 to 45 percent humidity. A lot of the success of dry-aging has to do with air circulation, temperature, and humidity levels. We have a digital thermometer in our dry-aging fridge that tells us all of this. At home, you can easily make things like the lavender-aged beef on page 46 in the crisper drawer of your regular refrigerator, but if you want to get serious about dry-aging, it's worth investing in a designated fridge for this purpose and monitoring it accordingly. What's perfect at the Bea may not be perfect in your environment, so don't feel discouraged if you need to experiment a bit with the conditions.

SMOKING: Smoky flavors are heavily imprinted on my brain and in my palate, likely as a result of having grown up in the Pacific Northwest. Some of my fondest memories take place around a campfire on the beach with my family, roasting crabs and marshmallows and eating everything with our hands. When I taste things that have that smoky flavor and depth, it feels like home.

A few recipes in this book call for cold-smoking meat. I cannot recommend a handheld smoking gun highly enough. You can buy one online for less than $100. They are small, simple, and allow you to infuse the exterior of food with a smoky flavor in minutes.

To cold-smoke food using a smoking gun, place whatever you're smoking in a metal or glass container with a tight-fitting lid, or tightly wrap with foil. Open the container very slightly, just enough to insert the tip of the smoking gun and fill it with cold smoke, then cover and allow the meat (or anything else) to sit and absorb the smoky flavor. This usually takes between 20 and 30 minutes, depending on the size of the food. I have also included suggestions for the appropriate wood to use in every recipe that calls for smoking, as different woods impart different flavors.

CARTOUCHE: I often call for covering a dish that simmers for extended periods with a cartouche, which is a simple parchment paper lid that helps slow the rate of evaporation and protects ingredients from exposure to air, which can dry them out. It is sometimes used under an actual lid. You can make one by cutting a sheet of parchment paper into a round or rectangle to fit the size and shape of the pot you are using.

SCALPING GARLIC: Leaving the root end of a head of garlic intact, slice the top of the head off, exposing just the tops of the cloves. Leave the papery skins on.

SEASONING TO TASTE: Recipes that do not call for specific amounts of salt and pepper should be seasoned to taste. Taste frequently throughout cooking to get to know your own palate and preferences.

ACKNOWLEDGMENTS

TO MY FATHER, ROY: Thank you for giving me the love of food, family, and life. Your unwavering love and support for all my decisions, no matter how you felt, allowed me to make mistakes, learn, grow, and ultimately succeed. I hope that I make you proud, I hope that you love this book, and that you are happy. I love you, Daddy. You are missed every single day.

To my beautiful cousin and business partner **MELISSA MERRILL:** I love you beyond words. Thank you for being my biggest fan, my biggest supporter, and my greatest friend. Who would have thought that two girls picking blackberries and secretly getting their ears pierced at the age of eight would turn into a partnership that would see us purchasing a piece of

New York history? Your PoPo, your mother, and my father are looking down on us, smiling. Thank you for believing in me and our family.

To my brothers, **CONRAD** and **CHAD:** Thank you for always supporting the insane ideas, for being present at every event, for pushing me harder, and for always reminding me where we come from. Daddy would be so proud to see how close we are today. I love you both beyond words.

To my mother, **NANCY:** Thank you for giving me the love of fashion, the verve for living life, and the passion for travel and adventure.

To my family, **STACI, HOLLY, ROD, BEKAH, LEXI, SEAN, JON, JOE, COCO, GAIL, BRANDON, AUNTIE WENDY, AUNTIE VI, UNCLE JIMMY, AUNTIE RUBY, JESSICA, NATHAN, PAUL,** and

THE ENTIRE MAR, LUKE, LIN, and CHOW CLANS: Thank you for raising me, for nurturing me, for feeding my mind, body, and soul. It takes a village to raise a child, and we have raised each other, generation after generation. I love you all.

To my darling **PATRICK LAFRIEDA:** Thank you for your unwavering support, love, and encouragement, without which I would not be who I am today.

To my amazing assistant **PATRICIA HOWARD:** You have been a rock for me and the keeper of my sanity. You've been invaluable during the creation of this book and our business. I am so excited to see where your future goes, my dear.

To my writer, partner in crime, and great friend **JAMIE FELDMAR:** I am so happy that we found each other for this project. This is truly a labor of love that I am so proud to share with you, and I certainly hope this will not be the last. Thank you for telling the story of me and the Beatrice in the most beautiful words that I could have imagined. I love you, my dear.

To my agent, **ALISON FARGIS:** Thank you for believing in me before anyone else knew who I was. For taking a chance on someone who'd not yet found her voice, for pounding the pavement with me and for me, for shouting from the rooftops the story of the Beatrice, and for truly believing in the core of who I am, for better or for worse, and for finding a platform for it to sing.

To our photographer, **JOHNNY MILLER:** You are truly a genius. The art that you have created in this book is more than I could have ever dreamed of. Thank you for stepping into our world, living, eating, breathing, the Beatrice. You truly have created a window into how we eat, drink, live, and love. I am so proud of what we have created together.

To my great friend, my soul sister, and my brilliant stylist, **ANNEBET DUVALL:** Without your talent, vision, and unwavering support and love I would be in rags. Your vision has taken me on the most beautiful journey, filled with the most beautiful things. I am honored and lucky to have you in my life, and my restaurant. Thank you for your tireless work on this book.

To my publicist, **JESSE GERSTEIN:** Thank you for your support, your patience, your enthusiasm, and your unwavering belief in what we do. I am so grateful that Melissa and I found you when we did. Your tireless work has helped pave the way to where we are today.

To creative director and designer **MARYSARAH QUINN:** Thank you for your vision, your kindness, your understanding, your sense of humor, and your immense talent. Without your support, this book would not be what it is today. Thank you for understanding the weird, the quirky, the moodily beautiful world that I live in, and helping me to share it with everyone.

To my publisher, **AARON WEHNER:** Thank you for believing so ardently in our vision, our food, our restaurant, especially when no one else saw how tremendous coloring outside the lines could be.

To my editor, **AMANDA ENGLANDER:** Thank you for giving us an opportunity to share our story with the world, and for what it is—raw, gritty, and darkly beautiful.

To **JANA BRANSON, DAVID HAWK, KATE TYLER,** and **STEPHANIE DAVIS:** Thank you for your tireless attention to detail and the promotion of our book. I could not have asked for a better team.

To **CHRIS TANIGAWA** and **PHILIP LEUNG:** Thank you for your brilliant behind-the-scenes work to make this book as beautiful as it is.

To **JUSTIN CONOLY** and **REBECCA JURKEVICH:** You are an amazing team and together with **JOHNNY** and **DUNCAN BURGIN,** I can't believe we made such amazing magic happen in the kitchen and on the page.

To my managers, **SCOTT FELDMAN** and **ALI WALD:** Thank you for your work, your support, and your encouragement. You truly understand who I am and what I represent. Thank you for always allowing me to stay true to that.

MY CHOSEN FAMILY IS ESSENTIAL TO UNDERSTANDING HOW I GOT TO WHERE I AM TODAY. IT TAKES A VILLAGE TO RAISE A CHILD AND SO, TOO, DOES IT TAKE ONE TO RAISE A RESTAURANT. Thank you to the people behind the Beatrice Inn, whose work, love, passion, talent, and drive make our restaurant what it is: **NICOLE AVERKIOU** and **LUCERO RAMALES,** you are not only my souschefs but also my sisters. **NICOLE:** To have lived through four restaurants with you, to have cooked on several continents with you, to live this life with you, has been my honor. I know that if I needed to bury a body tomorrow, you would rent the car and bring the shovels. You truly are one of the most talented live-fire

meat cooks I have ever had the privilege to work with, and you also have one of the biggest hearts I have ever encountered. **LUCERO:** You are my rock. Your quiet, calming nature grounds me. Thank you for always telling it like it is, and being tough as hell. You show us all how it's done, and I hope all of our cooks aspire to be as true as you are. My loves, this business and my sanity would cease to exist without either of you.

WILLIAM SORVILLO, you are one of the most insightful people I have ever met. I wish I was a fraction as cool as you are: charming, good-looking, and you can DJ the hell out of a playlist. I often walk through the dining rooms, and people are at their tables singing and dancing because you've set the tone. Thank you for being my confidant, my advisor, and my family.

ANTANAS SAMKUS, I have come to see you as a brother. I love watching you make magic behind the bar with your team, **CAMILO, JOSÉ, JOHN,** and **DOMINGO,** especially when the line to get a drink is eight deep. Thank you especially for writing all of the cocktail recipes in this book. Thank you for your fashion and for your friendship. I love you, my brother.

ALLISON LEE, thank you for being a guiding light, a shoulder to cry on, a person to vent to, and a figure of unwavering support for me and my team.

MARIUSZ ZURAWSKI, MISHU, you truly are a teddy bear, giving me a hug when I walk in every day. Thank you for treating me, my family, and the Beatrice as your own. There is no one whom I trust more in this business then you, my brother. You have built a beautiful thing to be proud of.

MOHAMED SONOGO, I love how much you care about our food and our family. Thank you for being the voice of reason and of authority. There are few with as big a heart as you, my darling.

There are more members of my team, past and present, that have become my family: **JORDAN LUKE, CELIO TAMANIS, DUNCAN BURGIN, DIANA LEE, REMY JIMENEZ,**

DYCOTA ROBINSON, AARON CHANG, VIRGINIO ORTEGA, CARLOS RUÍZ, MIGUEL URBANO, PATRICIO SALDANA, MELISSA CARUSO, JOE REED, ADAMA ZORNE, OSCAR TORRES, BYRON LOPEZ, JASON BOWELL, RICHARD VACHINO, ARTURO ZAMUDIO, DOMINGO PEREZ, VIRGINIO ORTEGA, MAUN RAHMAN, CARLOS HURTADO, ANTONIO GONZALES, JORGE ESCUDERO, MEGAN HIGGINS, JESSICA KOTULA, KYLE RIDDINGTON, THERA CLARK, NATHAN WOODEN, RICHARD LEFTIG, KEN EBERLE, EMMA ARANGO, BYRON LOPEZ, NAHIYAN FARUQUE, JOSÉ FLORES, JULIO MARIN, EDUARDO ZENTENO, KOGBA KODJOVI, JOHN FILBY, JABRIA HENDRYX-EVANS, LUQMAN JINADU, JOSÉ VELECELA, JACINTO CASTRO, RUBEN TACUEPIAN ROMERO, STEPHEN KOENIGSAMEN, SOULEYMAN SOW, BETO AGUILAR, SEBASTIAN MORALES, ANTONIO PEREZ, CHELLA VICENTE, ALLISON GIBSON, STESHA MARCON, KEITH LARRY, ROBERT AMBURN, KEVIN HUFFMAN, JAYMEE WISE, JOSH COPELAND, and JACQUELINE WESTBROOK. I thank each and every one of you for what you bring and have brought into my business and my life every day.

To our amazing purveyors, especially HENRY SMULWITZ, LUIS ROZZO, FRANCESCA & MARCO BASSI and the team at LAFRIEDA MEATS: Thank you for your support and embarking on our never-ending quest to find the best products.

TO OUR INCREDIBLE GUESTS AT THE BEATRICE: Thank you. When we bought this restaurant in 2016, I was both nervous and excited to share our vision with you. The darkly romantic, beautifully violent, primal notions that we create within our tiny kitchen are not for the faint of heart. And yet you've embraced us, our oddities, our weirdness, our genius, and our vision. My team and I thank you from the bottom of our hearts, we would be nothing without your patronage.

And finally, to the real lady of the house, LADY BEATRICE: Thank you for listening to my requests, for granting them, for taking care of the family that is housed under your roof, and for allowing us all to be a part of a chapter in your tremendous history in New York Motherfucking City.

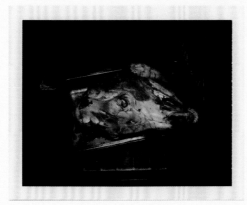

INDEX

Library of Congress Cataloging-in-Publication Data
Names: Mar, Angie, author.
Title: Butcher and beast: mastering the art of meat/Angie Mar; with Jamie Feldmar;
photographs by Johnny Miller.
Description: First edition. | New York: Clarkson Potter/Publishers, 2019 |
Includes index.
Identifiers: LCCN 2018061292 | ISBN 9780525573661 (hardcover) | ISBN
9780525573678 (ebook)
Subjects: LCSH: Cooking (Meat) | Seasonal cooking. | LCGFT: Cookbooks.
Classification: LCC TX749 .M2575 2019 | DDC 641.6/6—dc23
LC record available at https://lccn.loc.gov/2018061292.

ISBN 978-0-525-57366-1
Ebook ISBN 978-0-525-57367-8

Printed in China

Book design by Marysarah Quinn
Cover photographs by Johnny Miller

10 9 8 7 6 5 4 3 2 1

FIRST EDITION